Patterns
in Household Demand
and Saving

Constantino Lluch
Alan A. Powell
Ross A. Williams

Patterns in Household Demand and Saving

with contributions by
Roger R. Betancourt, Howard Howe, and Philip Musgrove

Published for the World Bank
Oxford University Press

Oxford University Press

NEW YORK OXFORD LONDON GLASGOW
TORONTO MELBOURNE WELLINGTON CAPE TOWN
IBADAN NAIROBI DAR ES SALAAM LUSAKA ADDIS ABABA
KUALA LUMPUR SINGAPORE JAKARTA HONG KONG TOKYO
DELHI BOMBAY CALCUTTA MADRAS KARACHI

© *1977 by the International Bank
for Reconstruction and Development / The World Bank
1818 H Street, N.W., Washington, D.C. 20433 U.S.A.*

Library of Congress Cataloging in Publication Data

Lluch, Constantino.
  Patterns in household demand and saving.
  Bibliography: p. 261
  1. *Consumption (Economics)* 2. *Supply and demand.*
3. *Economic development.* I. *Powell, Alan A., joint
author.* II. *Williams, Ross A., Joint author.*
III. *International Bank for Reconstruction and Develop-
ment.* IV. *Title.*
HB805.L58   339.4'1   77-3442
ISBN 0-19-920097-1
ISBN 0-19-920100-5 *pbk.*

Preface

In 1972 a research program on patterns of demand and saving in the development process was initiated at the Development Research Center of the World Bank. The project was conceived as a systematic examination of the consumption and savings behavior of households in countries at different levels of development. It was believed that inter- and intracountry comparisons of such behavior might yield empirical regularities useful for broad characterizations of the development process.

The pioneering attempts to discover patterns in economic development (including household demand and saving) were those of Clark (*The Conditions of Economic Progress,* 1940) and Kuznets ("Quantitative Aspects of the Economic Growth of Nations," I–X, *Economic Development and Cultural Change,* 1956–67). Later researchers have attempted to extend this work to take advantage of improvements in the data base and in econometric techniques over the past decade or so. The most notable recent contribution is that by Chenery and Syrquin (*Patterns of Development, 1950–1970*), who make intercountry comparisons of ten basic processes of accumulation, resource allocation, and income distribution. The present work is more limited in scope, but by concentrating on household demand and saving in some detail it complements the broader treatment of Chenery and Syrquin. Our analysis differs from previous work on household behavior in that it allows for a joint treatment of saving and the allocation of expenditure. This is made possible through the use of Lluch's extended linear expenditure system (ELES).

The first phase of the project was devoted primarily to the development of methodology with some exploratory empirical work. Much of this has been published elsewhere. In the second phase the adopted model, ELES, was fitted to time-series (national accounts) data for seventeen countries and cross-section data for eight countries spanning the development spectrum. The results are presented in this book; the theoretical model and estimation techniques are given in chapter 2 in outline form only.

International comparisons, particularly those which involve cross-section data on individual households, require the advice and assistance of a large number of people at various stages of inquiry: not least in obtaining data, in carrying out computations, and in presenting results. Most of the cross-section studies represent the output of joint research with agencies in the various countries. The work on the Republic of Korea in chapter 5 was undertaken in cooperation with the Special Research Office of the Bank of Korea, and we are particularly indebted to the director, K. S. Park, for assistance. The Korean data themselves were generously provided by S. K. Chang, Director of the Bureau of Statistics, Economic Planning Board, Korea, and we were also considerably helped by J. Y. You of the bureau. The Mexican study in chapter 6 represents in part the output of joint research with Dirección General Coordinadora de la Programación Económica y Social, Secretaría de la Presidencia, Mexico. We are greatly indebted to our collaborators José Luis Aburto and Gabriel Vera for their assistance with data and analysis of results and to Leopoldo Solis and Carlos Bazdresch for their constant support and encouragement. Chapter 7 was written in conjunction with the ECIEL program (Estudios Conjuntos sobre Integración Económica Latinoamericana). The Yugoslavian data were obtained through the World Bank study, "Small Holder Development Strategies: A Case Study in Yugoslavia," undertaken by the Agriculture and Rural Development section of the World Bank's Central Projects Staff; Graham Donaldson and Peter Hazell of the World Bank provided much assistance here. The national accounts data were assembled by Rita Parrilli and Sandra Hadler; Richard Berner kindly provided disposable income estimates for Italy.

In carrying out computations we enjoyed the invaluable services of John Chang throughout the life of the project; Alexander Meeraus provided advice on computing problems. Orani Dixon assisted in the preparation of the monograph with her usual combination of charm and skill.

Although all three authors have interacted on each chapter, the prime responsibility for authorship is as follows: chapters 1, 2, 3, and 10, Lluch, Powell, and Williams; chapter 4, Lluch and Williams except the section on Taiwan, which was written by Williams assisted by John Chang; chapters 5 and 6, Lluch and Williams; chapter 9, Williams. Earlier versions of parts of chapters 3 and 5 appeared in the *Economic Record, Bank of Korea Quarterly Economic Review,* and the *Review of Economics and Statistics.* Chapters 7 and 8 were written by consultants—chapter 7 by Howard Howe and Philip Musgrove, chapter 8 by Roger Betancourt—who also provided us with useful insights in writing our own chapters. The bulk of the editorial work was done by Williams. Needless to say, the work does not necessarily reflect the views of the World Bank.

Some important acknowledgments remain. Monash University generously granted extended study leave to Powell and Williams, and throughout the life of the project we have benefited substantially from discussions with colleagues in the World Bank. Particular thanks are due to Montek Ahluwalia, Bela Balassa, Hollis Chenery, John H. Duloy, Roger Norton, Yung Rhee, Sang Mok Suh, and Jean Waelbroeck. Other valuable comments have been provided by Colin Clark, Ken Clements, and Nico Klijn. Jane Carroll edited the final manuscript for publication.

CONSTANTINO LLUCH
ALAN POWELL
ROSS WILLIAMS

February 1977

Contents

Tables

Glossary of Symbols

The symbols used throughout the book are identified here to facilitate reading the empirical results of chapters 3–10 without frequent cross-references to chapter 2. The general rule is that Greek letters denote parameters and elasticities, while Latin letters denote variables. Except where explicitly noted, unsubscripted symbols in the text refer to vectors, the typical elements of which are shown by the corresponding subscripted symbols listed below. In the presentation of the empirical results, the use of a hat (ˆ) indicates a parameter estimate, but in chapter 2 this symbol also indicates the operation of converting a vector into the corresponding diagonal matrix. The following list excludes notation for stochastic specification.

Greek symbols (parameters and elasticities)

α_i intercept for the ith commodity in cross-section estimating equations for ELES (extended linear expenditure system)

α_i' intercept for the ith commodity in cross-section estimating equations for LES (linear expenditure system)

α intercept in ELES cross-section aggregate consumption function

β_i marginal budget share for the ith commodity

β_i^* marginal propensity to consume the ith commodity

γ_i "origin" parameter for the ith good in Klein-Rubin utility function; may be interpreted as subsistence or committed consumption of the ith commodity

γ_i^* value of subsistence or committed consumption of ith good in cross-section analysis measured at the price prevailing at the time of the household survey

δ subjective rate at which consumers discount future utility

η elasticity of total consumption expenditure with respect to income

η_s elasticity of saving with respect to income

η^i elasticity of total consumption expenditure with respect to the price of the ith good

η_i total expenditure elasticity of demand for the ith good

$\tilde{\eta}_i$ income elasticity of demand for the ith good

η_{ij} uncompensated elasticity of demand for the ith good with respect to the price of the jth good; total expenditure assumed fixed

$\tilde{\eta}_{ij}$ uncompensated elasticity of demand for the ith good with respect to the price of the jth good; income assumed fixed

η_{ij}^* compensated elasticity of demand for the ith good with respect to the price of the jth good under LES

$\tilde{\eta}_{ij}^*$ compensated elasticity of demand for the ith good with respect to the price of jth good under ELES

θ parameter used in calculating permanent income measures. It is used in two ways: in the appendix to chapter 8, as a correction factor which converts the stock formulation into a flow formulation; in the last section of chapter 4, as a scale parameter

λ parameter of extrapolative tendencies used in calculating measures of permanent income; its interpretation in chapter 8 differs from that in chapter 4

λ_i parameter which, for the ith good, measures the effects of family size on γ_i

μ marginal propensity to consume

ξ scale parameter used in defining permanent income in the last section of chapter 4

ξ_i elasticity of the household savings ratio (and of saving) with respect to the price of the ith good

π expected general rate of inflation

ρ the market rate of interest

σ expected rate of growth of income (in the appendix to chapter 8)

$-\phi$ supernumerary ratio, that is, the ratio of uncommitted expenditure to total expenditure

ω total expenditure elasticity of the marginal utility of total expenditure, that is, the Frisch parameter

ω^* income elasticity of the marginal utility of income

Latin symbols (variables)

f family size

f_h family size of hth household; f_i in chapter 2 is the ith partial utility within a directly additive utility framework

p_i price of the ith good

P index of general consumer prices

q_i quantity purchased of the ith good

s household saving

s' household savings ratio

$u(\ )$ utility function

u value of utility function

$U(\ )$ intertemporal utility function

v_i expenditure on the ith good at current prices

v total consumption expenditure at current prices

v^* total consumption expenditure in real terms

w_i average budget share of the ith good

y personal disposable income at current prices

y^* personal disposable income in real terms

z permanent income

z^* permanent income defined in terms of current and past real income

z_f dummy variable representing household size; $f = 1, 2$ for small and large households respectively

General Perspectives

The world bank has for several years encouraged applied economic studies designed to facilitate the implementation of development policy in its less developed member countries. These studies have sometimes focused on immediate problems specific to a particular country or to groups of countries; at the other end of the spectrum, the Bank has also supported work designed to broaden and deepen knowledge of the basic development process. The present study falls into the latter category.

The Role of Demand in Economic Development

Economic development is best conceived as an economywide process. The distribution of growth over different types of economic activity and of income over socioeconomic groups is basic to this process. Quite apart from the direct interest which the detailed picture undoubtedly will have for the policymaker, there is a growing consensus among economists that reliable perspectives on economic development are unlikely to be obtainable from models which do not describe the structure of basic demand and supply forces evolving in the economy.

This book represents a broad attack on the role of demand in economic development. It is designed to complement the work of the Bank and other researchers on flexible economy-wide models of developing countries. In crudest outline, the domestic economy in such models consists of a final demand sector and a productive (or input-output) sector. Rewards to capital and labor (of different skill levels) are determined by productivity. The possession of capital or skills thus determines the distribution of personal income, perhaps with modification by taxation and other government policies, such as those designed to change the skill distribution through public vocational training programs. The final demand due to private consumption expenditure is then determined by this personal income distribution and by prices, which are themselves determined by the combined interaction of the myriad of forces at work within the economy. Together with investment demand and government spending, personal consumption expenditures present final demands on the productive sector, which, in meeting these demands, generates wages and profits, completing the cycle.

Household demand as a link in this chain is important for a number of reasons: First, since the commodity composition of personal demand varies with prices and income, it follows that an economy with growing per capita GNP may require a changing balance among its productive activities. Economic planning must cater to this change.

Second, because the import and export content of consumer goods varies, a changing pattern of demand may have implications for external trade policy and for international financial management.

Third, governments may wish to redistribute income to improve general welfare. Such a change will affect the structure of aggregate consumer demand in ways that will need to be anticipated.

Fourth, domestic savings need to be mobilized to make feasible the growth targets of developing nations. Since savings are the surplus of income over consumption, a proper understanding of demand behavior necessarily implies an addition to knowledge concerning savings behavior.

Fifth, until recently, the bulk of models of economic development have been based on the assumption that commodity prices are of little or no significance in determining the crucial aspects of economic behavior. The oil crisis may or may not constitute a convincing rebuttal of this proposition, but investigation of the role of prices remains high on the list of priorities in economic development modeling. Prices cannot be investigated meaningfully without also examining the structure of demand.

Sixth, the price of food is a politically sensitive issue in developing countries. The behavior of food prices under various conditions of shortage or glut depends on the responsiveness of consumers' demand to the price of food. Used with due care, the results of this study give some guidelines as to the likely orders of magnitude for the relevant responses in a typical developing country at a given stage of development.

The starting point for our characterization of demand and savings patterns was the work of Clark (1940) and Kuznets (1962). On the basis of data from several countries, these two authors documented changes in the commodity composition of demand as real per capita income grew. Clark (1957) drew some generalizations about the structure of the demand for food and, in less detail, other consumer goods based on international as well as intracountry data. Houthakker (1965) made an exhaustive analysis of national accounts data for Western European countries. This was followed by further international comparison studies by Goldberger and Gamaletsos (1970), Weisskoff (1971), Gamaletsos (1973), and Parks and Barten (1973). These studies failed to detect systematic patterns in demand structure which could be related to the stage of economic development.

The present monograph differs from previous work in two ways: first, savings and demand patterns are treated within a single integrated framework; second, all of the consumer's demand decisions are modeled simultaneously, using the demand systems approach. Although this approach is not unique, none of the earlier works used it in the context of a data base widely dispersed over the development spectrum. With the use of relatively powerful techniques of estimation, this difference in approach was sufficient to reveal some systematic tendencies in demand and savings behavior.

Specific questions of some importance were identified early in the work. (a) Can the behavior of an average consumer be characterized in terms of a relatively small set of explanatory variables, and, if so, how important are relative prices as part of that set? (b) At different levels of per capita GNP are there systematic patterns in the responsiveness of the average consumer's demand behavior to changes in prices and income? (c) Can "subsistence expenditure" be measured, and what are the implications of such measures? (d) How many consumer "types" (groups of homogeneous consumers with important differences in expenditure and savings behavior) emerge in the analysis of particular countries?

These questions were analyzed at various levels of generality and with different bodies of data. Overall patterns were first ascertained using time series of per capita disposable income, per capita total consumption expenditure, its allocation over broad expenditure categories, and prices from the United Nations national accounts for up to seventeen countries, covering a broad range of GNP per capita. More detailed intracountry patterns were ascertained from cross-section data for eight countries on the same variables, plus other socioeconomic characteristics of the household relevant for consumption and savings behavior (for example, age and occupation of head of household, family size and location). In both overall and intracountry patterns, it was thought important to limit the scope of analysis to larger categories of expenditure such as food, clothing, and housing. This decision was made partly for technical economic and econometric reasons, but in any event it is consistent with an emphasis on patterns of expenditure on basic human needs and, in particular, with the central role that food expenditure must be assigned in any study of development.

Principal Research Findings

The results of our research are grouped below by the type of data from which they are obtained: national accounts, aggregated cross sections over time, and cross sections proper.

National Accounts

The research findings for aggregate data are summarized first, without regard for the effects of population size and composition. National accounts data have been used to fit systems of demand equations for an average consumer in the seventeen countries and sample periods given in table 3.2 for eight commodities. Estimates have been obtained for eight marginal budget shares, giving the percentage allocation among commodities of an additional unit of total expenditure, and for the basic needs or subsistence level of consumption for each commodity at base-year prices, as well as for the percentage of an additional unit of disposable income that is consumed in the fourteen countries for which income data were available. The responsiveness of consumer demand for each of the eight commodity groups to income and price changes can be computed on the basis of these estimates.

As noted, our analysis allows for a joint treatment of saving and the allocation of expenditure. The goodness of fit, precision of estimates, and ability of the fitted system to predict the average saving ratio at mean sample values make the system an adequate tool to characterize broad tendencies in both household saving and the allocation of expenditure. It is somewhat less reliable in characterizing savings than in characterizing demand behavior.

The key determinants of the demand for a good are total expenditure (or income), the price of the good, and the price of food. Other cross-price effects can be ignored for most practical purposes.

The results reported in chapter 3 indicate that: (a) If total expenditure or "income" per capita is increased by one currency unit in low-income countries, it is allocated approximately as follows: 39 percent to food, 12 percent to housing, 9 percent to transport, and 7 percent to clothing, with a third going to other goods and services. For high-income countries the comparable figures are: 21 percent each to housing and transport, 17 percent to food, and 8 percent to clothing, with a third again going to other goods and services. (Low-income countries are defined as those with a GNP per capita of between $100 and $500 when expressed in 1970 U.S. prices, and high-income countries are those with a GNP per capita of over $1,500.) (b) In low-income countries a 10 percent decrease in the price of food has about the same effect on the demand for food as a 7 percent increase in total expenditure; in high-income countries the effect of such a price fall is equivalent to about an 8 percent increase in total expenditure. (c) When the price of food falls this releases income for purchasing other goods. A 10 percent fall in the price of food in low-income countries would lead to an expansion in the demand for other goods equivalent to a rise of about 5 percent in total expenditure. The corresponding figure for high-income countries is around 2.5 percent. (d) In low-income countries the demand for a commodity other than food is about twice as responsive to the price of food as it is to the price of the commodity itself. The reverse is true for high-income countries.

Disposable income and the price of food are important determinants of savings behavior, as shown in chapter 4. The model yields adequate predictions of the household savings ratio, but it has a systematic tendency to underpredict by an average of 10 percent of the actual ratio. A pattern in the responsiveness of the average household saving ratio to changes in the price of food is quite apparent. The percentage decline in savings expected to result from a one percent rise in the price of food has the following average values at different levels of GNP per capita in 1970 U.S. dollars: $100–500, 1.8; $500–1,000, 1.0; $1,000–1,500, 0.8; $1,500–2,500, 0.6; $2,500 and over, 0.3.

Under certain assumptions (which cannot be accepted uncritically), the estimated system yields also a measure of the subsistence consumption "bundle" in each country. For given levels of income and prices the subsistence consumption bundle determines the minimum level of consumption expenditures which an average consumer in each country studied regards as necessary. This basic level could obviously be used to define poverty: the poor part of the population would then include all households with per capita income below the subsistence consumption expenditure for the average consumer. Although our results are not robust enough to justify their uncritical application to welfare analysis, the relative magnitudes of estimated subsistence expenditures do offer some guidance on these issues, however qualified.

With these qualifications in mind, the following statements can be made on the basis of work reported in chapter 4: (a) Total subsistence expenditure as a proportion of per capita GNP falls as GNP per capita increases. At different levels of GNP per capita, the average ratio is as follows: $100–500, 62 percent; $500–1,000, 56 percent; $1,000–1,500, 46 percent; $1,500–2,500, 37 percent; $2,500 and over, 25 percent. (b) Food subsistence expenditure is about 63 percent of the total subsistence expenditure for the per capita GNP interval $100–500. For all other values of GNP per capita it is about 50 percent. (c) These relationships for food and for total subsistence expenditure fit the data well and can be used to infer the order of magnitude of the cost of purchasing a socially accepted minimal consumption bundle in countries lacking expenditure allocation and price data in the national accounts.

Aggregated Cross Sections over Time

The degree of usefulness of a statistical average depends in part upon the homogeneity of its components. The concept of an average consumer (that is, one with an average income) is a major abstraction in dualistic economies: in the extreme, almost nobody receives the average income of an income distribution with two peaks. It follows that different categories of consumers must be distinguished when distributional considerations are a basic concern. The present project reflects this concern through the analysis of bodies of data other than national accounts. In this part of the work, the concept of an average consumer for the economy as a whole is abandoned and the composition of the population is explicitly considered in its effects upon demand and savings patterns.

The first body of evidence to bear on different patterns of expenditure and saving within an economy is contained in a series of annual averages of household expenditure data for different groups of the population. Such data exist for a rural-urban breakdown for Korea.[1] The relevant results, and their relation to the work based on national accounts, are given in chapter 5. There is evidence of considerable dualism in demand and savings patterns of rural and urban consumers in Korea not accounted for by income differences alone. For farmers, the estimated responsiveness of food expenditure to changes in the total size of the consumer's budget is almost twice the value for urban dwellers. Farmers consume only about 46 percent of any increase in disposable income, whereas urban dwellers consume about 81 percent, but the cost of subsistence is about 50 to 60 percent of income for both groups. The estimated system is shown to be a useful tool to predict the savings ratio of rural and urban consumers and its variation over time.

Economic analysis of rural-urban migration and generation of savings in Korea can benefit from the work summarized above. More generally, this work indicates that household disaggregation by location yields results on different patterns of expenditure and savings that are of practical importance and cannot be accounted for by income differences alone.

Cross Sections

Purely cross-section data on individual households are the basis of additional work on consumer types. Determinants of behavior other than income and prices can be explicitly considered. In some cases, price information is available in the form of territorial price indexes. But in general it is not available, and price effects have to be inferred either from strong theoretical specification or from parallel work using time-series data.

In all, household budget data (cross sections) were available for Korea, Mexico, Yugoslavia, and Chile and for one major city in each of Colombia, Ecuador, Peru, and Venezuela. The scope and budget of the project did not extend to the collection of household data nor to the editing of existing raw data into a consistent form for the computer. The selection of countries therefore depended partly on chance, partly on the degree of interest shown by the relevant officials in countries which had consumer surveys on record, and partly on the work of other researchers and research programs.

A summary of all the cross-section studies would defeat the aim

1. Throughout the book, references to Korea are to the Republic of Korea, otherwise known as South Korea.

of this chapter of providing a succinct account of the entire work. The most noteworthy determinants of demand and savings behavior are family size, location, and the socioeconomic class and age of the household head. To illustrate these features and give the general flavor of our findings the examples of Chile, Mexico, and Yugoslavia are used here.

In chapter 8, different patterns of expenditure and savings for 3,542 households included in the Cost of Living Survey for Central Chile, January 1964, have been analyzed. The households are classified by urban-rural location and, within each locality, by age and occupational status of head. Current income and family size are used to explain demand patterns in each subclass.

To be emphasized are the independent roles of age and location as determinants of consumption and savings behavior. In particular the Chilean data suggested that, for urban households, with any increase in income the proportion saved decreases with income per capita for households with a relatively young head; it increases with income per capita for households whose head is older. The average ratio of saving to income for the older category is more than twice the value for the younger; in both cases, this average savings ratio increases with income. For both urban and rural households total subsistence expenditure always increases with income for each age group considered separately. A similar but less pronounced phenomenon is observed for estimated subsistence expenditure on food.

In the case of Mexico, the 1968 nationwide survey of 5,608 households was split into thirty-two relatively homogeneous groups. The variables used as the basis for these categories were, first, place of residence (Mexico City, rural, or other urban); second, socioeconomic class (workers, entrepreneurs, technocrats, and others); third, family size (large families are those with more than five persons; small have five or less); and finally, age of household head ("young" is defined as less than 45 years of age; "old" as 45 or older).

The following conclusions emerged: (a) Income and family size exert an important influence on the proportions in which an additional unit of income would be allocated among the five commodity groups distinguished (food, clothing, housing, durables, other). These income effects are strong enough to show up even within socioeconomic classes. (b) Some economies of size seem to accrue to families in that subsistence expenses, per capita, are estimated to be lower for large families than for small families. (c) Subsistence expenditures are lower for households in lower socioeconomic classes.

(d) Place of residence (rural or urban) seems to exert only a negligible effect on the responsiveness of demand for the five commodities to changes in income level. Some systematic differences in responses to prices, however, may occur. (e) Place of residence does exert a modest but significant influence on the percentage of any increase in disposable income which is consumed: 89 percent for rural households, as against 75 percent for urban households.

By contrast, the Yugoslavian data, which were drawn from the 1972 annual farm survey, did not offer scope for analysis based on the socioeconomic characteristics of households. The data did, however, present an opportunity to explore the possibility of regional differences in demand and savings behavior. The sample was cross-classified by region (Serbia, Voyvodina, and Kosovo) and by type of farming activity. A six-commodity split of the consumption of farm households was available. A striking feature was the relative uniformity of the structure of demand responsiveness across both regions and farm types. This apparent uniformity of the behavior of rural households suggests that the urban-rural dichotomy used elsewhere in the study may not be a bad approximation in capturing important sources of difference in demand behavior in developing countries. Although savings behavior did vary across regions and farm types, the variation was adequately explained by income differences alone. In particular, as the per capita income of Yugoslavian farm households increases from 5,000 to 10,000 dinars, on average the fraction of income saved increases from 28 to 43 percent. The comparatively high magnitudes of both these figures seems to reflect the internal financing of farm production and the difficulty of separating the production and consumption accounts in farm households. This apparent tendency toward thrift on the part of farm households is confirmed by Korean evidence discussed in chapter 5.

All our cross-section work confirmed the following key findings obtained using time-series data:

1. The percentage of an increase in income which is spent on food is highest at low income levels.
2. The demand for a commodity is much more responsive to changes in its own price at high income levels than at low income levels.
3. A change in the price of food has an effect on both saving and the allocation of expenditure, but this effect is much more important at low income levels than at high income levels.
4. Estimates of total subsistence expenditure and subsistence

expenditure on food increase with income but at a slower rate than income itself.

Limitations of the Study

The methodology followed throughout this study (that is, the extended linear expenditure system) leans heavily on certain developments in the modern theory of demand. Although the implementation is new, the basic ideas involved can be traced back to Pigou (1910). Regarding consumer demand for a commodity he thought that its responsiveness to price changes would likely be related in a fairly straightforward way to its responsiveness to changes in income. This suggestion was followed up by Friedman (1935) and finally incorporated rigorously into demand theory by Houthakker (1960). It needs to be emphasized here that this methodology is based on rather strong assumptions about the underlying preferences which determine the market behavior of consumers. There is a consensus in the economics profession that this approach is valuable for the interpretation of demands for broad groups of commodities, but undoubtedly conclusions based on an uncritical acceptance of the methodology would lead to error in some circumstances.

For many of the sets of data analyzed here, information on prices is either lacking or of dubious quality. The advantage of the extended linear expenditure system in this context is that the income responsiveness of demand for commodities and of saving is sufficient to imply how demand would respond to prices. To a very great extent it is this implicit responsiveness of demand to prices which is reported in this work, especially in the cross-section studies. It follows that if more or better price data become available our estimates should be checked for plausibility and either revised or abandoned, as indicated. The degree of consistency evident between our estimates of the responsiveness of the demand for food to its own price and estimates from other studies based on different data and approaches is relatively high, however, and this lends some modest support to the validity of the method.

There may be room for improvement among other aspects of the methodology—the treatment of the demand for durable goods comes immediately to mind—but of at least equal importance are limitations in the quality of the data. More or less by accident in our routine analysis of national accounts data we discovered cases where the data had been, to a large extent, fabricated. Household budget studies conducted in highly literate developed countries and using highly trained enumerators inevitably pose serious conceptual and practical problems in the manipulation, editing, and interpretation of data. This problem is ineluctably worse in less developed countries. Lacking the detailed local knowledge necessary to do otherwise, however, we have had to take at face value the edited data supplied to us, except in the case of the South American studies reported in chapter 7. Because much of the cross-section data were supplied to us with the helpful cooperation of local officials, the more obvious pitfalls have perhaps been avoided, but independent evaluations of the reliability of the data were generally not available.

To sum up: all due care has been taken, but no responsibility accepted for the uncritical application of our results.

1
Introduction

THE FOCAL POINT OF THIS STUDY is the evolution of the structure of consumer preferences as a function of economic development. Since per capita GNP is the single most commonly used indicator of the level of economic development it is used as a classification index for discerning patterns in household demand and savings behavior. Economic development is, however, accompanied by phenomena such as urbanization, structural shifts in the composition of output and employment, and changes in age structure and family composition. To take into account the multidimensional nature of economic development we also examine how demand and savings parameters respond to changes in a number of socioeconomic and demographic variables.

The demand and savings responses given most emphasis are: (a) the allocation of total consumption expenditure at the margin, that is, marginal budget shares, (b) price and total expenditure (or income) elasticities, (c) marginal and average propensities to save (and consume), and (d) the elasticities of household saving with respect to changes in relative prices. In addition, we estimate parameters which, with a generous interpretation, may be said to represent subsistence expenditures.

All the measures mentioned are relevant for analyzing economic development. Hypotheses on household savings behavior occupy a central role in growth models and in models of dualistic economic development, usually through alternative specification of savings

1

patterns by source of income.[1] The response of the pattern of consumption to changes in income is an important element in the theories of balanced growth developed by Rosenstein-Rodan (1943) and Nurkse (1959) and in the unbalanced growth models which have developed from Lewis (1954, 1955). Movements in consumption patterns are also incorporated into the more recent models of structural change of Chenery (1960, 1965), Taylor (1969), and Kelley, Williamson, and Cheetham (1972). In the latter work the notion of subsistence occupies a key role, as it does in Lewis's model.

Estimation of price elasticities of demand requires more justification because in development literature they are customarily assumed to be relatively unimportant.[2] This is so for the models of balanced and unbalanced growth discussed above. Mathematical programming models of economic development have also traditionally assigned prices a low role.[3] At an empirical level the importance of prices depends both on numerical estimates of elasticities and on observed or likely movements in relative prices. The substantial movement in relative consumer prices over the past few years suggests a greater role for price effects in development models. Theoretical and empirical support for the importance of relative prices in economic development has recently been produced by Kelley, Williamson, and Cheetham (1972).[4]

Much information already exists on the relative shift in demand from primary to industrial goods as per capita incomes increase.[5] It is recognized that this shift partially explains the increase in the share of industrial goods in total output as incomes rise. Chenery (1960), while emphasizing the importance of supply considerations, noted that changes in final demand also have effects of some importance on intermediate demands for industrial goods. To these income effects, Kuznets (1966) added price effects, observing that

1. See, for example, Pasinetti (1962, 1974).
2. For recent summaries of the literature which emphasize the role of this assumption, see Chenery (1975) and Chenery and Syrquin (1975).
3. Typically, piece-wise linearizations or informal iterative procedures are needed to maintain the internal consistency of prices within programming models. For a particularly ingenious example of the former approach within a one-period agriculturally oriented linear program, see Duloy and Norton (1973). A number of representative programming models are contained in Chenery (1971); excellent surveys of the literature are contained in Blitzer, Clark, and Taylor (1975).
4. See also Cheetham, Kelley, and Williamson (1974).
5. See Clark (1940), Houthakker (1957), Kuznets (1962).

the relative price changes brought about by technological advance may produce differential effects on the various categories of final demand.

Kelley (1969), however, has argued that a simple comparison of demand patterns at different levels of income may mask the individual effects on demand of the various changes which accompany economic development. Systematic changes in population growth, age structure, family size, and degree of urbanization may be at least as important as income effects and, furthermore, may offset them. An aim of this study is to isolate these specific effects by using detailed data on household budgets. Only by obtaining these disaggregated estimates is it possible to evaluate the (demand) effects on development of alternative policy mixes.

We would hope that, ultimately, our findings would be incorporated into price-responsive economywide development models.[6] The model used in this book facilitates such incorporation by endogenizing saving: the choice between saving and consumption is directly linked with the decision regarding allocation of expenditure. This feature of the model permits an examination of the effect of changes in relative prices on saving.

Previous Studies

The two pioneering studies relating the level and structure of consumption to economic development are those of Clark (1940) and Kuznets (1962). The latter confined his conclusions to broad descriptive statements about the share of consumption in total product. This share did not vary greatly, although there was a tendency for it to be higher in low-income countries. Kuznets also noted marked cross-country differences in the structure of private consumption expenditures. These differences were similar to those found in intracountry cross-section studies but differed from results obtained using long time series within countries. Kuznets rationalized his findings in terms of basic social forces: urbanization and changes in technology, in organization of economic units, and in values. Clark attempted to detect systematic variations in demand elasticities

6. In addition to Kelley, Williamson, and Cheetham (1972), for recent developments in this field see also Johansen (1974), Chenery and Raduchel (1971), Taylor and Black (1974), Lluch (1974a), Blitzer (1975), and Norton (1975).

as a function of per capita GNP.[7] He found that the income elasticity
for food declines as living standards rise.

Chenery and Syrquin (1975) have updated and extended the
work of Clark and Kuznets, using more sophisticated statistical techniques and a much larger data base. They found that private consumption expenditure comprises a smaller proportion of GDP as
income levels rise, but this is more than accounted for by a substantial
fall in the share of food, so that the share of nonfood private
consumption in GDP increases. Gross domestic saving was found to
form an increasing percentage of GDP as development proceeds, but
household saving was not considered separately.

In the studies by Clark, Kuznets, and Chenery and Syrquin, the
analysis of household demand and saving forms only a relatively
small part of a larger search for the "stylized facts" about economic
development. A number of other studies have been concerned solely
with international differences in the structure of demand. Comparisons using national accounts data have been carried out by
Houthakker (1965), Goldberger and Gamaletsos (1970), Weisskoff
(1971), Gamaletsos (1973), and Parks and Barten (1973). These
studies failed to detect patterns in estimated parameters of demand
which could be related to the stage of economic development.
Working with double logarithmic models and Western European
data, Houthakker (1965, p. 287) concluded: "The price elasticities,
in particular, show no uniformity at all." Goldberger and Gamaletsos
(1970, p. 385), using similar data but a model derived from an
additive utility function, came to a similar conclusion: "The elasticities show considerable variation across countries, uniformity being
particularly lacking for price elasticities." In none of these studies,
however, did the selected countries span the development spectrum,
and only Weisskoff included less developed countries in the sample.
Patterns discerned by cross-section studies of demand behavior have
tended merely to confirm Engel's law, that is, income elasticities of
demand for food are shown to be less than unity, although
Houthakker (1957) noted some tendency for the expenditure elasticity of food to be lower at higher income levels.

Comparisons of aggregate consumption functions for countries
at all levels of economic development have been made by Yang
(1964) and for developed countries by Oksanen and Spencer (1973).
The literature on savings functions for developing countries has

7. See the 3d edition of Clark's *The Conditions of Economic Progress*
(1957), ch. 8.

been summarized by Mikesell and Zinser (1973). Their conclusions are rather negative in that they find (p. 19) "no consensus in support of any of the major hypotheses formulated (and tested) for the developed countries," although they confirm the Kuznets and Chenery and Syrquin finding that average saving tends to increase with per capita income.[8] Mikesell and Zinser conclude (p. 19) with the plea that greater knowledge of saving propensities of different categories of transactors, such as households and farmers, is needed for better policy guidance. An aim of the present work is to provide such information for both savings and demand parameters.

Analytical Framework

The potential set of variables influencing demand and savings parameters includes income, prices, the size and composition of families, age of household head, and the location and socioeconomic class of households. Since we also want to measure all cross-price effects, a model in which all variables enter all equations in an unrestricted manner is clearly not feasible. The methodology used throughout the book is derived from the neoclassical theory of consumer choice. At a very general level, this confines the explanatory variables used in estimation to income and prices. Other relevant explanatory variables (where allowed for) are introduced as criteria for subdividing data prior to estimation.[9] Thus a given set of estimates, such as price and income elasticities, will be interpreted in the light of what other variables are being held constant.

Limiting explanatory variables to income and relative prices does not of itself reduce the problem of estimation to one of manageable proportions. A common approach to estimation at this stage is to fit demand equations one at a time—indeed, the earliest dawning of econometrics was in the attempts of Moore (1914) and Shultz (1938) to estimate single equations purporting to describe market demand. While this approach has the advantage of simplicity, the presence in time-series samples of a large degree of collinearity among relevant predetermined variables—the price of the particular good, the prices of its substitutes and complements, and income—makes precise estimation of coefficients difficult and often impossible.

8. They also note that the average savings rate is positively associated with rates of growth of GNP.

9. Except in chapters 7 and 8, where family size appears directly as an explanatory variable in estimation.

The present study follows the newer stream of development in which the demand relations for an exhaustive list of the items in the consumer's budget are modeled simultaneously. In the older single-equation approach, the basic difficulty is one of asking too much from too few data. To put it slightly differently, the data are not equal to the information load demanded by the estimation procedure. The only solution possible is to increase the supply of usable information. For this there are two sources: further observations on the variables and a priori information generated by economic theory.

The collection of additional data is generally ruled out for many reasons. First, and most obviously, data collection is always costly. Second, time-series data can be augmented only by the passage of time, but usually the analysis cannot be arbitrarily postponed. Third, with the near collinearity of time-series observations, data equal to the task of estimation might involve impossibly long periods. Ineluctably, only one practical remedy remains, namely, the use of extraneous information. For an economist the obvious source is economic theory, which contributes to the estimation process by imposing constraints among the parameters to be estimated.

But why should this information derived from economic theory be tied to a systems rather than a single-equation approach? In microeconomic theory the constructs which tie economic relationships together are (a) an objective function or maximand and (b) a set of economic, financial, or institutional constraints. Behavioral relations are seen as generated by the optimization of (a) subject to (b). Given their common parentage, it is no surprise that the various behavioral relations in a microeconomic model are highly interrelated. Two obvious examples are the interrelations among factor demands in the theory of the firm[10] and the interrelations among the demand functions for different goods in the theory of the consumer.[11] The latter provides the methodological focus of this book. Although some small part of the information coming from economic theory could be implemented within a single-equation framework, efficient use of the information requires a systems approach.

A point still at issue in the literature is the degree of reliance to be placed on a priori restrictions. At one end of the spectrum is the view that such restrictions are a logical consequence of the way

10. The seminal work is Marschak and Andrews (1944).
11. See Slutsky (1915) and Hicks (1939).

in which the model is specified, and consistency requires that the estimates adhere to them. At the other extreme, the restrictions are treated with diffidence, even skepticism. Each economic theoretical restriction is regarded as a testable hypothesis. If the restricted model fits "significantly" worse than an unrestricted one, the restrictions are scrapped. The trouble with this approach is that, by putting the status of the restrictions in doubt, it once again places a large (often impossibly large) information load on the data—back to square one.[12]

A recent development by Byron (1974) takes an intermediate position. The economic theoretical restrictions are assumed to be correct *on average*. Stochastic terms now appear on the restrictions as well as on the demand equations. Although Byron's approach is attractive it was beyond the resources available to the present study and in any event became available very late in the life of this project. Economic theoretical constraints in this study, consequently, are uniformly treated as *exact*.

The restrictions we impose on the demand system are of three types. First are those which ensure that the "adding-up" property holds, that is, that the sum of expenditures on individual commodities is equal to total expenditure. These restrictions do not require that consumers maximize an objective function. A second set of restrictions follows from maximization of a general utility function subject to a budget constraint. These involve homogeneity of degree zero of the demand functions and symmetry of the income-compensated cross-price effects.[13] The third set of restrictions depends on the assumption that the underlying utility function is directly additive. That is to say, it is postulated that a "representative consumer's" utility function can be written (possibly after a monotonic transformation) as the sum of a set of individual partial utility functions each having as its only argument the quantity of a particular good. It is assumed that the additional satisfaction or utility obtained from consuming an additional unit of a commodity does not depend on the level of consumption of other commodities.

This tightly restricted analytical framework permits estimation of a large number of demand and savings responses at the risk of imposing incorrect a priori restrictions on the relations among them. In the light of our use of an additive system, the importance of these restrictions is reduced by confining estimation to broad commodity

12. A variety of conflicting results have been obtained in empirical testing of the validity of restrictions. They are summarized in Barten (1975).

13. Sanderson (1974) has derived a similar set of restrictions without introducing the concept of a utility function.

groups, where the assumption of additive utility has greater validity.[14] The maximum number of commodities considered here is eight.[15] Experimental sensitivity analysis on the level of commodity aggregation is reported in chapter 4.

Aggregation over Consumers

Neoclassical theory of demand refers to the optimizing behavior of an individual consuming unit. Consistent aggregation of demand equations over consumers requires strong assumptions, unlikely to be met in practice.[16] Nevertheless, demand systems are most commonly fitted to the most aggregate data, namely, time series of national accounts aggregates. This procedure is usually justified in terms of obtaining average estimates of demand and savings parameters for the "representative" consumer. This practice is followed in chapters 3 and 4 where annual time-series data on a standard UN classification of consumption expenditures are analyzed separately in each of seventeen countries with per capita GNPs as widely disparate as possible. Estimates of demand and savings behavior are therefore obtained for representative consumers at different levels of economic development, as measured by real income.

National accounts data offer no scope for determining the effects of income distribution, region, family size, or other socioeconomic factors. These require household budget study data. But how finely should one disaggregate by consumers? If the disaggregation is too great the results become unwieldy, difficult to interpret and to incorporate into economywide models. Stylized facts are what is sought and not the measurement of fine differences in consumer preferences. Households with substantially different demand and savings behavior should be grouped separately, however, so that the effects of planned

14. In summarizing the empirical evidence Barten (1975) concludes (p. 51): "The various conditions [i.e., restrictions] are more acceptable for a limited set of equations than for a finer breakdown."

15. Except in chapter 4, where results for Korea are presented for twelve commodities solely for comparative purposes. Deaton (1974, 1975) has shown that additivity is extremely restrictive at a high level of disaggregation (he uses thirty-seven commodities), and even for eight commodities care must be exercised in interpreting results.

16. See Theil (1954) and Green (1964). Barten (1974) adopts a more optimistic view and concludes (p. 8) that "there exists a *prima facie* case in favour of the analogy between the properties of derivatives of individual demand equations and those of average demand equations."

or expected structural changes can be measured. Within Dixon's (1975) general equilibrium framework, for example, the number of separate representative consumers needed for accurate modeling depends on identifying socioeconomic groups which are internally homogeneous with respect to marginal budget shares.

We proceed to throw light on the question of the optimum number of representative consumers by sequentially breaking down the population from the single representative consumer of chapters 3 and 4. Since dualistic models form an important part of the theoretical literature on economic development, the most natural first step is to disaggregate into two representative consumers: rural and urban. In chapter 5 time series of cross-section aggregates for Korea are used to determine whether any differences noted in the structure of consumer preferences between rural and urban consumers are statistically or economically significant. We also search for possible distortions introduced into the national accounts results as a consequence of working at a higher level of aggregation.

The rural-urban dichotomy is also explored for Mexico (chapter 6) using a single budget study. Then household survey data for Korea, Mexico, and six other countries, mostly in Latin America, are examined at a more disaggregated level. These results are contained in chapters 5 to 9. Representative consumers are defined according to criteria such as socioeconomic class, family size and age of household head, as well as location. In Mexico, for example, demand and savings responses for thirty-two different representative consumers are estimated. In all cases we look for systematic variation in demand and savings behavior among different representative consumers and note instances of similar behavior.

Plan of the Book

Chapter 2 sets out the basic economic model underlying the empirical analysis, namely, the extended linear expenditure system.[17] Alternative interpretations of the estimating equations are offered. For convenience the expressions used throughout the book for calculating elasticities and other economic measures are assembled in this chapter. The stochastic specification adopted is also set out here, and estimation procedures for both time-series and cross-section data are briefly discussed.

17. See Lluch (1973a).

Chapter 3 contains a comparison of separately fitted national accounts time-series data for seventeen countries using an eight-commodity breakdown. The chapter commences with a discussion of the data base (the median sample size is fourteen years). In presenting empirical estimates, attention is concentrated on the basic parameters of the model and on total expenditure and price elasticities. In all cases we search for systematic movements in estimates with the level of GNP per capita. In chapter 4 the results are extended; the same data base is used as in chapter 3, but the level of commodity aggregation is varied. Estimates of subsistence expenditure are considered, as well as the ability of the model to predict household saving. In addition, dynamic versions of the model are discussed and estimated using data from Taiwan.[18]

Korean data at three different levels of consumer disaggregation are discussed in chapter 5. The three sets of data analyzed are: a time series of national aggregates, a time series of cross-section means for rural and urban households respectively, and individual household data at a point in time. Regional price indexes are used in estimating price responses from the household data.

Chapters 6, 7, 8, and 9 deal with household budget studies undertaken in a number of selected low-income countries in recent years. Estimates of income and price elasticities from budget studies are particularly useful for less developed countries because frequently national accounts data is either unavailable or unsuitable. Chapter 6 is devoted to analyzing the 1968 nationwide survey in Mexico. Chapter 7 compares results for large urban centers in selected Latin American countries: Colombia, Ecuador, Peru, and Venezuela. Chile is considered separately in chapter 8. In chapters 7 and 8 there is some discussion of the effects of introducing measures of permanent income into the model. Finally, demand and savings behavior of farm households in Yugoslavia is analyzed in chapter 9. In each country, households in the surveys were cross-classified, to the extent allowed by the data, by region and socioeconomic and demographic features.

Chapter 10 presents an overview and summary of our findings plus our conclusions and perspectives for further research in the area.

18. The Republic of China is referred to throughout the book as Taiwan.

2
Methodology

In this book, the basic tool to model household decisions on savings and the allocation of expenditure is a single linear demand system with current disposable income and prices as the explanatory variables. The model is quite stringent, and its implications must be clarified from the outset. Also, it needs to be supplemented with econometric specification and methods before it is applied to data.

The purpose of this chapter is to set out all these aspects of the basic model. In the first section the system is analyzed in deterministic terms; in the second section the system is specified stochastically and the methods of estimation are given.

The Extended Linear Expenditure System (ELES)

To begin the formulation of ELES all possible determinants of saving and expenditure allocation are put aside except for current disposable income and prices. Location, household size, and the age, education, and occupation of household members are among the factors that are ignored for the moment. Some will be taken into account in later chapters; others will not be considered in this book.

Formulation

Household decisions are assumed to be made on a per capita basis, and the problem facing the household is put in the following terms: Given a spendable amount per unit of time, to be called per capita disposable income (y), and a set of n commodities (whose quantities are denoted $q_1, ..., q_n$) with prices $(p_1, ..., p_n)$, how much is actually spent on each commodity, $v_i = p_i q_i$, $(i = 1, ..., n)$, so that total expenditure is $v = \Sigma v_i$; and how much is saved, $s = y - v$.

We assume that the answer is given by

$$(2.1) \qquad v_i = p_i \gamma_i + \beta_i^* (y - \Sigma p_j \gamma_j)$$

for all $(i = 1, ..., n)$, where (γ_i, β_i^*) are parameters to be estimated. System (2.1) will be called the extended linear expenditure system, ELES. Its counterpart in the applied demand literature (where v is considered exogenous), is the well-known linear expenditure system, LES.[1] In fact (2.1) contains LES: Add all the expenditure equations, v_i, to obtain

$$(2.2) \qquad v = (1 - \mu)\Sigma p_j \gamma_j + \mu y$$

where $\mu = \Sigma \beta_i^*$; from (2.2) obtain an expression for y in terms of v, and substitute it into (2.1). The result is LES,

$$(2.3) \qquad v_i = p_i \gamma_i + \beta_i (v - \Sigma p_j \gamma_j)$$

where $\beta_i = \beta_i^*/\mu$. The sense in which ELES is "extended" relative to LES is then apparent: ELES allows for the endogenous determination of total consumption expenditure, v.

In LES the β_i are marginal budget shares $(\partial v_i/\partial v)$, that is, marginal propensities to consume out of total expenditure, so that $\Sigma \beta_i = 1$. In ELES the β_i^* are marginal propensities to consume out of income, so that $\Sigma \beta_i^* = \mu$, the aggregate marginal propensity to consume. The γ_i parameters which appear in both LES and ELES may be interpreted as representing basic needs, committed consumption, or subsistence quantities, if they are positive, and $\Sigma p_j \gamma_j$ as total committed or subsistence expenditure. In LES the quantity $(v - \Sigma p_j \gamma_j)$ may be thought of as "supernumerary" expenditure, which is allocated among commodities in the proportions β_i $(i = 1, ..., n)$. In ELES $(y - \Sigma p_j \gamma_j)$ represents supernumerary income.

Figure 1 is a useful graphical representation of (2.1) that considers the two-commodity case and uses elementary concepts from demand analysis. A utility function $u(q_1, q_2)$, $q_i > \gamma_i$, is assumed to exist, and two of its indifference curves are shown. (The specific form of u implied by (2.1) and (2.3) will be discussed in the section on ELES and utility.) The linearity of (2.1) in income means that for each set of prices the income expansion path DF is a

---

1. See Klein-Rubin (1947–48), Geary (1950–51), Samuelson (1947–48), and Stone (1954).

Figure 1.   ELES: The Two-Commodity Case

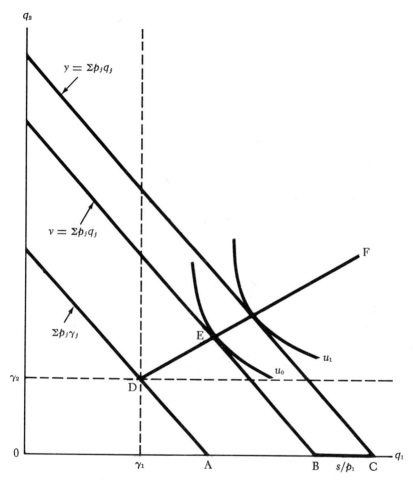

straight line from (γ_1, γ_2), and the indifference map is homothetic to this point. If all income were spent on commodity 1, the amount OC would be consumed. According to (2.1), the value of BC is put aside for future consumption, and the value of OB is then allocated among the two commodities so that E is the chosen bundle, with a utility level u_0.

Why is the value of BC saved? It apparently results in a utility loss; without saving, the utility level u_1 could be reached. The answer to this puzzle is simple. Figure 1 shows that maximization of $u(q_1, q_2)$ subject to the income constraint $\Sigma p_j q_j = y$ cannot yield (2.1) and therefore something else must be being maximized.

Two possibilities have been advanced. The first is that (2.1) represents optimal behavior at the beginning of a consumption plan (Lluch, 1973a). The plan is defined as the maximization of the present value of utility, $u(t) = u(q_1(t), q_2(t))$, $0 < t < \infty$, discounted at the fixed rate $\delta > 0$, subject to the constraint that the present value of expenditure cannot exceed initial wealth. This initial wealth has two components: nonhuman wealth that yields an income flow at the rate ρ, the rate of interest; and human wealth, the flow of expected labor income over the plan, discounted to the present at the rate ρ. To justify the interpretation of (2.1) as behavior at $t = 0$ the plan needs further restrictions: (a) $u(t)$ is specified as an additive logarithmic function of the Klein-Rubin type (see below); (b) expectations about prices and the interest rate are stationary; (c) the present value of expected changes in labor income is zero.

The second possibility was pointed out by Betancourt (1973) and elaborated independently by Howe (1975). Suppose that saving enters directly into the instantaneous utility function $u(q_1, q_2, s)$, which is also specified as a Klein-Rubin logarithmic function, but with committed saving set at zero ($\gamma_s = 0$).[2] Instantaneous utility maximization, subject to the constraint $\Sigma p_j q_j + s = y$, also yields (2.1) for any income concept, y.

From the point of view of this book, either of these possibilities can be chosen—or neither, in which case ELES is considered just a descriptive device to organize data on household saving and expenditure allocation. We favor the first interpretation. It appears to give more content to ELES[3] and also to open avenues for further work.[4]

2. This has similarities with the original Klein-Rubin (1947–48) formulation. They state: "Some of the X_i [our q_i] may be future commodities (savings), and the corresponding p_i are the prices of the commodities properly discounted to the present" (p. 84n).

3. For example, the marginal propensity to consume μ is interpreted as δ/ρ under the intertemporal derivation of (2.1). Thus if $\delta = \rho$, $s = 0$. The condition $s > 0$ is needed for the atemporal, but not the intertemporal, interpretation of ELES.

4. Some of which has already been carried out. See Klijn (1974) for alternative ELES specifications allowing for time varying ρ and δ; for finite horizons, Klijn (1974), Mattei (1973); for discrete time formulations, Betancourt (1973), Powell (1974); for the introduction of adjustment costs, Clements, Evans, Ironmonger, and Powell (1975); for the treatment of durables, Dixon and Lluch (1975); for the introduction of accumulated consumption into the utility function, Lluch (1974b).

The second interpretation is a terminal one: Nothing much can be said afterward.

Once BC in figure 1 is justified, questions about ELES begin in earnest. They boil down to the fact that ELES can be decomposed into (2.2) and (2.3), and therefore combines the virtues and defects of LES with a modified Keynesian consumption function:[5]

$$v/P = (1 - \mu) \, \Sigma\gamma_j + \mu \, (y/P),$$

which is just a rearrangement of (2.2) in which the price level is defined as $P = \Sigma p_j \gamma_j / \Sigma \gamma_j$. In the consumption function, the marginal propensity to consume appears in the intercept term as well as in its conventional role as the coefficient of real income (y/P).

Why use ELES instead of LES in applied work? Or, for that matter, why apply either when more general and flexible demand systems are available? The use of a linear system derived from an additive utility function was elaborated upon in the Introduction. This book does not deal with model generalizations for a given body of data. Rather the emphasis is on broad-based patterns and regularities as seen from the viewpoint of a fixed simple model, both in order to make generalizations about the data and to learn more about the limitations of the given model. Once the premium on simplicity is established, so is the use of the linear system without lags proposed here.

The focus on ELES rather than LES in estimation is justified as follows. One of the crucial concerns here is whether relative prices matter, and if so how much, in decisions regarding household saving and expenditure allocation. The effect of relative prices on saving cannot be measured at all with LES. The price effects on expenditure allocation, for a given total expenditure, would be identical in ELES and LES if the parameter estimates coincided. But attaching a stochastic specification to (2.1) rather than to (2.3) may alter the estimated values of parameters. Experience indicates that such changes in these values are substantial and that the γ estimates are more stable and exhibit more regularities across countries under the ELES specification (see chapter 3). Obtaining the best γ estimates possible is of particular importance because they determine price effects.

A further justification of ELES as against LES is that (2.2) enables

5. In the sense that total consumption expenditure is a function of current income. Notice that market disequilibrium and the distinction between notional and actual demand are *not* necessary to obtain (2.2), which is therefore not a Keynesian function in the sense that Clower (1965) would have it.

the identification of $\Sigma p_j \gamma_j$ in the absence of price data (or variation in prices) if $\mu \neq 1$. This fact will be amply used in chapters 5 to 9 to obtain price elasticities from cross-section samples.

Some caveats remain. With a static Keynesian-type consumption function and a linear system with no lags, no distinction between short and long runs is possible.[6] Also, in this linear system behavior is completely characterized by the focus D and the slope of DF in figure 1. The disadvantage of this simplicity is that there is limited room for price substitution. These linear systems are taken as local approximations and are distinguished from the global as follows: In time-series applications, linearity is assumed to be good enough for per capita time series up to about fifteen years for each country in the sample. In cross-section applications, linearity is considered good enough for homogeneous consumer groups, which are defined on the basis of a mixture of art, data, and preliminary empirical results. All applications are limited to broad commodity aggregates, in part so as not to stretch too much the additivity assumption (see the section on ELES and utility), in part to focus on food expenditure, an important aspect of this work.

Elasticity Formulas

For convenience all relevant elasticity formulas for (2.1) are given in this section together with their relationship to formulas for (2.3)— the ones obtained assuming constancy of total expenditure. Simple scalar transformations relate both sets of elasticities, and empirical results will focus on formulas relating to (2.3), for the purpose of comparison with those in the literature on consumer demand systems. Differences in results for the same body of data can, of course, be attributed solely to differences in the estimated values of parameters.

Each set of elasticities is expressed in two forms: in terms of a function, the supernumerary ratio, $-\phi$,

$$(2.4) \qquad\qquad -\phi = (v - \Sigma p_j \gamma_j)/v,$$

and in terms of individual parameters and data (tables 2.1 and 2.2).[7] The following notation is used: w_i denotes the average budget share, v_i/v; η_i, the expenditure elasticity of demand for the ith commodity; (η_{ij}, η_{ij}^*), the uncompensated and expenditure-compensated price

6. Except for a brief departure in chapter 4. Note that in the time-series work only annual data are used.

7. Table 2.2 also includes other elasticity formulas developed in later sections of this chapter.

Table 2.1.   *LES and ELES Elasticity Formulas in Terms of the Supernumerary Ratio*

LES	ELES
$\eta_i = \beta_i/w_i$	$\tilde{\eta}_i = \eta\eta_i$
$\eta_{ij} = \begin{cases} \phi\eta_i - \eta_i w_i(1 + \phi\eta_i), & i = j \\ -\eta_i w_j(1 + \phi\eta_j), & i \neq j \end{cases}$	$\tilde{\eta}_{ij} = \begin{cases} \mu\eta_{ii} + (1 - \mu)\phi\eta_i, & i = j \\ \mu\eta_{ij}, & i \neq j \end{cases}$
$\eta_{ij}^* = \begin{cases} \phi\eta_i(1 - \beta_i), & i = j \\ -\phi\eta_i\beta_j, & i \neq j \end{cases}$	$\tilde{\eta}_{ij}^* = \eta_{ij}^*$
	$\eta^i = (1 - \mu)(1 + \phi\eta_i)w_i$
	$\eta = \mu - (1 - \mu)\phi$

elasticities for a change in the jth price, with given total expenditure; $(\tilde{\eta}_i, \tilde{\eta}_{ij}, \tilde{\eta}_{ij}^*)$, the corresponding income elasticity of demand and the uncompensated and income-compensated price elasticities, given disposable income; (η, η^i), the elasticities of total consumption expenditure with respect to income and the ith price. The concepts of expenditure and income compensation under LES and ELES are discussed in the next section.

The LES elasticity formulas (η_{ij}, η_{ij}^*) given in table 2.1 can be expressed more compactly in matrix notation. Let $\{\eta_{ij}\}$, $\{\eta_{ij}^*\}$ denote the corresponding matrices. Then $\{\eta_{ij}\} = \phi\hat{\eta} - \eta(w' + \phi\beta')$, and $\{\eta_{ij}^*\} = \phi(\hat{\eta} - \eta\beta')$, where (η, w, β) are column vectors with typical elements (η_i, w_i, β_i), and where a prime denotes transposition, while a hat ($\hat{}$) indicates the corresponding diagonal matrix. Notice that $\hat{w}\{\eta_{ij}^*\} = \phi(\hat{\beta} - \beta\beta')$, a symmetric matrix. Also, the following is immediate,

(2.5)
$$\phi = \frac{tr\{\eta_{ij}^*\}}{\Sigma(1 - \beta_j)\eta_j},$$

so that the larger the value of ϕ, in absolute terms, the larger the sum of the substitution-effect components of own-price elasticities. In this sense ϕ measures the average price responsiveness in system (2.3).[8]

The rigidity in price responses allowed by LES is apparent from

8. See also Sato (1972).

Table 2.2. *Annotated Formulas for Demand Elasticities in LES and ELES*

Description	Model	Formula	Comments
Elasticity of demand for good i with respect to:			
Income	ELES	$\bar{\eta}_i = \mu\beta_i y/v_i$	Always positive since no inferior goods are allowed. Would be unity if all $\gamma_j = 0$ or if $\mu = 1$ and $(\beta_i/\beta_i) = (p_r\gamma_i/p_r\gamma_i)$ for all i and j; see figure 2.1.
Total expenditure	LES, ELES	$\eta_i = \beta_i/w_i$	Always positive as above. Would be unity if all $\gamma_j = 0$ or if $(\beta_i/\beta_i) = (p_r\gamma_i/p_r\gamma_i)$ for all i and j.
Prices Uncompensated			
Own	LES	$\eta_{ii} = (1-\beta_i)\dfrac{p_i\gamma_i}{v_i} - 1$	Strictly less than unity in absolute value except when γ_i is negative and sufficiently large in absolute value. If "necessities" are associated with positive γ_i's, the own price elasticity of a necessity cannot exceed 1 in absolute value.
	ELES	$\bar{\eta}_{ii} = (1-\mu\beta_i)\dfrac{p_i\gamma_i}{v_i} - 1$	
Cross	LES	$\eta_{ij} = -\beta_i\gamma_j p_j/v_i$	In the absence of negative γ's, ordinary cross-price elasticities are negative, indicating that income effects swamp substitution effects.
	ELES	$\bar{\eta}_{ij} = \mu\eta_{ij}$	
Compensated			
Own	LES, ELES	$\eta_{ii}^* = -(1-\beta_i)\left(1 - \dfrac{p_i\gamma_i}{v_i}\right)$	Unambiguously negative provided actual spending on ith good, v_i, exceeds subsistence expenditure, $p_i\gamma_i$.
Cross	LES, ELES	$\eta_{ij}^* = \beta_j\left(1 - \dfrac{p_i\gamma_i}{v_i}\right)$	Unambiguously positive (indicating net substitutability) provided v_i exceeds $p_i\gamma_i$.

18

Description	Model	Formula	Comments
Elasticity of total expenditure with respect to			
Income	ELES	$\eta = \mu y/v$	Ratio of marginal to average savings propensities.
Price of good i	ELES	$\eta^i = (1-\mu)p_i\gamma_i/v$	In the usual case, when $\mu < 1$ and $\gamma_i > 0$, has positive sign.
Elasticity of saving with respect to:			
Income	ELES	$\eta_s = y/(y - p'\gamma)$	Unambiguously greater than 1 for $p'\gamma$ (cost of the subsistence bundle) positive.
Prices[a]	ELES	$\xi_i = -p_i\gamma_i(1-\mu)/(y-v)$	Unambiguously negative provided the marginal and average propensities to consume are less than 1.
Frisch parameter	LES, ELES	$\omega = -v/(v - p'\gamma)$	The elasticity of the marginal utility of total expenditure with respect to total expenditure, equal to the negative of the inverse supernumerary ratio. With $p'\gamma$ positive, asymptotically approaches -1 from below as total expenditure gets larger.
Substitution elasticities	LES, ELES	$\sigma_{ij} = \overset{*}{\eta}_{ij}/w_j = -\eta\eta_j/\omega$	Unambiguously positive, since no inferior goods are allowed and since ω is required to be negative.

Note: A full glossary of symbols may be found at the front of the book. Symbols used in this table are: β_i, the marginal budget share of the ith commodity in total expenditure; γ_i, the basic needs or subsistence amount of the ith commodity; μ, the marginal propensity to consume; p_i, the price of the ith commodity; v_i, the expenditure on the ith commodity; v, total expenditure; $w_i = v_i/v$, the average budget share of the ith commodity; y, income. In all cases, the commodity subscript i runs from 1 through n.

a. ξ_i may also be interpreted as the price elasticity of the average savings ratio, $(y - v)/y$.

19

the formulas for price elasticities. If $\phi < 0$ and $0 < \beta_i < 1$, conditions required by the utility specification (see the following section), then from the LES formulas in table 2.1 $\eta_{ij}^* > 0$, for all $i \neq j$, so that all goods are net substitutes. In addition, if $\gamma_i > 0$ $(i = 1, ..., n)$ table 2.2 indicates that $-1 < \eta_{ii} < 0$, and $\eta_{ij} < 0$, $i \neq j$, that is, demand is price inelastic and all goods are gross complements. Rigidity in income responses is also apparent. Marginal budget shares are constant and, if $\beta_i > 0$, inferior goods are ruled out.

All these restrictions imply that the model is to be used with caution, because inferences from it should be adequate only for broad commodity groups and a limited range of variability in total expenditure. It is argued here that this limited model is useful for the purposes of this book. In particular, it focuses attention on a neglected contribution of demand analysis to the literature on development theory and planning: the influence of relative prices. If much of this influence consists of the income effects of price changes, there is no reason to ignore them. In particular, the price aspects of Engel's law should be explored. One aspect is apparent from $\eta_{i1} = - \eta_i(1 + \phi\eta_1)w_1$ (where the subscript 1 denotes food), as given in table 2.1. Because the food budget share, w_1, is large at low levels of income, η_{i1} is likely to be relatively important in development planning.

Both the limitations and strengths of LES and ELES have their roots in their implied utility specification. This aspect of the model is analyzed in the next section.

ELES and Utility

It is well known that LES can be derived from utility maximizing behavior, if the utility function is directly additive, namely,

$$u(q) = \Sigma f_i(q_i),$$

with the additional specification

$$f_i(q_i) = \beta_i \log (q_i - \gamma_i); \quad q_i > \gamma_i, \ \beta_i > 0, \ \Sigma\beta_j = 1,$$

for all $(i = 1, ..., n)$.[9] Samuelson (1947–48) has emphasized that this is the only function that would yield (2.3). By implication, $\Sigma f_i[q_i(t)]$ is also the only function that would yield ELES (2.1), when imbedded into an intertemporal utility maximization problem

9. See Geary (1950–51) and Samuelson (1947–48). The restriction $q_i > \gamma_i$ is required for the utility function to be defined. Then for marginal utilities to be positive the β_i must be positive.

of the type specified in Lluch (1973a). The direct utility functional associated with this problem is

$$U[q(t)] = \int_0^\infty e^{-\delta t} \Sigma f_i[q_i(t)]dt$$

with

$$f_i[q_i(t)] = \beta_i \log [q_i(t) - \gamma_i]; \; q_i(t) > \gamma_i, \; \beta_i > 0, \; \Sigma\beta_j = 1.$$

Notice that the γ parameters are assumed to be constant in the consumer plan.[10]

It follows that we are incurring all costs and benefits associated with additive utility functions, in particular that all price responses can be expressed in terms of the income elasticities and just one additional term, ϕ. This implication of additivity was first noted by Frisch (1959) and Houthakker (1960), and emphasized by Sato (1972). For our purposes, it is reflected in the complete formal equivalence between formulas for η_{ij} in table 2.1 and the ones given by Frisch and Sato. The difference in table 2.1 is, of course, one of parameterization: what we consider constant over the relevant range of observations or which particular additive utility specification we choose.[11] Our choice is based on simplicity.[12] It is emphasized again

10. See Lluch (1974b), for a formulation in which the γ_i's are specified as linear functions of accumulated consumption of the ith commodity.

11. There are other additive utility specifications which produce more flexible demand structures. The class has been explored by Pollak (1971), Johansen (1969), and Sato (1972); some have been applied empirically by Gamaletsos (1973) and Brown and Heien (1972). Sato's contribution is particularly noteworthy. He justifies the widely used double-log systems as approximations to demand systems obtained from an additive utility specification—a generalized constant elasticity of substitution function. He also presents a balanced discussion of pros and cons associated with alternative parameterizations. More recently Deaton (1974 and 1975) has argued against *all* additive utility specifications. Central to his argument is that η_{ii}/η_i is approximately constant across commodities under additivity (which requires w_i and β_i to be of order $1/n$, where n is the number of commodities); and the joint occurrence of $n_i < 0$ and $n_{ii} > 0$ for 9 of the 37 commodities considered. His use of the double-log form to test the approximation overlooks Sato's contribution, where η_{ii}/η_i is exactly constant. Deaton's results illustrate the difficulties that may arise with additive models at fine levels of commodity disaggregation, although he ignores the fact that the parameter estimates may violate the utility specification for many other reasons: use of total consumption as explanatory variable, assumption of no serial correlation in errors, estimation methods, or absence of lags, to list a few. See chapter 3 below for additional evidence on the approximation.

12. For some extensions of ELES using alternative utility specifications, see Lluch (1973b).

that, if $\mu \neq 1$, ELES permits identification of the additional term ϕ in the absence of price data or price variation, given that average and marginal propensities to consume are related to ϕ (using 2.2): $v/y = [1 - \phi(1 - \mu)/\mu]^{-1}$, and therefore

$$(2.6) \qquad -\phi = \frac{\mu}{v/y} \frac{1-v/y}{1-\mu} = \frac{\eta}{\eta_s}.$$

Under ELES the supernumerary ratio has then an added interpretation as the ratio of the income elasticities of consumption, η, and saving, η_s.

The choice of a specific form of the utility function raises several questions: How seriously do we consider (2.1) a device to estimate utility function parameters? How do we interpret changes in parameter estimates across countries and within countries, and across consumer groups? How much should we dwell upon the indirect utility implications of ELES (among them, for instance, the interpretation of $1/\phi$ as the expenditure elasticity of the marginal utility of expenditure and the construction of true indexes of the cost of living)? The position taken on these questions is straightforward: ELES is a convenient tool, in applied consumption analysis, for a task parallel to parameter estimation in Cobb-Douglas production functions. Both tasks can be accepted or rejected on similar grounds and are viewed as useful steps in the process of accumulating empirical evidence. We therefore proceed to make statements on the basis of (2.1) and its associated utility functional, making full use of the postulated model with some elementary cautions. In keeping with the limitations of linearity, its use is confined to broad commodity groups and to the "center of gravity" of samples.

The empirical results that follow provide information for comparing parameter values of the direct and indirect utility functions associated with ELES, both across and within countries. Referring to figure 1, we shall analyze how D and the slope of DF change with economic development, in particular for the case of food and non-food. For a given level of development we shall be concerned with how they change across homogeneous consumer groups.

An examination of the indirect utility function of ELES yields important theoretical results. First, all the well-known propositions associated with LES (treated exhaustively, for example, in Goldberger, 1967, and Goldberger and Gamaletsos, 1970) hold. In particular, $\eta_{ii}^* - \eta_{ii} = \beta_i$ $(i = 1, ..., n)$, so that the β_i's have both the interpretation of marginal budget shares and the own-price expenditure compensation term. Also, the expenditure elasticity of the marginal utility of expenditure, ω, which is a constant under many additive utility specifications,[13] is the function

$$(2.7) \qquad\qquad \omega = 1/\phi,$$

with ϕ as defined in (2.4).

Second, ELES contains also an income compensation concept, which is equivalent to expenditure compensation in LES. The indirect utility function associated with the intertemporal interpretation of ELES is a linear transformation of the LES indirect utility function, with identical coefficients for the relevant differentials.[14]

Third, under ELES we can define the income elasticity of the marginal utility of income, ω^*, as the linear transformation of ω,[15]

$$(2.8) \qquad\qquad \omega^* = \mu\omega - (1 - \mu).$$

It follows from (2.8) and the definition of η in table 2.1 that the income elasticity of total consumption expenditure can be expressed as

$$(2.9) \qquad\qquad \eta = \omega^*/\omega.$$

From (2.6) to (2.9) it follows also that the income elasticities of saving and of the marginal utility of income are the same in absolute value, that is, $\omega^* = -\eta_s$. Both ω^* and ω will be used in the following chapters for intercountry comparisons of utility functions.

ELES and Saving

Hicks (1946, p. 177) wrote: "By eschewing *utility* we were able to sharpen the edge of our conclusions in economic statics; for the same reason we shall be advised to eschew *income* and *saving* in economic dynamics. They are bad tools, which break in our hands."

Hicks's advice is ignored in this book, and this of course is done at the cost of also ignoring all complications associated with the definition of income and saving. Pushed aside are problems associated with durable consumption goods, endogenous changes in tastes, unfulfilled expectations on prices and income, and uncertainty. Also, under the intertemporal interpretation of ELES, (2.1) is obtained only

13. See, again, Frisch (1959) and Sato (1972). We shall refer to ω as the Frisch "parameter."
14. For details see Powell (1974), pp. 119–21.
15. If the indirect utility functional $G(y,p)$ is differentiated with respect to y, $G_y = \delta^{-1} (y - p'\gamma)^{-1}$. Expressing the marginal utility of income in flow terms and converting to elasticity form yields $\omega^* = -y (y - p'\gamma)^{-1}$. This can be rewritten, using (2.2) and (2.7), as (2.8).

if the present value of the time derivative of expected labor income is zero, an assumption whose empirical importance is not easy to evaluate.[16]

In spite of all this, we consider it fruitful to proceed to applications as a first step toward a fuller integration of applied work on demand systems and aggregate consumption functions. The resulting model of savings is static, since all intertemporal aspects of behavior have been reduced to relations at a given time and involve only current values of income and prices. The model is attractive for its simplicity: Saving is positive, zero, or negative according to whether the marginal propensity to consume is smaller than, equal to, or larger than one (see equation 2.10). The payoff is the identification of price elasticities in cross sections, a payoff derived from the utility structure imposed and the ex post identity $s = y - v$.

The theory of saving put forward here is based on "impatience": the marginal propensity to consume is the ratio of the subjective rate of discount to the rate of interest, that is, $\mu = \delta/\rho$, so that $s \gtreqless 0$ as $\delta \lesseqgtr \rho$.[17] This differs from Fisher's solution of the savings problem under certainty, which requires the equality of the rate of interest and the marginal rate of time preference as an equilibrium condition.[18] It also differs from permanent income and life-cycle formulations, where zero interest rate and absence of time preference are compatible with positive saving.[19] We assume additivity over commodities at a point in time and, intertemporally, over utilities; we then concentrate attention on behavior at the beginning of a consumption plan, which is assumed to exist,[20] with (real) time seen as the sequence of initial points of plans.

Whether the price paid is too high and the tools indeed break in our hands, can be judged after the empirical results are available. It is of interest to proceed to applications, given the added role assigned to factors that traditionally were considered relevant only from the point of view of the allocation of total expenditure, which previously was considered as exogenous. In particular, γ estimates

---

16. An attempt is made in chapter 4 in the section on Taiwan.

17. In ELES only if $\rho > \delta$, that is, if $\mu < 1$, will the consumption of commodities along an optimal path increase over planning time. Yaari (1964) earlier showed this to be true in the context of a single-commodity optimal growth model.

18. See Fisher (1930), pp. 510–13.

19. See, for example, Fama and Miller (1972), pp. 43–44.

20. Existence in a broader context is shown by Uzawa (1968), who assumes that δ depends upon current utility.

are seen to be relevant also for savings behavior. Two examples of this are given, both drawn from (2.2), which it is convenient to rewrite as

$$(2.10) \qquad\qquad s = (1 - \mu)(y - \sum_j p_j \gamma_j).$$

If $s' = 1 - v/y$, the average propensity to save, the following relationship between s', μ, and ω may be derived from (2.10):

$$(2.11) \qquad\qquad s' = \frac{1}{1-\psi}; \quad \psi = \frac{-\omega\mu}{1-\mu}.$$

Thus the Frisch parameter, which is a function of the γ's, and the marginal propensity to consume jointly determine the average savings ratio under ELES.

The second example refers to the effect of changes in p_1, the price of food, on s'.[21] The magnitude of this effect depends upon the γ_1 estimate. The measure used is the elasticity of the average savings ratio with respect to the price of food as given by

$$(2.12) \quad \xi_1 = \frac{p_1}{s'}\frac{\partial s'}{\partial p_1} = -p_1\gamma_1(1-\mu)/s = -\gamma_1(1-\mu)/s^*$$

where $s^* = s/p_1$, that is, the real value of saving in terms of its purchasing power over food.[22]

The γ_1 estimates play an important role in the subsistence bundle, as shown below, and this results in an important empirical regularity in ξ_1 as income increases.

Stochastic Specification and Estimation Methods

In outlining the economic assumptions which underly our chosen model, we eliminated subscripts for the unit of observation to simplify presentation. Full econometric specification, however, requires precise statements as to which parameters are assumed to be constant over the sample data and a complete description of the error structure. In this section these requirements are met, and the methods used to obtain estimates of the parameters of the model are then described.

21. The effect on saving of a change in import prices has been the subject of considerable debate in the literature on international trade; for a convenient summary see Johnson (1968), pp. 164–66.

22. Because income is exogenous the same formula applies for the elasticity of total saving with respect to food price.

Stochastic Specification

In the stochastic specification of ELES we treat the deterministic formulation (2.1) as reflecting the mean value of commodity expenditures conditional on given values of the exogenous variables, prices and income. Thus we append to (2.1) additive errors with zero means.[23] In general, variances and covariances of the error terms are assumed to be stationary.[24] This stochastic representation of ELES may be written as

$$(2.13) \qquad v_{it} = p_{it}\gamma_i + \beta_i^*(y_t - \sum_{j=1}^{n} p_{jt}\gamma_j) + e_{it}$$

$$(2.14) \quad E(e_t) = 0, E(e_t e_t') = \Omega, \text{ and } E(e_t e_{t'}') = 0, t \neq t'$$

where i denotes commodities ($i = 1, ..., n$), t denotes sample observations ($t = 1, ..., T$), e_t is a vector of error terms $(e_{1t}, ..., e_{nt})'$, and Ω is an $n \times n$ positive definite variance-covariance matrix of errors across equations (commodities). In addition, e_t is assumed to come from a multivariate normal distribution. In the context of a time series t represents time periods (years), and assumption (2.14) rules out serial correlation in the errors.[25] In a cross-section context t represents households, and (2.14) rules out correlation of the errors across consumers. The explanatory variables (p_{it}, y_t) are taken to be nonstochastic or, if stochastic, independent of e_{it}.

Summing (2.13) over commodities yields the stochastic counterpart of the ELES aggregate consumption function (2.2):

$$(2.15) \qquad v_t = (1 - \mu) \sum_{i=1}^{n} p_{it}\gamma_i + \mu y_t + \epsilon_t$$

where $\epsilon_t = \sum_{i=1}^{n} e_{it}$, $E(\epsilon_t) = 0$, $E(\epsilon_t^2) = \iota'\Omega\iota$, and ι is a vector of units.

23. In atemporal models such as LES, stochastic terms have sometimes been incorporated into the utility function (see Pollak and Wales, 1969; Barten, 1968). Byron (1974) has recently considered making stochastic the parameter restrictions which are implied by utility theory. Our stochastic formulation, apart from being simpler to estimate, seems more appropriate in view of the fact that (2.1) may be derived from alternative problem formulations.

24. The exception is chapter 8 where the error terms are assumed to possess these properties only after transformation of the variables.

25. The treatment of serial correlation is discussed in Lluch and Williams (1975a). For a thorough discussion of serial correlation in allocative models such as LES, see Berndt and Savin (1975).

In parameterizing the model the marginal propensity to consume, μ, is assumed to be constant over the sample data. If the intertemporal utility-maximizing interpretation of ELES is adopted, then constancy of μ implies constancy of the ratio of the subjective rate of discount to the rate of interest, that is, of δ/ρ. This would appear to be a valid assumption for our cross-section work, which considers only groups of homogeneous consumers at a given time. With time-series data, however, the rate of interest will vary. Thus to assume constancy of μ is to assume that δ varies proportionally with ρ. This assumption may produce a misspecification bias if the model is fitted for long periods, but the bias is likely to be less important for the relatively short periods considered in this analysis. In any event, our time-series results should be interpreted as pertaining to the sample mean values of δ/ρ.[26]

Following (2.13) and (2.14), the stochastic representation of LES (2.3) is written as

$$(2.16) \qquad v_{it} = p_{it}\gamma_i + \beta_i\left(v_t - \sum_{j=1}^{n} p_{jt}\gamma_j\right) + u_{it}$$

$$(2.17) \qquad E(u_t) = 0, E(u_t u_t') = \Lambda, \text{ and } E(u_t u_{t'}') = 0, t \neq t'$$

where $i = 1, ..., n; t,t' = 1, ..., T; u_t = (u_{1t}, ..., u_{nt})'$; and Λ is an $n \times n$ singular variance-covariance matrix of errors. Singularity of Λ follows from the property $\iota'u_t = 0$. Joint normality of the errors is again assumed.

In the first section of this chapter it was shown that deterministically ELES may be decomposed into LES and an aggregate consumption function. The stochastic version of LES obtained in this way is most easily seen by eliminating y_t from (2.13) and (2.15). The error term

---

26. Powell (1973a) estimated an ELES consumption function using U.S. annual data in which δ and ρ were estimated separately. The individual estimates of δ and ρ were very sensitive to model specification but the ratio of δ/ρ was relatively stable. Iacono (1976) has obtained similar findings in the context of ELES (and extensions) fitted to quarterly Australian data. An alternative parameterization is to make the rate of interest a variable and the subjective rate of discount a parameter to be estimated. Such an approach is adopted by Lluch (1974c). Using U.S. annual data for 1947–59 he finds that this parameterization improves the precision of the γ estimates compared with the parameterization which treats μ as a constant. Lluch finds differences in the point estimates of β and γ for durables, but overall fit is similar for the two models. A difficulty with this approach for developing countries lies in choosing an appropriate interest rate and obtaining time-series data.

on LES now becomes

(2.18) $u_{it} = e_{it} - \beta_i \epsilon_t$

for all i and t. If ELES (2.13) is the postulated model, equations (2.15) and (2.18) clearly imply that for LES there exists contemporaneous correlation between u_{it} and the stochastic explanatory variable v_t, that is,

$$\text{plim } T^{-1} \sum_{t=1}^{T} v_t u_{it} \neq 0 \quad (i = 1, ..., n).$$

Conventional maximum likelihood (ML) methods of estimation of LES would therefore not be appropriate. Thus there are statistical reasons for expecting the estimates of β and γ obtained using ELES (2.13) to differ from those obtained using LES (2.16).

The maintained hypothesis in this book is ELES. The parameter estimates reported are all obtained using this formulation, except for a few countries in chapter 3 where suitable time-series data on income were not available and LES estimates are given. In applications of ELES and LES to common sets of time-series data, ELES estimates were preferred, for reasons discussed in chapter 3. In cross-section work there are additional methodological reasons for preferring ELES which are discussed below.

Time-Series Estimation

Both ELES (2.13) and LES (2.16) involve cross-equation restrictions on the parameters; in both cases all the γ_i occur in all equations. The demand systems must be estimated as a whole by methods which impose the cross-equation constraints. The procedure followed is direct maximization of the likelihood functions associated with the systems (2.13) and (2.16). In the case of ELES, the logarithm of the likelihood function may be written as

(2.19) $L(e; \beta^*, \gamma, \Omega) = -\dfrac{nT}{2} \ln 2\pi - \dfrac{T}{2} \ln|\Omega| - \dfrac{1}{2} \sum_{t=1}^{T} e_t' \Omega^{-1} e_t.$

In the case of LES, an attempt to use (2.19) to write down the corresponding likelihood function would involve replacing β^*, e_t, and Ω^{-1} by β, u_t, and Λ^{-1} respectively. Such a function is not defined, however, since Λ is a singular matrix: $\iota' u_t = 0$ and $\iota' \Lambda = 0$. A number of authors have shown that the solution is to omit one equation (results being invariant to the equation dropped) and use the constraint $\sum_i \beta_i = 1$ to obtain the β estimate for the excluded equation.[27] Thus if LES is the maintained hypothesis, the log-likelihood function to be maximized is

$$(2.20) \quad \tilde{L}(\tilde{u}; \tilde{\beta}, \gamma, \tilde{\Lambda}) = \frac{(n-1)T}{2} ln2\pi - \frac{T}{2} ln|\tilde{\Lambda}| - \frac{1}{2} \sum_{t=1}^{T} \tilde{u}_t'\tilde{\Lambda}^{-1}\tilde{u}_t$$

where a tilde denotes deletion of entries for the nth equation; $\tilde{u}$ and $\tilde{\beta}$ are $n-1$ vectors and $\tilde{\Lambda}$ is an $(n-1) \times (n-1)$ symmetric matrix of error covariances.

The maximum likelihood estimates of β^*, γ, and Ω are those which maximize (2.19); the ML estimates of $\tilde{\beta}$, γ, and $\tilde{\Lambda}$ are those which maximize (2.20). The log-likelihood functions (2.19) and (2.20) are nonlinear in the parameters and were maximized using the modified Gauss-Newton method with analytical derivatives. The basic program used was the general nonlinear extremization package written by Bard (1967).[28]

In this way maximum likelihood estimates of β^* and γ are obtained for ELES and of β and γ for LES. Under ELES, ML estimates of μ and β are obtained from the relationships

$$(2.21) \quad \mu = \sum_{j=1}^{n} \beta_j^*$$

$$(2.22) \quad \beta_i = \beta_i^*/ \sum_{j=1}^{n} \beta_j^* = \beta_i^*/\mu \quad (i = 1, ..., n).$$

Asymptotic estimates of the variance-covariance matrices of estimated parameters in (2.13) and (2.16) were obtained from the Hessian of the log-likelihood function evaluated at estimated parameter values.[29]

27. See Barten (1969), Parks (1969, 1971), Powell (1969), Solari (1969, 1971), and Deaton (1975). The problem is common to demand systems in which total expenditure, rather than income, is exogenous and the budget constraint holds exactly at all observations.

28. In earlier work (see Lluch and Powell, 1975), LES estimates were obtained using LINEX, a LES specific program written by Carlevaro and Rossier (1970). The method used follows that of Solari (1969) and is similar to that of Parks (1971). In test runs LES parameter estimates obtained using Bard's program and LINEX were the same to five significant figures. There was some tendency for the standard errors of parameters to be a little smaller using Bard's method (of the order of 2 to 5 percent) owing to a slightly different specification of the Hessian. Although the likelihood functions for LES and ELES are virtually isomorphic (see Powell, 1974, pp. 123–24), they are sufficiently different to prevent the use of LINEX for the estimation of ELES.

29. See, for example, Dhrymes (1970), pp. 133–36. The procedure is spelled out in detail for LES in Parks (1971) and Deaton (1975).

For ELES, let $\Sigma_{\beta^*\beta^*}$, $\Sigma_{\beta^*\gamma}$, and $\Sigma_{\gamma\gamma}$ denote the asymptotic variance-covariance matrices of order n for the (β^*, γ) estimates. The $(2n + 1)$ asymptotic variance-covariance matrix of the (μ, β, γ) estimates is then given by

$$
\begin{bmatrix}
\iota'\Sigma_{\beta^*\beta^*}\iota & \mu^{-1}\iota'\Sigma_{\beta^*\beta^*}J' & \iota'\Sigma_{\beta^*\gamma} \\
 & -\mu^{-2}J\Sigma_{\beta^*\beta^*}J' & \mu^{-1}J\Sigma_{\beta^*\gamma} \\
 & & \Sigma_{\gamma\gamma}
\end{bmatrix}
$$

where $J = (I - \beta\iota')$, and I is an $n \times n$ unit matrix.[30]

For LES, the variance of the omitted element of β, β_n, is obtained from var $\hat{\beta}_n = \iota' \Sigma_{\tilde{\beta},\tilde{\beta}}\iota$ where the hat ($\hat{\ }$) denotes estimated value and $\Sigma_{\tilde{\beta},\tilde{\beta}}$ is the $(n - 1)$ asymptotic variance-covariance matrix for the $\tilde{\beta}$ estimate.

In situations where the nonlinear procedure did not converge, ELES estimates were obtained by ruling out contemporaneous covariances in the errors and assuming homoscedasticity across equations, that is, we assume

$$(2.23) \qquad E(e_t e_t') = \Omega = \sigma_e^2 I.$$

In the case of LES estimates we assume

$$(2.24) \qquad E(\tilde{u}_t \tilde{u}_t') = \tilde{\Lambda} = \sigma_u^2 I.$$

These procedures amount to a systems least squares (LS) approach and are in the tradition of earlier empirical work using LES.[31]

Cross-Section Estimation with Price Variation

In a given economy at a given time, different consumers may pay different prices for the same goods. Regional differences may exist, for example, in the price of food or housing. Subgroups of consumers, however, are likely to face the same or very similar prices. The model

---

30. For the relevant asymptotic expression, see, for example, Goldberger (1964), p. 125.

31. See Stone (1954) and Goldberger and Gamaletsos (1970). We estimate LES by systems least squares in a manner which permits a ML interpretation and therefore direct calculation of standard errors of parameters (see Parks, 1971). The difficulty with the ML interpretation is that since $\iota' u_t = 0$, theoretically all covariances cannot be zero. Specification (2.24) implies that the relationship $\iota'\Lambda = 0$ is preserved through nonzero covariances in the last row and column of Λ. The parameter estimates we report for LES, LS, in chapter 3 are the same as those obtained using the least squares option of LINEX, except for some small changes in the γ estimates for the Philippines.

estimated in chapter 5 assumes that households in the sample can be divided into nine regional groupings. Within each group all households are assumed to face identical prices, but among groups relative price differentials are used. Thus for this application ELES (2.13) may be written as

$$(2.25) \qquad v_{ih} = p_{ih_g}\gamma_i + \beta^*_i(y_h - \sum_{j=1}^{n} p_{jh_g}\gamma_j) + e_{ih}$$

where i denotes commodities $(i = 1, ..., n)$, h denotes households $(h = 1, ..., H)$, g denotes regions $(g = 1, ..., G)$, and $p_{ih_g} = p_{ig}$ for all $h_{\epsilon}g$ $(i = 1, ..., n)$.[32] Since all error covariances across households are already ruled out, the error specification (2.14) is unchanged,[33] as are the estimation methods for ELES described in the preceding section.

Cross-Section Estimation in Absence of Price Data

As explained above, ELES enables all price elasticities to be estimated in the absence of price data.[34] The assumption that all consumers face identical prices is required, however, and for this reason we restrict estimation to groups of households where this assumption is not likely to be grossly violated. In particular, we do not pool data for urban and rural households.

Under the assumption that $p_{ih} = p_i$ $(i = 1, ..., n)$, where i denotes goods and h households, the $p_i\gamma_i$ terms become independent of the unit of observation and may be replaced by γ^*_i $(i = 1, ..., n)$, where γ^*_i measures subsistence expenditure in prices prevailing at the time of the household survey. It should be noted that in comparing γ^* values across different groups of consumers, for example rural and urban, at a given time, the estimates will reflect any differences in prices paid by the various groups.

ELES (2.13) may now be written as

$$(2.26) \qquad v_{ih} = \alpha_i + \beta^*_i y_h + e_{ih}$$

32. LES could be rewritten in a similar manner but it is not estimated.
33. Replacing the subscript t by h.
34. The estimation of ELES from household budget data was first implemented by Belandria (1971); theoretical aspects of the procedure were systematized by Powell (1973b, 1974). Further contributions have been made by Betancourt (see chapter 8) and Howe and Musgrove (see chapter 7).

where $i = 1, ..., n$ goods; $h = 1, ..., H$ households;[35] and

$$\alpha_i = \gamma_i^* - \beta_i^* \sum_{j=1}^{n} \gamma_j^*.$$

The error specification remains classical, that is, (2.14) with h replacing t as a subscript.

The associated ELES aggregate consumption function is

$$(2.27) \qquad\qquad v_h = \alpha + \mu y_h + \epsilon_h$$

where $\alpha = \sum_{i=1}^{n} \alpha_i = (1-\mu) \sum_{i=1}^{n} \gamma_i^*$ and $\epsilon_h = \sum_{i=1}^{n} e_{ih}$.

Elimination of y_h from (2.26) and (2.27) yields LES:

$$(2.28) \qquad\qquad v_{ih} = \alpha_i' + \beta_i v_h + u_{ih}$$

where $\alpha_i' = \alpha_i - \beta_i \alpha = \gamma_i^* - \beta_i \Sigma \gamma_j^*$ and $u_{ih} = e_{ih} - \beta_i \epsilon_h$.

The system (2.26) is one of identical regressors in which every left-hand variable is regressed on the same set of exogenous variables. It follows that estimation of each of its equations by ordinary least squares (OLS), commodity by commodity, is equivalent to systems maximum likelihood estimation.[36]

Maximum likelihood estimates of β_i $(i = 1, ..., n)$ and μ are obtained from the estimates of β_i^* using (2.21) and (2.22);[37] ML estimates of γ^* and $\Sigma \gamma_i^*$ are obtained from α_i and β_i^* using the following relationships:[38]

$$(2.29) \qquad \sum_{i=1}^{n} \gamma_i^* = (1 - \sum_{i=1}^{n} \beta_i^*)^{-1} \sum_{i=1}^{n} \alpha_i = (1 - \mu)^{-1} \sum_{i=1}^{n} \alpha_i$$

$$(2.30) \qquad \gamma_i^* = \alpha_i + [\beta_i^*(1 - \sum_{j=1}^{n} \beta_j^*)^{-1} \sum_{j=1}^{n} \alpha_j] = \alpha_i + \beta_i^* \sum_{j=1}^{n} \gamma_j^*.$$

35. The elasticity formulas in table 2.2 should also be reparameterized by replacing $p_i \gamma_i$ with γ_i^*.

36. Retaining the assumption that the e_{ih} are joint normally distributed. On all this see Zellner (1962); Goldberger (1964), pp. 207–12; and Dhrymes (1970), pp. 153–61.

37. This μ estimate is identical to that obtained from estimating (2.27) by OLS.

38. Under LES it is not possible to unscramble estimates of the individual γ_i^*.

The $2n$ variance-covariance matrix of $(\hat{\alpha}, \hat{\beta}^*)$, which will be denoted by Σ_{α,β^*}, is obtained from

$$(2.31) \qquad \Omega \otimes (X'X)^{-1}$$

after appropriate rearrangement of the rows and columns, where X is the $H \times 2$ matrix of explanatory variables in (2.26) and $\otimes$ denotes the Kronecker product. The elements, σ_{ij}, of the error variance-covariance matrix Ω are estimated as

$$\hat{\sigma}_{ij} = (H - 2)^{-1} \sum_{h=1}^{H} \hat{e}_{ih}\hat{e}_{jh} \qquad (i, j = 1, ..., n)$$

where $\hat{e}$ denotes estimated residuals from (2.26). The asymptotic variance-covariance matrices of order n for $\hat{\beta}$ and $\hat{\gamma}^*$ are given by

$$\Sigma_{\beta,\beta} = \mu^{-2}(I - \beta\iota') \Sigma_{\beta^*,\beta^*} (I - \iota\beta')$$

and

$$\Sigma_{\gamma^*,\gamma^*} = (N|\iota'\gamma^*N) \Sigma_{\alpha,\beta^*}\left(\frac{N'}{\iota'\gamma^*N'}\right)$$

where Σ_{β^*,β^*} is the $(n \times n)$ variance-covariance matrix for $\hat{\beta}^*$ and $N = [I + (1 - \mu)^{-1}\beta^*\iota']$. It follows that var $\hat{\mu} = \iota'\,\Sigma_{\beta^*,\beta^*}\iota$, and var $\Sigma\hat{\gamma}_i^* = \iota'\,\Sigma_{\gamma^*,\gamma^*}\iota$. The variances of $\hat{\mu}$ and $\Sigma\hat{\gamma}_i^*$ may also be obtained from ordinary least squares estimation of the aggregate consumption function (2.27). The two methods yield identical estimates of the variances.

In some empirical work we ignore covariances across equations (commodities) and assume that Ω in (2.31) is diagonal. The variances across equations are, however, allowed to differ. That is, we assume

$$(2.32) \qquad E(e_{ih}e_{jh}) \begin{array}{ll} = \sigma_i & i = j. \\ = 0 & i \neq j. \end{array}$$

In this case the matric Σ_{β^*,β^*} is diagonal. The estimated variances of the estimates of μ and $\Sigma\gamma_i$ are no longer identical with those obtained from OLS estimation of (2.27).

The basic cross-section equations (2.26) are, of course, linear Engel curves with income as the explanatory variable. There has been considerable discussion in the literature as to how the parameters of Engel curves should be estimated to avoid bias. Summers' (1959, p. 121) starting point is that "In estimating the parameters of Engel curves, the assumption is made universally that a household's expenditure on the goods and services in its budget depend upon its income (and possibly other variables), but that its income does not depend upon its expenditures." He then proceeds to formulate an $(n + 2)$ simultaneous equation model, which is formally equivalent to our equations (2.26) and (2.27) plus the identity $v = \Sigma v_i$. Using the arguments outlined by us in the section on stochastic specification above, he shows that ordinary least squares estimates of Engel curves with total expenditure as the explanatory variable (our equation 2.28) will yield parameter estimates which are biased and inconsistent.[39] In our terminology, ELES is the maintained hypothesis, from which it follows that LES estimates are biased.

It is also argued, however, that measured or recorded income is not the appropriate income variable to use in cross-section analysis.[40] These arguments all reduce to one of errors in variables, whether they be based on the inaccuracy of household responses or failure to take account of normal or permanent income.

To overcome the problem of errors in variables, Liviatan (1961) proposed that consistent estimates of marginal budget shares be obtained by estimating Engel curves, with total expenditure as the explanatory variable, using the method of instrumental variables with measured income as the instrument. But this method is identical to our own, which estimates the β_i^* from Engel curves, with income as the explanatory variable, and μ from the aggregate consumption function,[41] and then divides to obtain estimates of β_i. More formally,

$$\hat{\beta}_i = \frac{\sum_h v_{ih} y_h}{\sum_h v_h y_h} = \frac{\sum_h v_{ih} y_h}{\sum_h y_h^2} \bigg/ \frac{\sum_h v_h y_h}{\sum_h y_h^2} = \hat{\beta}_i^* / \hat{\mu}$$

where the expression after the first equality sign is Liviatan's instrumental variable estimator of β_i and the next expression corresponds to our method (all variables are now assumed to be deviated from sample means). This provides a strong reason for concentrating on estimates of β_i rather than β_i^* in presenting results. Of course the

39. Summers' article was a response to the classic work of Prais and Houthakker (1955). The latter were aware of such biases but deemed them to be relatively unimportant (p. 63). Prais (1959) subsequently showed that the biases average out over commodities; Powell (1973a) has derived a similar result in the context of ELES and LES and worked out expressions for biases on individual β_i.

40. See, for example, Friedman (1957), Prais and Houthakker (1955), Liviatan (1961, 1964).

41. Recall that this is equivalent to using $\hat{\mu} = \sum_i \hat{\beta}_i^*$.

argument regarding errors in variables still applies to estimates of μ, and in the text we endeavor to point out where biases may be important. Similarly, the presence of errors in variables implies the existence of biases in the estimates of the γ_i, which should be borne in mind when considering estimates of price elasticities.[42]

42. In chapters 7 and 8 some comparisons are made with model estimates obtained by directly introducing considerations of permanent income into the definition of income used as the explanatory variable in ELES.

3

International Patterns in Demand Parameters and Elasticities: Evidence from the National Accounts

As THE STARTING POINT for our empirical investigation we examine the demand and savings behavior of the representative consumer for each of seventeen countries spanning the development spectrum. To this effect we fit LES and ELES to aggregate national accounts data for each country. Attention is focused on how marginal budget shares and the expenditure and price elasticities vary with the level of GNP per capita.

Data Considerations

In order for intercountry comparisons of demand and savings behavior to be useful for broad characterizations of the development process, it is necessary to include countries at all levels of economic development. Previous international comparisons using time-series data have focused exclusively either on developed countries (Houthakker 1965; Goldberger and Gamaletsos, 1970; Parks and Barten, 1973) or on developing countries (Weisskoff, 1971).

The basic data requirements for estimating models (2.13) and (2.16) are national accounts estimates in current and constant prices (in order to derive implicit price indexes) at the chosen eight-commodity level of aggregation (see table 3.1). In addition, personal

Table 3.1.   *Classification of Eight Commodities*
Used in Time-Series Analysis

Commodity number	Commodity title used in text	Commodities in UN national accounts statistics[a]
1	Food	Food, beverages, and tobacco
2	Clothing	Clothing and other personal effects
3	Housing	Household operation, rent, water, fuel, and light
4	Durables	Furniture, furnishings, and household equipment
5	Personal care	Personal care and health expenses
6	Transport	Transport and communication
7	Recreation	Recreation and entertainment
8	Other services	Miscellaneous services (financial services, education and research, and other)

a. The definitions used are those given in the United Nations, *Yearbook of National Accounts Statistics* (1969). In the data for West Germany and Taiwan, commodities 3 and 4 are combined. Motor vehicles are included in transport, and meals away from home are included in recreation.

disposable income data is required for ELES estimation.[1] The data must be available for a sufficient number of years to permit econometric estimation. The basic data source was the United Nations *Yearbook of National Accounts Statistics*, supplemented where necessary by national accounts publications of individual countries.[2]

Initially twenty-one countries were selected which satisfied the above requirements and provided a reasonably even spread over the development spectrum. Two of these were subsequently found to exhibit hidden data peculiarities: Budget shares remained constant over the sample in Peru,[3] and implicit price indexes were the same for each good in Ecuador.[4] Estimation problems led to dropping

1. In the empirical work presented in this chapter, permanent and measured income are assumed to be the same; in the context of Lluch (1973a) the present value of expected changes in labor income is zero. In chapter 4 we present results for Taiwan in which four different measures of permanent income are used. ELES estimates are similar in all cases.

2. Population figures were obtained from UN *Demographic Yearbook* and International Monetary Fund (IMF), *International Financial Statistics, 1972 Supplement.*

3. Yielding expenditure elasticities of unity, own-price elasticities of minus one, and zero cross-price elasticities—a heaven for believers in Cobb-Douglas utility functions.

4. The price indexes for the Philippines also show very little differential variation, and model estimates should be treated with due care.

Table 3.2. Characteristics of the Sample of Seventeen Countries

Country (1)	Sample period (2)	Sample midpoint (3)	National currency unit (NCU) (4)	Per capita GNP at midpoint of sample period in 1970 U.S. dollars[a] (5)	Per capita personal disposable income at midpoint of sample period		Per capita private consumption at midpoint of sample period		Implicit conversion ratio between NCU at sample midpoint and 1970 U.S. dollars (NCU per U.S. dollar)[c] (10)
					NCU's[b] (6)	1970 U.S. dollars (7)	NCU's[b] (8)	1970 U.S. dollars (9)	
Korea	1955–68	1962	Won	142	108[e]	115	112[e]	120	0.9366[e]
Thailand	1960–69	1964	Baht	148	1,952	115	1,729	102	16.96
Philippines	1953–65[d]	1961	Peso	161	—	—	407	125	3.248
Taiwan	1955–68	1962	New Taiwan dollar	216	4,598	146	5,099	162	31.50
Jamaica	1959–68	1964	Jamaican dollar	541	273	436	271	432	0.6266
Panama	1960–68	1964	Balboa	564	—	—	390	447	0.8723
South Africa	1955–68	1962	Rand	596	260	461	226	401	0.5637
Greece	1958–68	1963	Drachma	676	13,883	564	12,325	501	24.61
Ireland	1955–68	1962	Irish pound	1,014	220	564	209	779	0.2682
Puerto Rico	1955–67	1961	U.S. dollar	1,023	220	820	683	828	0.8250
Italy	1955–68	1962	Lira	1,207	4,124[e]	916	3,520[e]	782	4.503[e]
Israel	1959–68	1964	Israeli pound	1,468	2,917	1,228	2,513	1,058	2.376
United Kingdom	1955–68	1962	Pound	1,900	379	1,331	352	1,236	0.2847
Australia	1955–66	1961	Australian dollar	2,192	1,015	1,622	932	1,489	0.6259
West Germany	1955–68	1962	Deutsche mark	2,203	4,229	1,474	3,665	1,277	2.870
Sweden	1955–68	1962	Krona	2,962	7,023	1,956	6,083	1,694	3.590
United States	1955–68	1962	U.S. dollar	3,669	2,030	2,481	1,840	2,249	0.8182

— Data unavailable or unsatisfactory.

a. Per capita GNP for 1970 as reported in *World Bank Atlas 1972*, projected backward to sample midpoints using growth rates from the same source.

b. *Sources:* UN *Yearbook of National Accounts Statistics, National Accounts of OECD countries, 1953–69*, and country national accounts.

c. Per capita GNP in NCU's at sample midpoint divided by column 5. *Source:* International Monetary Fund, *International Financial Statistics, 1972 Supplement*. Column 10 is used to derive columns 7 and 9.

d. Years 1954, 1956, 1957, 1959 omitted.

e. 10^3 NCU's.

Sri Lanka and Chile from the sample.[5] We thus report results for seventeen countries, which are listed in table 3.2 together with general characteristics of the data. The mean values of average budget shares are given in table 3.3, changes in average budget shares in table 3.4, and price and income movements over sample periods in table 3.5. Suitable income data is available in thirteen cases.[6] The countries are listed in order of GNP per capita at sample midpoints in 1970 U.S. dollars. The level of per capita GNP covered by the data ranges from about $150 (Korea and Thailand) to near $4,000 (United States). Table 3.2 also contains per capita estimates of total consumption expenditure and personal disposable income at sample midpoints in both national currencies and 1970 U.S. dollars. There are of course well-known difficulties involved in converting values to a common currency unit,[7] but here it is done for broad illustrative purposes and as an aid in the interpretation of results. The models themselves are always fitted separately for each country with data expressed in the national currency. In the majority of cases the period of estimation is 1955–68, giving fourteen observations. All the low-income countries are located in East Asia, a limitation in coverage that should always be borne in mind when making comparisons of demand (and savings) behavior at different income levels.

Parameter Estimates

For the fourteen countries in table 3.2 for which personal income data exists, ELES (2.13) was fitted to national accounts data on per capita expenditures, per capita personal disposable income, and (implicit) prices using an eight-commodity breakdown.[8] The results ob-

5. LES estimates for Sri Lanka failed to converge; those for Chile were obtained only for least squares, which produced extreme outliers for the γ estimates and a supernumerary ratio greater than one (see Lluch and Powell, 1975). Data limitations prevented ELES estimation in both cases.
6. Income data is available for Panama, but personal saving was found to be negative in each year of the sample period. Because of concerns about the data it was decided to estimate only LES.
7. See, for example, the interchange between Balassa (1973, 1974) and David (1972, 1973).
8. In Lluch and Williams (1975c) the estimates obtained on fitting ELES are compared with LES estimates for the same or similar data. The two models lead to similar levels of overall fit (as measured by R^2) and similar estimates of the marginal budget shares, β_i, but ELES yielded γ estimates which were theoretically more acceptable (standard errors were roughly comparable). For these reasons we limit results to ELES, which in addition to estimates of β and γ give insight into savings behavior. The detailed LES results are available in Lluch and Powell (1975).

Table 3.3. *Average Budget Shares at Sample Mean Values*

Country	Sample period	Commodity							
		Food	Clothing	Housing	Durables	Personal care	Transport	Recreation	Other services
Korea	1955–68	0.599	0.104	0.114	0.028	0.042	0.047	0.044	0.022
Thailand	1960–69	0.576	0.084	0.080	0.032	0.056	0.079	0.075	0.018
Philippines	1953–65[a]	0.598	0.074	0.147	0.020	0.035	0.023	0.018	0.084
Taiwan	1955–68	0.563	0.055	0.183		0.057	0.018	0.026	0.097
Jamaica	1959–68	0.433	0.107	0.145	0.060	0.026	0.106	0.074	0.049
Panama	1960–68	0.455	0.074	0.167	0.064	0.047	0.094	0.075	0.023
South Africa	1955–68	0.368	0.118	0.167	0.078	0.048	0.132	0.047	0.041
Greece	1958–68	0.468	0.122	0.183	0.039	0.036	0.069	0.061	0.023
Ireland	1955–68	0.492	0.100	0.128	0.057	0.013	0.088	0.063	0.059
Puerto Rico	1955–67	0.356	0.106	0.153	0.069	0.069	0.123	0.088	0.037
Italy	1955–68	0.463	0.101	0.166	0.032	0.063	0.081	0.075	0.018
Israel	1959–68	0.319	0.094	0.192	0.074	0.066	0.073	0.081	0.100
United Kingdom	1955–68	0.397	0.107	0.183	0.066	0.023	0.109	0.075	0.040
Australia	1955–66	0.333	0.110	0.127	0.078	0.057	0.131	0.043	0.121
West Germany	1955–68	0.366	0.123	0.263		0.037	0.080	0.077	0.054
Sweden	1955–68	0.366	0.115	0.159	0.070	0.037	0.142	0.089	0.024
United States	1955–68	0.267	0.095	0.227	0.073	0.081	0.152	0.055	0.049

a. Excluding 1954, 1956, 1957, 1959.

40

Table 3.4. Changes in Average Budget Shares over the Sample Period

Country	Sample period	Commodity							
		Food	Clothing	Housing	Durables	Personal care	Transport	Recreation	Other services
Korea	1955–68	0.883	1.128	0.710	1.524	2.040	2.857	1.560	1.287
Thailand	1960–69	1.015	1.025	0.543	1.347	0.983	1.133	1.288	1.428
Philippines	1953–65	0.920	0.961	1.143	1.176	1.129	1.368	1.125	1.260
Taiwan	1955–68	0.870	0.841		1.184	1.290	1.923	1.186	1.303
Jamaica	1959–68	0.862	1.169	1.037	1.270	1.190	1.020	1.039	1.577
Panama	1960–68	1.046	0.987	0.885	1.100	1.067	0.857	1.114	0.913
South Africa	1955–68	0.929	0.825	1.025	0.955	1.269	1.270	0.978	1.295
Greece	1958–68	0.912	1.160	0.995	0.947	1.054	1.375	1.106	0.955
Ireland	1955–68	0.882	0.963	1.058	1.466	0.769	1.366	1.182	1.089
Puerto Rico	1955–67	0.745	1.070	0.968	1.061	1.328	1.385	1.485	1.533
Italy	1955–68	0.863	0.883	1.070	1.081	1.377	1.680	1.082	1.126
Israel	1959–68	0.791	0.951	1.109	1.148	1.031	1.600	1.250	1.029
United Kingdom	1955–68	0.807	0.852	1.182	0.925	1.210	1.494	1.084	1.893
Australia	1955–66	0.883	0.786	1.388	0.935	1.392	1.097	0.875	1.077
West Germany	1955–68	0.781	0.837		1.223	1.243	1.349	1.111	1.538
Sweden	1955–68	0.900	0.740	1.039	1.097	1.322	1.377	1.022	1.200
United States	1955–68	0.821	0.960	1.019	0.987	1.400	0.994	1.118	1.594

Note: Ratio of average budget shares in last year of sample to the one in first year of sample.

Table 3.5. Changes in Implicit Price Deflators and Income over the Sample Period

Country	Sample period	Prices									Income	
		Food	Clothing	Housing	Durables	Personal care	Transport	Recreation	Other services	Total	Money	Real
Korea	1955–68	5.617	6.802	4.329	5.102	8.771	5.208	6.097	6.849	5.707	8.187	1.435
Thailand	1960–69	1.338	1.017	0.789	0.863	1.127	1.005	1.245	1.199	1.183	1.599	1.351
Philippines	1953–65	1.416	1.419	1.415	1.418	1.420	1.411	1.401	1.417	1.416	1.678[a]	1.185[a]
Taiwan	1955–68	2.087	1.310	1.865		1.531	1.805	1.642	1.347	1.901	3.461	1.821
Jamaica	1959–68	1.303	1.210	1.633	1.002	1.261	1.044	0.750	1.912	1.235	1.609	1.302
Panama	1960–68	1.169	1.048	1.044	1.009	1.196	1.033	1.081	1.000	1.169	1.375[a]	1.176[a]
South Africa	1955–68	1.344	1.027	1.577	1.042	1.661	1.366	1.383	1.555	1.327	1.657	1.249
Greece	1958–68	1.293	1.127	1.172	1.069	1.282	1.206	1.057	1.071	1.207	2.144	1.776
Ireland	1955–68	1.512	1.122	1.677	1.506	1.189	1.503	1.602	1.736	1.495	2.198	1.470
Puerto Rico	1955–67	1.369	1.189	1.165	1.105	1.995	1.330	1.468	1.343	1.369	1.777[a]	1.298[a]
Italy	1955–68	1.388	1.326	1.607	0.979	1.736	1.344	1.697	1.724	1.449	2.737	1.889
Israel	1959–68	1.547	1.519	2.020	1.191	1.788	2.066	1.712	1.915	1.681	2.965	1.764
United Kingdom	1955–68	1.315	1.248	1.838	1.246	1.494	1.464	1.824	1.639	1.484	2.011	1.355
Australia	1955–66	1.291	1.165	1.709	1.054	1.414	1.240	1.379	1.394	1.316	1.593	1.211
West Germany	1955–68	1.248	1.298	1.524		1.533	1.168	1.349	1.706	1.360	2.432	1.788
Sweden	1955–68	1.683	1.340	1.650	1.262	1.449	1.569	1.730	1.618	1.574	2.276	1.446
United States	1955–68	1.272	1.234	1.248	1.074	1.485	1.219	1.358	1.751	1.275	1.761	1.381

Note: Ratio of implicit price deflators and per capita personal disposable income in last year of sample to first year of sample.

a. Per capita total consumption expenditure.

42

tained in this manner are supplemented by LES estimates for the three countries (Panama, Puerto Rico, and Philippines) in which suitable income data are not available.

Table 3.6 contains estimates of the marginal propensity to consume, μ, and marginal budget shares, β_i, together with estimates of their asymptotic standard errors. The method of estimation is given in each case; systems least squares results (LS) imply that full ML estimation failed to converge. Estimates of the γ parameters and associated standard errors are given in table 3.7. The units of measurement are national currencies at base-year prices. In table 3.8 these values are converted to 1970 U.S. dollars by using sample midpoint prices and the conversion ratios given in table 3.2.

Overall fit is high, as is to be expected from time-series data: The values of the coefficient of determination, R^2, exceed 0.95 in 103 of the 134 equations (see table 3.9).[9] Values of the Durbin-Watson d statistic, however, show fairly marked positive first-order serial correlation in the residuals of individual equations, and reported standard errors should be interpreted with due care.[10] Serial correlation is less marked on the equations for food and clothing (mean value of d is 1.4 in each case) and most pronounced in the case of personal care and other services (mean d values are around 0.9). Detailed results are given in table 3.10.

Estimates of the marginal propensity to consume range from 0.58 (Israel) to 0.93 (Korea); all are less than unity; all have relatively small standard errors. The values do not appear to move in any systematic way with GNP per capita. There is some evidence that the marginal propensity to save out of current income is higher in those countries with higher rates of growth in income. The rank correlation

9. Calculated as $R^2 = 1 - [\sum_t \hat{u}_{it}^2 / \sum_t (v_{it} - \bar{v}_i)^2]$ where $\hat{u}$ denotes residuals from expenditure equations. It is to be interpreted solely as a descriptive indicator of goodness of fit.

10. Again, the d statistic in this context is a descriptive indicator with unknown statistical properties. While LES and ELES tend to yield very similar d values, it has been shown in Lluch and Williams (1975a) that, for U.S. data at least, allowance for serial correlation does not substantially affect the point estimates obtained using ELES, but it affects LES estimates markedly.

Another form of potential error misspecification is the assumption of constant error variances over time, particularly as the dependent variables are in current prices. Two sets of ELES estimates obtained for Korea using data for 1963–72 in both current and real values yielded remarkably similar results for both parameter estimates and standard errors (the current price results are contained in table 5.15). This result is noteworthy in that the ratio of the consumer price index at sample end to sample beginning was 3.35 (compare table 3.5).

Table 3.6. Estimated Marginal Propensity to Consume (μ) and Marginal Budget Shares (β_i)

Country	Type of estimate[a]	μ	Food	Clothing	Housing	Durables	Personal care	Transport	Recreation	Other services
Korea	ELES, ML	0.928 (0.028)	0.434 (0.024)	0.069 (0.011)	0.085 (0.010)	0.077 (0.006)	0.074 (0.009)	0.146 (0.007)	0.078 (0.005)	0.038 (0.005)
Thailand	ELES, LS	0.759 (0.035)	0.482 (0.027)	0.101 (0.014)	0.013 (0.001)	0.052 (0.001)	0.052 (0.017)	0.123 (0.014)	0.150 (0.020)	0.028 (0.018)
Philippines	LES, LS	— —	0.311 (0.019)	0.055 (0.019)	0.267 (0.019)	0.044 (0.019)	0.060 (0.019)	0.056 (0.019)	0.030 (0.019)	0.176 (0.050)
Taiwan	ELES, ML	0.667 (0.011)	0.317 (0.017)	0.069 (0.015)	0.244 (0.009)		0.097 (0.009)	0.051 (0.003)	0.046 (0.002)	0.176 (0.007)
Jamaica	ELES, LS	0.922 (0.018)	0.249 (0.036)	0.208 (0.031)	0.103 (0.057)	0.159 (0.023)	0.060 (0.027)	0.161 (0.024)	0.150 (0.023)	−0.090 (0.067)
Panama	LES, LS	— —	0.418 (0.023)	0.081 (0.018)	0.113 (0.017)	0.113 (0.017)	0.044 (0.021)	0.085 (0.016)	0.127 (0.019)	0.019 (0.039)
South Africa	ELES, ML	0.621 (0.083)	0.295 (0.036)	0.164 (0.025)	0.066 (0.013)	0.115 (0.030)	0.049 (0.013)	0.206 (0.049)	0.046 (0.006)	0.059 (0.011)

Marginal budget share (β) (spanning header over Food through Other services)

Country	Model									
Greece	ELES, LS	0.810 (0.051)	0.341 (0.028)	0.168 (0.006)	0.175 (0.007)	0.050 (0.007)	0.048 (0.011)	0.107 (0.009)	0.083 (0.005)	0.028 (0.007)
Ireland	ELES, ML	0.846 (0.018)	0.315 (0.011)	0.134 (0.007)	0.108 (0.005)	0.114 (0.005)	0.014 (0.002)	0.170 (0.007)	0.075 (0.005)	0.070 (0.007)
Puerto Rico	LES, ML	— —	0.177 (0.009)	0.112 (0.004)	0.144 (0.004)	0.068 (0.004)	0.114 (0.007)	0.176 (0.007)	0.137 (0.004)	0.072 (0.004)
Italy	ELES, ML	0.790 (0.034)	0.401 (0.017)	0.087 (0.005)	0.171 (0.018)	0.069 (0.019)	0.066 (0.025)	0.117 (0.016)	0.070 (0.010)	0.019 (0.003)
Israel	ELES, LS	0.577 (0.020)	0.210 (0.011)	0.103 (0.011)	0.172 (0.014)	0.119 (0.010)	0.066 (0.013)	0.116 (0.014)	0.117 (0.013)	0.097 (0.014)
United Kingdom	ELES, ML	0.890 (0.011)	0.120 (0.016)	0.067 (0.007)	0.258 (0.039)	0.076 (0.017)	0.030 (0.003)	0.277 (0.011)	0.066 (0.010)	0.106 (0.020)
Australia	ELES, LS	0.796 (0.021)	0.143 (0.011)	0.050 (0.010)	0.220 (0.024)	0.082 (0.009)	0.133 (0.013)	0.224 (0.011)	0.009 (0.012)	0.138 (0.013)
West Germany	ELES, ML	0.807 (0.014)	0.243 (0.018)	0.096 (0.006)	0.321 (0.016)		0.045 (0.003)	0.116 (0.003)	0.085 (0.001)	0.094 (0.007)
Sweden	ELES, ML	0.810 (0.004)	0.278 (0.027)	0.071 (0.014)	0.145 (0.014)	0.079 (0.007)	0.052 (0.005)	0.253 (0.014)	0.097 (0.014)	0.024 (0.008)
United States	ELES, ML	0.836 (0.025)	0.090 (0.008)	0.108 (0.007)	0.206 (0.014)	0.106 (0.009)	0.137 (0.013)	0.174 (0.011)	0.065 (0.003)	0.113 (0.015)

45

a. LS: least squares; ML: maximum likelihood.

— Parameter does not occur in model.
Note: Asymptotic standard errors are given in parentheses.

Table 3.7. *Estimated Subsistence Minimums* (γ_i)

Country	Base year	Food	Clothing	Housing	Durables	Personal care	Transport	Recreation	Other services	Sum of γ_i
Korea	1965	130.5 (1.5)	22.8 (0.6)	21.0 (0.6)	3.9 (0.5)	7.6 (0.5)	4.3 (0.4)	7.2 (0.3)	3.2 (0.2)	200.5 (2.1)
Thailand	1962	623.5 (82.5)	68.0 (20.3)	179.2 (12.4)	15.6 (13.9)	57.8 (18.6)	37.9 (22.0)	6.5 (31.1)	8.7 (17.6)	977.2 (175.4)
Philippines	1955	192.3 (22.7)	23.1 (4.1)	40.6 (19.5)	5.2 (3.3)	9.8 (4.5)	6.0 (4.1)	5.0 (2.3)	22.7 (13.0)	304.8 (73.0)
Taiwan	1966	2,562.9 (37.8)	175.6 (4.9)		588.8 (22.4)	157.2 (16.6)	20.8 (5.4)	71.9 (4.9)	228.9 (14.9)	3,806.1 (73.0)
Jamaica	1960	72.2 (8.0)	-0.5 (6.6)	20.0 (7.3)	-6.2 (3.9)	-1.5 (4.0)	5.9 (4.1)	-1.2 (3.0)	20.8 (6.2)	109.5 (27.9)
Panama	1960	86.4 (28.2)	12.3 (6.4)	42.2 (7.2)	1.2 (6.2)	8.9 (5.3)	18.9 (5.4)	2.7 (9.1)	4.9 (8.8)	177.5 (62.0)
South Africa	1958	71.3 (3.9)	22.2 (2.4)	33.5 (1.0)	13.8 (2.3)	8.3 (0.8)	22.0 (3.6)	8.7 (0.6)	6.6 (0.8)	186.3 (14.5)

	Year									
Greece	1958	3,000.0 (870.8)	277.2 (398.8)	936.9 (409.6)	107.4 (155.4)	73.6 (171.0)	57.5 (275.5)	137.0 (209.2)	69.3 (112.2)	4,658.8 (2,572.0)
Ireland	1963	84.5 (3.1)	12.6 (1.0)	21.1 (1.1)	5.1 (1.2)	1.7 (0.2)	8.3 (1.7)	8.8 (0.9)	8.6 (0.8)	150.8 (9.5)
Puerto Rico	1963	156.8 (13.6)	11.4 (6.4)	27.6 (7.3)	10.2 (3.5)	-17.9 (10.1)	-13.4 (11.2)	-17.1 (9.0)	-15.7 (4.3)	141.9 (60.0)
Italy	1963	844.9 (169.9)	182.1 (37.7)	245.5 (112.1)	-46.6 (27.1)	98.6 (86.2)	50.1 (79.8)	129.3 (50.6)	24.3 (15.3)	1,528.2 (515.0)
Israel	1964	652.3 (10.7)	165.0 (8.2)	397.1 (12.9)	117.4 (8.2)	122.5 (9.0)	116.5 (10.7)	136.4 (9.9)	190.1 (10.5)	1,897.2 (52.8)
United Kingdom	1963	117.2 (3.6)	24.7 (1.4)	12.4 (12.1)	7.7 (3.6)	1.8 (0.6)	-18.8 (4.8)	13.5 (2.6)	-7.5 (5.1)	151.1 (20.9)
Australia	1966	302.9 (7.7)	93.3 (4.5)	58.0 (18.7)	46.0 (4.1)	10.3 (8.6)	52.8 (8.7)	43.7 (5.3)	79.4 (8.8)	686.5 (52.2)
West Germany	1954	579.1 (65.2)	164.5 (22.5)		96.0 (69.5)	13.4 (9.8)	-10.4 (20.8)	44.9 (14.3)	-32.7 (22.9)	854.7 (194.8)
Sweden	1959	973.3 (331.0)	379.5 (45.7)	360.8 (180.5)	101.4 (69.2)	12.2 (6.2)	-140.4 (277.5)	136.1 (131.2)	43.4 (53.1)	1,866.3 (1,107.4)
United States	1963	416.1 (18.9)	67.2 (14.3)	224.3 (47.3)	28.0 (12.0)	12.4 (36.3)	110.2 (33.3)	38.5 (13.6)	-25.2 (35.2)	871.6 (20.1)

Note: Measured in national currency units (NCU's) per capita in base-year prices, except for Korea and Italy where the units are 10^2 NCU's. Asymptotic standard errors are given in parentheses.

Table 3.8. Estimates of per Capita Subsistence Expenditure $(p_i \gamma_i)$ at Sample Midpoint in 1970 U.S. Dollars

Country	Sample midpoint	Food	Clothing	Housing	Durables	Personal care	Transport	Recreation	Other services	Total	$-\bar{\phi}$
Korea	1962	68.7	11.7	13.7	1.9	3.7	3.6	4.2	2.7	110.3	0.097
Thailand	1964	36.9	3.9	7.2	0.9	3.4	2.2	0.4	0.5	55.5	0.467
Philippines	1961	69.1	8.3	15.4	1.9	3.5	2.2	1.8	8.2	110.3	0.096
Taiwan	1962	74.3	5.4	17.5		4.9	0.7	2.1	7.5	112.3	0.241
Jamaica	1964	127.7	-1.1	39.9	-10.1	-2.4	8.8	-1.8	41.2	202.5	0.520
Panama	1964	105.8	14.1	49.1	1.4	11.2	22.9	3.1	5.6	213.2	0.536
South Africa	1962	133.9	38.9	66.9	25.0	17.4	42.8	17.2	14.0	356.0	0.151
Greece	1963	137.1	11.5	41.7	4.5	3.3	2.6	5.6	2.9	209.2	0.583
Ireland	1962	309.8	45.9	76.1	18.6	6.3	29.8	31.7	30.9	549.2	0.269
Puerto Rico	1961	183.0	13.6	32.5	12.2	-20.6	-16.7	-20.0	-18.5	165.5	0.794
Italy	1962	172.6	38.1	51.8	-10.1	19.8	10.7	26.5	4.9	314.3	0.569
Israel	1964	274.5	69.4	167.1	49.4	51.6	49.0	57.4	80.0	798.5	0.189
United Kingdom	1962	405.3	85.7	41.4	27.0	6.3	-67.1	46.0	-25.6	519.5	0.574
Australia	1961	424.3	141.1	76.1	75.6	14.1	77.0	59.9	108.6	976.7	0.351
West Germany	1962	230.4	65.7	40.9		6.1	-3.9	18.7	-15.8	342.2	0.701
Sweden	1962	313.4	116.5	106.5	31.1	3.8	-43.1	43.3	13.3	584.8	0.649
United States	1962	501.5	81.9	270.8	34.3	14.9	134.9	46.1	-29.5	1,055.0	0.539

Note: Conversions made by multiplying each γ_i in table 3.7 by the value of the corresponding p_i at the sample midpoint and then dividing by the implicit conversion factors given in the last column of table 3.2.

48

Table 3.9. Coefficients of Determination (R^2) for Fitted Models

Country	Food	Clothing	Housing	Durables	Personal care	Transport	Recreation	Other services
			Commodity					
Korea	0.9988	0.9945	0.9959	0.9896	0.9866	0.9928	0.9914	0.9698
Thailand	0.9791	0.9581	0.9720	0.9184	0.9253	0.9510	0.9595	0.9209
Philippines	0.9958	0.9830	0.9891	0.9663	0.9940	0.9627	0.9968	0.9625
Taiwan	0.9950	0.9927	0.9933		0.9289	0.9516	0.9786	0.9852
Jamaica	0.9313	0.9453	0.9734	0.9598	0.8475	0.9292	0.9304	0.9520
Panama	0.9762	0.9273	0.9334	0.9142	0.9289	0.6882	0.9575	0.8473
South Africa	0.9876	0.8645	0.9948	0.8162	0.9711	0.9040	0.9834	0.9640
Greece	0.9966	0.9907	0.9834	0.8908	0.8571	0.9792	0.9698	0.5700
Ireland	0.9975	0.9772	0.9954	0.9868	0.7656	0.9898	0.9875	0.9756
Puerto Rico	0.9929	0.9911	0.9952	0.9698	0.9841	0.9870	0.9937	0.9702
Italy	0.9957	0.9807	0.9969	0.5283	0.9268	0.9439	0.9892	0.9803
Israel	0.9980	0.9795	0.9960	0.8401	0.9944	0.9879	0.9900	0.9925
United Kingdom	0.9983	0.9925	0.9869	0.9178	0.9963	0.9638	0.9948	0.8773
Australia	0.9938	0.9531	0.9797	.8687	0.9724	0.9804	0.8974	0.9882
West Germany	0.9774	0.9850	0.9890		0.9864	0.9954	0.9983	0.9847
Sweden	0.9980	0.9751	0.9913	0.9700	0.9835	0.9914	0.9917	0.8887
United States	0.9923	0.9855	0.9813	0.9695	0.9834	0.9727	0.9945	0.9844

Table 3.10. *Durbin-Watson* d *Statistics for Fitted Models*

				Commodity				
Country	*Food*	*Clothing*	*Housing*	*Durables*	*Personal care*	*Transport*	*Recreation*	*Other services*
Korea	2.24	2.29	1.06	2.09	1.23	0.88	1.76	0.83
Thailand	1.64	1.29	0.57	0.74	0.89	1.30	1.54	0.76
Philippines	1.46	1.02	1.76	1.81	0.69	0.61	2.41	0.63
Taiwan	1.31	1.75		1.92	0.36	0.73	0.68	1.04
Jamaica	1.41	2.35	1.34	1.09	1.85	2.40	1.04	1.39
Panama	1.80	2.23	1.04	2.37	1.06	0.72	2.49	1.26
South Africa	1.39	0.76	1.10	0.84	0.55	0.78	0.89	0.72
Greece	0.58	1.43	0.85	0.35	0.37	0.75	0.66	0.29
Ireland	1.54	2.15	1.42	1.48	0.55	1.86	1.02	0.94
Puerto Rico	1.46	1.35	1.15	0.95	1.16	0.84	1.23	1.29
Italy	1.03	0.66	0.98	0.24	0.15	0.30	0.26	0.76
Israel	1.53	2.18	1.50	2.05	1.77	1.41	1.93	2.29
United Kingdom	1.07	1.13	0.75	0.59	1.01	0.40	1.29	0.53
Australia	1.38	1.28	0.90	0.87	1.04	1.57	0.38	1.00
West Germany	0.32	0.89		0.66	0.70	1.30	1.33	0.71
Sweden	1.12	0.54	0.69	0.60	0.90	1.53	1.16	0.68
United States	2.15	0.75	0.22	0.44	0.26	2.27	0.65	0.69

coefficient between $1 - \mu$ and the annual average rate of growth of real per capita personal disposable income over the sample period is 0.34. The coefficient is 0.60 if South Africa is excluded, a result significantly different from zero at the 5 percent level, although the former result is not.

The estimated marginal budget shares, β_i, are all positive as required except in one case (Jamaica, other services), where the value is not significantly different from zero. In only six other cases is the ratio of the β_i estimate to its standard error less than 2, and all but one of these fall in the categories of recreation and other services.

In order to discern patterns in the β estimates we first average values for countries at similar levels of economic development as measured by the sample midpoint of GNP per capita in 1970 U.S. dollars. Second, we regress parameter estimates on the common logarithm of GNP per capita.[11] Both sets of results (see table 3.11) show that the marginal budget share for food decreases markedly as GNP per capita rises, whereas the β estimates for housing and transport rise with income. The marginal budget share for food at the highest income levels is only half that for the low-income countries: 0.18 for per capita GNP over \$1,500, 0.39 for per capita GNP less than \$500. The exact opposite is true for housing and transport. No strong patterns emerge for other commodities, although there is some tendency for the marginal budget share for durables to increase with income,[12] and that for clothing is highest at middle income levels.[13]

The γ estimates are determined with considerably less precision than the β estimates. Thirty-three of the 110 ELES estimates of γ_i are less than twice their standard errors (in absolute terms), as are twelve of the twenty-four LES estimates. Fifteen of the γ estimates are negative, but Jamaica and Puerto Rico account for eight of these. For the basic commodities, food, clothing, and housing, however, the γ estimates behave as "subsistence" parameters—all estimates but one (clothing, Jamaica) are positive. These γ values increase with levels of GNP per capita (see table 3.8), but more precise quantification of this phenomenon is left until chapter 4.

At mean values the sum of the γ estimates is always less than actual consumption expenditure, as required by the underlying utility

11. Notice that the regressions preserve the identity $\Sigma\beta = 1$ at any level of GNP per capita.

12. Recall that expenditure on motor vehicles is included in transport not durables.

13. Note the low value for the Durbin-Watson d statistic, which suggests a curvilinear relationship between β_3 and per capita GNP.

Table 3.11. *Relation between Marginal Budget Shares (β_i) and Level of GNP per Capita*

Item	Food	Clothing	Housing	Durables	Personal care	Transport	Recreation	Other services
Mean values of β_i								
GNP per capita[a]								
100–500	0.386	0.074	0.122	0.074	0.071	0.094	0.076	0.105
500–1,000	0.351	0.138	0.118	0.092	0.047	0.133	0.085	0.035
1,000–1,500	0.276	0.109	0.149	0.093	0.065	0.145	0.100	0.065
1,500 and over	0.175	0.078	0.209	0.090	0.079	0.209	0.064	0.095
Overall mean	0.286	0.096	0.155	0.087	0.068	0.150	0.080	0.079
Regressions of $\beta_i = a + b \log_{10}$ GNP per capita[b]								
a	0.805[c]	0.081	−0.049	0.040	0.030	−0.092	0.097	0.089
	(0.132)	(0.059)	(0.102)	(0.042)	(0.058)	(0.088)	(0.064)	(0.088)
b	−0.179[c]	0.005	0.070[d]	0.016	0.013	0.083[c]	−0.006	−0.004
	(0.045)	(0.020)	(0.035)	(0.014)	(0.020)	(0.030)	(0.022)	(0.030)
R^2	0.531	0.005	0.228	0.084	0.029	0.354	0.005	0.001
d	2.45	1.00	2.36	2.41	2.50	2.32	2.60	1.78

Note: Based on table 3.6; Jamaica excluded. ($\beta_3 + \beta_4$) divided 1:1 for Taiwan, 2:1 for West Germany.

a. In 1970 U.S. dollars at sample midpoints.
b. Standard errors in parentheses. Data ranked in order of increasing GNP per capita so that Durbin-Watson d statistic indicates appropriateness of functional form.
c. Significant at 5 percent level.
d. Significant at 10 percent level.

theory. The mean values of the supernumerary ratio, $-\phi$, which express the excess of total consumption expenditure over the γ sum as a percentage of the former, are given in the last column of table 3.8. For all countries and all time periods there are only three instances in which the γ sum exceeds actual total consumption expenditure: the first year of the sample for Korea, Philippines, and Israel, where the difference never exceeds 4 percent of total consumption expenditure.

Total Expenditure and Price Elasticities

Estimates of total expenditure elasticities evaluated at sample mean values are given in table 3.12, uncompensated own-price elasticities in table 3.13, and cross-price elasticities for food in table 3.14. Total expenditure elasticities for food are always less than one; those for clothing and housing fall about evenly on either side of one. For the remaining commodities the values tend to exceed unity. All estimates of price elasticities satisfy the underlying utility theory requirements (compensated and uncompensated own-price elasticities negative, compensated cross-price elasticities positive) except for Jamaica, where the negative β value for other services produces a positive own-price elasticity and negative compensated cross-price elasticities. (For this reason we exclude Jamaica when searching for patterns.) Under LES the own-price elasticities exceed one in absolute value whenever the corresponding γ_i estimate is negative. This arises in fifteen cases, eight of them in the categories of transport and other services for countries with a per capita GNP of over $1,000 a year.

Our results show fewer problems than those encountered by authors working outside the demand systems framework. In the double-logarithmic functions fitted by Houthakker (1965) and Weisskoff (1971) only uncompensated own-price elasticities are estimated. Weisskoff's signs are implausible in 28 percent of the cases (6 commodities, 16 countries); Houthakker's in 31 percent (5 commodities, 14 countries). Using LES, Goldberger and Gamaletsos (1970) obtained estimates of uncompensated own-price elasticities which have correct signs in all cases, but the compensated own-price elasticities fail to meet utility requirements in 31 percent of the cases, at mean values (5 commodities, 12 countries). Parks and Barten (1973), however, obtained elasticity estimates which always have correct signs.

Table 3.12. *Total Expenditure Elasticities*

Country	Food	Clothing	Housing	Durables	Personal care	Transport	Recreation	Other services
Korea	0.72	0.66	0.74	2.76	1.76	3.12	1.78	1.71
Thailand	0.84	1.20	0.16	1.61	0.93	1.57	1.99	1.55
Philippines	0.52	0.75	1.82	2.23	1.72	2.39	1.69	2.08
Taiwan	0.57	1.26		1.33	1.69	2.77	1.76	1.81
Jamaica	0.58	1.95	0.71	2.67	2.35	1.52	2.03	−1.83
Panama	0.92	1.08	0.68	1.77	0.92	0.90	1.69	0.87
South Africa	0.80	1.39	0.40	1.47	1.02	1.56	0.98	1.44
Greece	0.73	1.37	0.96	1.28	1.35	1.55	1.37	1.22
Ireland	0.64	1.33	0.85	2.02	1.07	1.92	1.21	1.19
Puerto Rico	0.49	1.06	0.94	0.98	1.70	1.43	1.57	1.93
Italy	0.87	0.86	1.03	2.17	1.04	1.44	0.93	1.09
Israel	0.66	1.10	0.90	1.61	0.99	1.59	1.44	0.97
United Kingdom	0.30	0.62	1.41	1.14	1.35	2.53	0.89	2.63
Australia	0.43	0.45	1.73	1.06	2.34	1.70	0.22	1.14
West Germany	0.66	0.78		1.22	1.21	1.45	1.12	1.74
Sweden	0.76	0.62	0.92	1.13	1.43	1.78	1.09	1.03
United States	0.34	1.14	0.90	1.45	1.69	1.14	1.18	2.31
Mean values[a]								
100–500	0.66	0.97	1.01	1.98	1.53	2.46	1.81	1.79
500–1,000	0.82	1.28	0.68	1.51	1.10	1.34	1.35	1.18
1,000–1,500	0.67	1.09	0.93	1.70	1.20	1.60	1.29	1.30
1,500 and over	0.50	0.72	1.24	1.20	1.60	1.72	0.90	1.77
Overall	0.64	0.98	1.00	1.58	1.39	1.80	1.31	1.54

a. Class intervals refer to GNP per capita at sample midpoints in 1970 U.S. dollars as given in column (5) of table 3.2. Jamaica is excluded.

54

Table 3.13. *Own-Price Elasticities*

Country	Food	Clothing	Housing	Durables	Personal care	Transport	Recreation	Other services
Korea	-0.47	-0.13	-0.15	-0.33	-0.23	-0.40	-0.24	-0.20
Thailand	-0.68	-0.21	-0.09	-0.76	-0.46	-0.76	-0.94	-0.73
Philippines	-0.35	-0.12	-0.40	-0.25	-0.22	-0.27	-0.19	-0.34
Taiwan	-0.41	-0.35	-0.49		-0.46	-0.68	-0.45	-0.54
Jamaica	-0.47	-1.01	-0.43	-1.33	-1.21	-0.82	-1.05	1.13
Panama	-0.70	-0.62	-0.44	-0.95	-0.52	-0.53	-0.92	-0.47
South Africa	-0.38	-0.34	-0.12	-0.31	-0.20	-0.39	-0.19	-0.27
Greece	-0.62	-0.83	-0.64	-0.76	-0.80	-0.92	-0.82	-0.72
Ireland	-0.43	-0.44	-0.31	-0.60	-0.30	-0.60	-0.38	-0.37
Puerto Rico	-0.50	-0.86	-0.78	-0.80	-1.28	-1.11	-1.21	-1.49
Italy	-0.70	-0.54	-0.66	-1.22	-0.62	-0.84	-0.56	-0.63
Israel	-0.31	-0.29	-0.31	-0.39	-0.24	-0.38	-0.36	-0.26
United Kingdom	-0.27	-0.49	-0.86	-0.68	-0.78	-1.33	-0.54	-1.45
Australia	-0.27	-0.20	-0.69	-0.42	-0.85	-0.69	-0.09	-0.48
West Germany	-0.60	-0.59	-0.90		-0.86	-1.01	-0.80	-1.20
Sweden	-0.64	-0.44	-0.65	-0.76	-0.93	-1.11	-0.73	-0.68
United States	-0.26	-0.66	-0.59	-0.81	-0.92	-0.68	-0.66	-1.22
Mean values[a]								
100–500	-0.48	-0.30	-0.28	-0.46	-0.34	-0.53	-0.46	-0.45
500–1,000	-0.57	-0.60	-0.40	-0.67	-0.51	-0.61	-0.64	-0.49
1,000–1,500	-0.40	-0.53	-0.52	-0.75	-0.61	-0.73	-0.63	-0.69
1,500 and over	-0.41	-0.46	-0.74	-0.71	-0.87	-0.96	-0.56	-1.01
Overall	-0.47	-0.46	-0.51	-0.65	-0.60	-0.73	-0.57	-0.69

a. Class intervals refer to GNP per capita at sample midpoints in 1970 U.S. dollars as given in column (5) of table 3.2. Jamaica is excluded.

55

Table 3.14. Cross-Elasticities with Respect to Food Price

Country	Clothing	Housing	Durables	Personal care	Transport	Recreation	Other services
Korea	-0.37	-0.41	-1.55	-0.98	-1.74	-0.99	-0.95
Thailand	-0.42	-0.06	-0.57	-0.33	-0.55	-0.70	-0.53
Philippines	-0.42	-1.03	-1.27	-0.98	-1.36	-0.96	-1.18
Taiwan	-0.61	-0.65		-0.82	-1.35	-0.85	-0.88
Jamaica	-0.59	-0.22	-0.81	-0.71	-0.46	-0.62	-0.55
Panama	-0.25	-0.16	-0.41	-0.21	-0.21	-0.39	-0.20
South Africa	-0.45	-0.13	-0.48	-0.33	-0.51	-0.32	-0.47
Greece	-0.37	-0.26	-0.35	-0.36	-0.42	-0.37	-0.33
Ireland	-0.54	-0.35	-0.82	-0.44	-0.78	-0.49	-0.49
Puerto Rico	-0.23	-0.20	-0.21	-0.36	-0.31	-0.34	-0.41
Italy	-0.20	-0.24	-0.51	-0.25	-0.34	-0.21	-0.26
Israel	-0.31	-0.25	-0.45	-0.28	-0.45	-0.40	-0.27
United Kingdom	-0.20	-0.46	-0.37	-0.44	-0.83	-0.29	-0.86
Australia	-0.13	-0.49	-0.30	-0.66	-0.48	-0.06	-0.32
West Germany	-0.15	-0.24		-0.24	-0.28	-0.22	-0.34
Sweden	-0.12	-0.17	-0.21	-0.27	-0.33	-0.20	-0.19
United States	-0.25	-0.20	-0.32	-0.37	-0.25	-0.26	-0.50
Mean values[a]							
100–500	-0.46	-0.54	-1.01	-0.78	-1.25	-0.88	-0.89
500–1,000	-0.36	-0.18	-0.41	-0.30	-0.38	-0.36	-0.33
1,000–1,500	-0.32	-0.26	-0.50	-0.33	-0.47	-0.36	-0.36
1,500 and over	-0.17	-0.31	-0.29	-0.40	-0.43	-0.21	-0.44
Overall	-0.31	-0.33	-0.54	-0.46	-0.64	-0.44	-0.51

a. Class intervals refer to GNP per capita at sample midpoints in 1970 U.S. dollars as given in column (5) of table 3.2. Jamaica is excluded.

The relative importance of price effects for a given commodity can be measured by making use of the homogeneity property of the models: the sum of price and expenditure elasticities for a good is zero. If uncompensated cross-price elasticities are all negative, this leads to an unambiguous partitioning of income elasticities as the sum of the absolute values of the price elasticities. Apart from Jamaica, which we exclude, our cross-price elasticities are negative except in those cases where the γ_i estimates are negative. The exceptions are small enough in absolute value to be ignored, and table 3.15 gives estimates of the ratios of own-price and food cross-price elasticities to total expenditure elasticities for different levels of GNP per capita using average values obtained from tables 3.12, 3.13 and 3.14. Since for a given country the ratio of the food cross-price elasticity to the corresponding total expenditure elasticity is the same across commodities, only single average values are given for this ratio.[14]

The food cross-price elasticities at the lowest level of GNP per capita (the first row, table 3.15) amount to 50 percent of the expenditure elasticities for all goods and are roughly twice the own-price elasticities for nonfood goods. The exact opposite is true at middle income levels ($500–1,500): Own-price elasticities for nonfood are about half the total expenditure elasticities and about double the food cross-price elasticities. At the highest level of GNP per capita own-price elasticities dominate, centering around 60 percent of total expenditure elasticities. The sum of own-price and food cross-price elasticities as a percentage of expenditure elasticities are high (always at least 70 percent) and show little variation with per capita GNP. Below $1,500 all percentages lie in the range of 70 to 80, except for housing (81 to 85); above $1,500 the range is 79 to 88. Overall, the results imply that among cross-price effects that for food dominates, particularly at low levels of income. For this reason we do not present detailed estimates of other cross-price effects.

It has been argued by Deaton (1974, 1975) that additive demand systems in general, and LES in particular, tend to force the ratios of own-price elasticities to total expenditure elasticities to be the same for all goods. The results presented in table 3.15 offer only limited support for Deaton's hypothesis. There is a tendency for the ratios

14. It is a property of all directly additive models that $\eta_{ij}/\eta_i = k_j$; for all i and j, $i \neq j$ where k is a constant. Because our method of calculation uses averages from tables 3.12 and 3.14, the ratios are not exactly the same across commodities; we therefore average them to get the last column in table 3.15.

Table 3.15. *Percentage of Expenditure Elasticity Associated with Own-Price and Food-Price Responses*

GNP per capita (1970 U.S. dollars)	Own price								Food cross-price[a]
	Food	Clothing	Housing	Durables	Personal care	Transport	Recreation	Other services	
100–500	73	31	28	23	22	22	25	25	50
500–1,000	70	47	59	44	46	46	47	42	27
1,000–1,500	73	49	56	44	51	46	49	53	28
1,500 and over	82	64	60	59	54	56	62	57	24
Overall	73	47	51	41	43	41	44	45	34

Note: Ratio of (absolute) price elasticities to total expenditure elasticities using averages from tables 3.12, 3.13, and 3.14.

a. Ratio is same for all commodities.

to be similar in the case of nonfood categories at given levels of economic development; but the ratios for food and nonfood are quite different, except at the highest income levels, and the ratios differ considerably across GNP levels.

The preceding paragraphs examined the effects of changes in total expenditure and prices on demand for individual commodities. For ELES estimates it is also possible to look at the aggregate effects of changes in income and prices on total consumption expenditure. The relevant elasticities are presented in table 3.16 for each of the fourteen countries for which ELES was fitted. The relevant formulas are given in table 2.1. Note that the elasticities necessarily sum to unity. For the majority of countries the elasticity of consumption with respect to income, η, is around .90 to .95, and total consumption is fairly insensitive to changes in relative prices. By far the most important among the price effects is that of food. In Taiwan, South Africa, and Israel the influence of relative price changes is more important. In Taiwan, for example, the estimates imply that a one percent increase in per capita personal disposable income has the same effect on per capita total consumption as a 4.5 percent increase in the price of food.

In table 3.17 we attempt broad comparisons with elasticity estimates obtained by other researchers using time-series data. Average values are calculated for three levels of GNP per capita (low, middle, high) for countries that are categorized according to income levels at midpoints of our sample periods.[15] Countries are included only if they are common to both this and other studies. Comparisons are necessarily limited to three commodity groups for which the classification appears to be the same: food, clothing, and housing. At high levels of GNP the expenditure elasticities obtained from all studies are remarkably similar. Estimates for food all lie in the range of 0.5 to 0.6; for clothing the range is 0.8 to 0.9, and for housing 1.0 to 1.2. Our estimates of own-price elasticities are higher in absolute value than those obtained by Goldberger and Gamaletsos (1970) and Parks and Barten (1973). At both low and middle levels of income Weisskoff (1971) obtains expenditure elasticities which are a little higher for food and clothing than ours but substantially lower for housing. The price elasticities are similar for food and housing, but Weisskoff obtains higher estimates for clothing (in absolute value).

---

15. The sample periods used in the other studies are earlier than those used here, with the exception of the United Kingdom and United States in the Parks and Barten (1973) study.

Table 3.16. *Mean Income and Price Elasticities of Total Consumption Expenditure*

Country	η	η^1	η^2	η^3	η^4	η^5	η^6	η^7	η^8
Korea	0.935	0.040	0.007	0.008	0.001	0.003	0.002	0.003	0.001
Thailand	0.872	0.085	0.009	0.018	0.002	0.008	0.005	0.001	0.001
Taiwan	0.747	0.162	0.013	0.041		0.011	0.002	0.005	0.018
Jamaica	0.963	0.024	−0.000	0.007	−0.002	−0.000	0.212	−0.000	0.007
South Africa	0.678	0.122	0.035	0.060	0.023	0.016	0.038	0.015	0.012
Greece	0.920	0.051	0.005	0.015	0.002	0.002	0.001	0.002	0.001
Ireland	0.887	0.063	0.010	0.015	0.004	0.001	0.007	0.007	0.006
Italy	0.909	0.049	0.011	0.014	−0.001	0.005	0.003	0.008	0.001
Israel	0.657	0.118	0.032	0.068	0.022	0.023	0.022	0.025	0.035
United Kingdom	0.953	0.036	0.008	0.004	0.003	0.001	−0.006	−0.004	0.002
Australia	0.868	0.058	0.019	0.010	0.010	0.002	0.011	0.008	0.015
West Germany	0.942	0.038	0.011	0.007		0.001	−0.000	0.003	−0.002
Sweden	0.933	0.035	0.013	0.012	0.003	0.001	−0.004	0.005	0.002
United States	0.924	0.036	0.006	0.019	0.003	0.001	0.010	0.003	−0.002

Note: Superscripts on η refer to commodity numbers in table 3.1.

60

Table 3.17. *Comparison of Elasticity Estimates from Various Studies*

Elasticities	Low income 100–500[a]		Middle income 500–1,000[a]		High income 1,200 and over[a]			
	LPW[b]	W[c]	LPW[b]	W[c]	LPW[b]	H[d]	GG[e]	PB[f]
Expenditure								
Food	0.71	0.99	0.65	0.71	0.57	0.55	0.54	0.52
Clothing	1.04	1.59	1.42	1.80	0.81	0.80[g]	0.83	0.88
Housing	0.74	0.20	0.77	0.32	1.07	1.15	1.20	1.03
Own-price								
Food	−0.52	−0.41	−0.48	−0.18[h]	−0.47	−0.10[h]	−0.26	−0.27
Clothing	−0.36	−1.08	−0.70	−1.08[h]	−0.51	−0.42[h]	−0.21	−0.26
Housing	−0.24	−0.21	−0.50	−0.57	−0.69	−0.14[h]	−0.35	−0.36

a. GNP per capita in 1970 U.S. dollars. Countries included are: low income (Korea, Thailand and Taiwan); middle income (Jamaica, South Africa, Greece, Ireland, Puerto Rico); high income (Italy, United Kingdom, Sweden, United States).
b. Lluch, Powell, Williams estimates from tables 3.12 and 3.13.
c. Weisskoff (1971, p. 341) estimates.
d. Houthakker (1965, p. 286).

e. Goldberger and Gamaletsos (1970, p. 374, table 4).
f. Parks and Barten (1973, p. 851); own-price elasticities calculated using

$$\eta_{ii} = \eta^*_{ii} - \beta_i.$$

g. Excludes negative entry for Sweden.
h. Positive values included in average values shown.

Table 3.18. Regressions Across Countries of Expenditure and Price Elasticities against Logarithm of GNP per Capita

Commodity	Total expenditure elasticities			Own-price elasticities			Cross-elasticities with respect to price of food		
	a	b	R^2/d	a	b	R^2/d	a	b	R^2/d
Food	1.041ᵃ (0.289)	−0.138 (0.098)	0.123 1.96	−0.665ᵃ (0.265)	0.066 (0.090)	0.036 2.35			
Clothing	1.425ᵃ (0.488)	−0.153 (0.166)	0.057 1.32	−0.073 (0.358)	−0.135 (0.122)	0.080 2.40	−0.943ᵃ (0.176)	0.217ᵃ (0.060)	0.485 2.14
Housing	0.484 (0.706)	0.177 (0.240)	0.037 1.84	0.543 (0.321)	−0.361ᵃ (0.109)	0.438 2.62	−0.868ᵃ (0.373)	0.185 (0.127)	0.132 2.06
Durables	3.312ᵃ (0.682)	−0.597ᵃ (0.232)	0.322 2.72	−0.002 (0.411)	−0.224 (0.140)	0.154 2.83	−2.254ᵃ (0.426)	0.588ᵃ (0.145)	0.541 2.66
Personal care	1.254ᵇ (0.665)	0.046 (0.226)	0.003 2.27	0.617 (0.426)	−0.420ᵃ (0.145)	0.376 2.82	1.392ᵃ (0.345)	0.322ᵃ (0.117)	0.349 2.22
Transport	3.631ᵃ (0.869)	−0.630ᵃ (0.295)	0.245 2.21	0.221 (0.436)	−0.328ᵃ (0.148)	0.259 3.01	−2.608ᵃ (0.548)	0.679ᵃ (0.186)	0.486 2.31
Recreation	3.325ᵃ (0.501)	−0.695ᵃ (0.170)	0.510 2.28	−0.301 (0.527)	−0.092 (0.179)	0.018 2.88	−1.998ᵃ (0.209)	0.536ᵃ (0.071)	0.803 1.85
Other services	1.746ᵇ (0.859)	−0.069 (0.292)	0.004 2.59	0.556 (0.619)	−0.429ᵇ (0.210)	0.229 3.13	−1.627ᵃ (0.391)	0.384ᵃ (0.133)	0.373 2.29

a. Significant at 5 percent level.
b. Significant at 10 percent level.

Note: All regressions are of the form $\eta = a + b \log_{10} X$, where η is the relevant elasticity and X is GNP per capita at sample midpoint in 1970 U.S. dollars. The sample size is sixteen, Jamaica being excluded because some estimates do not satisfy the model specification. Standard errors are given in parentheses.

For the mean values listed in tables 3.12, 3.13, and 3.14 countries are grouped more naturally from the point of view of this study. The class intervals are the same as those used in table 3.11. Again, we also follow an alternative route in seeking patterns and regress elasticity estimates on the common logarithm of GNP per capita. These regression results are given in table 3.18.

The strongest pattern to emerge is the fall in absolute value of the cross-elasticities with respect to the price of food as GNP per capita increases. With the exception of housing, the coefficients of the log of GNP per capita are all significantly different from zero at the 5 percent level. The food cross-price elasticity for housing is relatively constant if the high value for the Philippines is excluded (mean value becomes −0.28). For the other six commodities, mean values at the highest income level ($1,500 and over) range from one-half (personal care and other services) to one-quarter (recreation) of the mean values at the lowest income level (below $500) (see table 3.14).

Own-price elasticities for food and recreation show little movement with income; mean values are −0.47 and −0.57 respectively. The own-price elasticity for clothing is noticeably lower in absolute value for countries with per capita GNP below $500; mean value here is −0.30 compared with −0.52 for countries with incomes above $500 (see table 3.13). For housing, personal care, and transport the absolute values of own-price elasticities increase significantly with income. In the case of housing, for example, the regression equation in table 3.18 implies an own-price elasticity of −0.29 at a per capita GNP of $200 a year compared with −0.65 at $2,000. The corresponding values for transport are −0.53 and −0.86. The price elasticity for other services is appreciably higher at GNP levels over $1,500 per capita; mean value for countries above this income level is −1.01 compared with −0.55 for countries with lower incomes.

The strongest patterns in total expenditure elasticities occur for recreation, durables, and transport, in that order. In each case the estimates decline significantly with income. The relevant regression equation in table 3.18 implies that for per capita GNP of $200 the expenditure elasticity of demand for recreation is 1.73, declining to 1.03 at a per capita level of $2,000. The corresponding figures for durables are 1.93, declining to 1.34; and for transport 2.18, declining to 1.55. There is some tendency for the expenditure elasticity for food to decline with GNP per capita, but the t value on the income variable is only 1.4—the regression line implies a value of 0.72 at per capita GNP of $200, falling to 0.59 at $2,000. For no commodity does the expenditure elasticity increase significantly with levels of GNP per capita.[16]

Key Patterns in Demand Responses

The previous sections dealt with how patterns of demand change in response to increases in per capita income and to changes in relative prices. Estimates were obtained of the effects of income on the propensity to allocate expenditure at the margin to groups of commodities and of the corresponding total expenditure elasticities. A comparison of patterns in the two measures (based on tables 3.11, 3.12, and 3.18) yields the following findings of significance:

(a) At lowest levels of GNP per capita ($100–500 expressed in 1970 U.S. dollars) nearly 40 percent of any increase in total expenditure is allocated to food. This figure falls to around 17 percent for the highest income countries. The average budget share for food, however, declines almost as fast as the marginal budget share. As a consequence, the expenditure elasticity for food falls only slightly as income levels increase; the overall average value is 0.64.

(b) For clothing the two measures of demand response to income change exhibit largest values for the middle income range ($500 to $1,000). Here our figures show that about 14 percent of total expenditure at the margin is allocated to clothing, and the total expenditure elasticity is around 1.3.

(c) The expenditure elasticity of demand for housing tends to vary somewhat irregularly around 1.0 with local factors appearing to be of some importance. The highest values of around 1.8 are recorded for countries at opposite ends of the income scale (the Philippines and Australia). The share of total expenditure allocated to housing at the margin, however, shows more of a tendency to increase with GNP per capita. It is around 12 percent at low income levels increasing to around 20 percent at high income levels.

(d) The marginal budget share for transport increases noticeably with income, whereas the expenditure elasticity falls with income. Since the elasticity is simply the ratio of the mar-

16. For a given country the weighted sum of total expenditure elasticities must be unity, where the weights are average budget shares. The apparent tendency exhibited in table 3.18 for this weighted sum to fall with "income" is explained by the tendency for personal consumption to be a lower percentage of GNP at higher levels of GNP per capita.

ginal to the average budget share, the differential movements are explained by a substantial increase in the average propensity to spend on transport as income levels rise.

(e) The expenditure elasticities for durables and recreation fall significantly as income levels rise; the marginal budget shares show much less variation, although for durables they are lower for the $100–500 income group at around 7 percent and for recreation they are lower for the highest income group at around 6 percent.

Among developing countries the effect on demand of changes in relative prices is dominated by changes in the relative price of food. At levels of per capita income between $100 and $500, a change in the relative price of food is estimated to have an effect on the demand for each of the other commodities equivalent in magnitude to half their respective expenditure elasticities.[17] For higher levels of income the ratio falls from a half to around a quarter. At income levels below $1,500 a 10 percent decrease in the relative price of food has about the same effect on the demand for food as a 7 percent increase in real total expenditure. The corresponding figure is about 8 percent for the highest income countries. The own-price elasticity for food itself, however, falls in absolute value only slowly from around −0.5 or −0.6 at low income levels to around −0.4 at high income levels.

For commodities other than food the stylized facts regarding the importance of price effects are estimated to be as follows: for GNP per capita of between $100 and $500 an increase of 10 percent in the relative price of a commodity has the same effect on demand as a decrease of about 2.5 percent in total expenditure, except for clothing where the effect is the same as a decrease of around 3.1 percent. At middle income levels ($500 to $1,500) an increase of 10 percent in the relative price of a commodity is equivalent to about a 5 percent decrease in total expenditure, although for housing the equivalent decrease is around 6 percent and for durables, 4.4 percent. At high income levels ($1,500 and over) own-price effects are about 60 percent of total expenditure effects for goods other than food. The absolute values of own-price elasticities for housing, personal care, transport, other services, and to a lesser extent durables increase with per capita GNP, although only for transport and other services do the absolute values exceed unity in individual countries at high income levels.

17. It is a property of the model that the ratio of the cross elasticity for good i, with respect to the price of good j, to the total expenditure elasticity for i is a constant for given j irrespective of i.

In any discussion of estimates of parameters and elasticities it is essential to evaluate the importance of a priori specifications imposed on the data by the chosen model and to note the precision of the estimates. As already stated, it is implicit in the chosen model, LES/ELES, that a simultaneous proportional decrease in the price of any one good and an increase in total expenditure has the same net effect on the demand for another good, irrespective of which good has its price decreased. Also, under LES and ELES all goods are net substitutes. Furthermore it is well known that LES frequently yields estimates with the following tendencies: total expenditure elasticities close to unity, own-price elasticities less than one in absolute value, the ratio of own-price to total expenditure elasticity similar for each good. There is no evidence that our results, which are estimated by a new procedure, are unduly affected by these tendencies, but the warning should be issued. It is clear, however, that greater weight should be attached to the estimates of the expenditure elasticities than to the estimates of price elasticities, not least because price elasticities are based on subsistence parameters, which were estimated with less precision than the marginal budget shares.

4
Subsistence and Saving: Further Time-Series Results

IN THE PREVIOUS CHAPTER EMPHASIS was given to time-series estimates of how households allocate expenditure at the margin and to estimates of total expenditure and price elasticities. The first two sections of this chapter continue with our interpretation of the results obtained using national accounts data but concentrate on estimates of subsistence expenditures and related measures such as the Frisch parameter. The third section is concerned with an examination of the ability of ELES to predict household savings behavior. Excluded from our analysis are the three countries for which savings data were unavailable. The last two sections are devoted to a more detailed examination of savings and demand behavior in Korea and Taiwan, using data for a longer time period than that used earlier.

Subsistence Expenditure

The γ parameters of the Stone-Geary utility function may be interpreted as measuring "subsistence" expenditure if they are positive. In the previous chapter it was observed that time-series estimates of the γ parameters for the basic necessities of food, clothing, and housing were, with one exception, positive. Among the other commodities, however, several negative values were encountered, and a number of estimates were not significantly greater than zero.

This section concentrates on the subsistence expenditure interpretation of the sum of the γ estimates, and on the γ estimates for food, clothing, and housing. It is of course possible to obtain estimates of these γ values of interest at lower levels of commodity disaggregation than that of the eight goods used in chapter 3. The most appropriate level of commodity disaggregation for additive models such as LES and ELES is not known precisely, but there is no reason for it to be the same for all countries in the sample. Hicks's (1946) composite commodity theorem is not of much help in approaching aggregation, because even though two commodities with collinear prices possess an unambiguous aggregate quantity index, they may not constitute a composite commodity which is plausible as an argument of an additive utility function.

Linear expenditure systems (considered as deterministic models) aggregate consistently if the price indexes used at higher levels of aggregation are obtained by weighting prices used at lower levels by the corresponding γ values (Stone, 1970; Powell, 1974). Since at each level we use implicit price indexes, where the weights reflect actual budget shares, consistent aggregation is lost; there is no point, therefore, in considering enforcement of consistency between γ estimates at different levels of aggregation.

We thus proceed in a pragmatic fashion and compare ELES results at four levels of commodity aggregation: the eight-commodity level used in chapter 3 (see table 3.1); a four-commodity level comprising food, clothing, housing (including durables), and other;[1] a two-commodity level comprising food and nonfood; and a single commodity. At the one-commodity level ELES reduces to a simple Keynesian consumption function,[2] and it is of some interest to compare the results with those of systems estimates. Aggregation to one commodity is of course unusual in the context of complete demand systems and is not permitted by LES, for example, which reduces to the identity $v_t = v_t$. Partly for this reason, but primarily because the next two sections consider results which are specific to ELES, we

---

1. Recall that durables include only household equipment and furnishings; for Taiwan and West Germany these items are always included in housing. "Other" comprises commodities 6 to 8 in table 3.1.

2. $v_t = (1 - \mu)P_t\gamma + \mu y_t$, where P is a general index of consumer prices. To illustrate the point raised in the previous paragraph, if a four-commodity classification is "correct," the price index used at the one-commodity level should be

$$\sum_{i=1}^{4} (p_i\gamma_i) \bigg/ \sum_{i=1}^{4} \gamma_i,$$

not an arbitrary P, such as an implicit deflator.

confine the sample in this chapter to the fourteen countries for which ELES estimation is possible.

Table 4.1 presents estimates of the sum of the γ parameters and associated "t ratios"[3] for aggregates of eight, four, two, and one commodities. The estimates have been converted to 1970 U.S. dollars at sample midpoints by the method used in chapter 3. For five countries (Korea, Taiwan, Ireland, Israel, and West Germany), the γ-sum estimates are quite stable across levels of commodity aggregation. Variability is most extreme for Jamaica, Italy, and Sweden. We use the criterion of highest t value to select the most appropriate level of aggregation for each country. Since in all cases except Italy and Sweden this corresponds to the γ-sum estimate with the lowest standard error, the procedure is equivalent to selecting the γ-sum value with the smallest confidence interval. There is a tendency for one level of aggregation in each country to yield a t ratio which substantially exceeds all others; where this does not occur, similar t ratios are associated with similar γ-sum estimates.

The selection procedure yields nine countries for which disaggregation to eight commodities appears preferable, three countries for the four-commodity level, and one each for the two- and one-commodity levels. At the two—and more especially the one—commodity level very small or negative values of the γ sum occur so that subsistence interpretation is not possible. Furthermore, precision is frequently low, with six out of the fourteen estimates at the one-commodity level less than twice their standard errors in absolute value. For the two countries (United Kingdom and Greece) in which the two lowest levels of disaggregation are preferred, very similar results are obtained at the four-commodity level, for both the γ-sum estimate and its standard error. Thus, aggregation to the two- and one-commodity levels gives no advantage for estimating ELES and appears to permit insufficient substitution between goods.

Per capita subsistence expenditure is now defined as the sum of positive γ estimates[4] for the most appropriate level of commodity

3. The term "t ratio" is used as shorthand for the ratio of the γ-sum estimate to the estimate of its asymptotic standard error in the base year. This value would differ slightly from a t ratio calculated at sample midpoint.
4. See Carlevaro (1971) for a justification of this procedure. At preferred levels of aggregation negative values occur for Italy, West Germany, Sweden, and the United States, all at the eight-commodity level. They always total less than 8 percent of the γ-sum estimates. For the United Kingdom the γ-sum estimate is used at the two-commodity level to permit direct comparison with the results for food in this chapter (the γ-sum estimates and t ratios are almost the same).

Table 4.1. *Estimates of γ sum at Sample Midpoints in 1970 U.S. Dollars for Different Levels of Commodity Disaggregation for Fourteen Countries*

Country	Sample midpoint	γ sum				t ratio[a]			
		8	4	2	1	8	4	2	1
Korea	1962	110	103	99	87	95.5	19.7	9.3	1.7
Thailand	1964	56	86	73	36	5.6	17.4	5.5	1.2
Taiwan	1962	112	112	111	112	52.2	36.3	35.4	34.7
Jamaica	1964	203	309	204	−27	3.9	11.9	1.6	−0.0
South Africa	1962	356	228	214	135	12.9	3.2	2.6	1.0
Greece	1963	209	339	343	339	1.8	20.4	21.7	21.1
Ireland	1962	549	564	564	569	15.9	18.2	17.6	18.2
Italy	1962	314	116	−75	−248	3.0	1.2	−0.8	−1.5
Israel	1964	799	794	793	797	35.9	31.0	24.8	26.0
United Kingdom	1962	520	913	929	944	7.2	18.7	19.2	21.5
Australia	1961	977	555	787	735	13.2	0.8	4.0	3.1
West Germany	1962	342	312	280	278	4.4	3.5	3.2	3.1
Sweden	1962	585	199	15	−238	1.7	0.8	0.0	−0.7
United States	1962	1,055	780	644	696	4.3	4.0	2.8	3.2

Note: 8, 4, 2, and 1 denote level of commodity aggregation. The eight-commodity results are from tables 3.7 and 3.8; the four- and two-commodity level results are all ELES, ML. Values in italics correspond to level of aggregation with highest *t* ratio for each country.

a. The ratio of the γ sum estimate to the estimate of its asymptotic standard error in the base year.

disaggregation, selected as above. The values are given in table 4.2. In addition, estimates of per capita subsistence expenditure on food, clothing, and housing are given for the same levels of aggregation as the γ-sum estimates.[5] Since our definition of housing here includes durables, at the eight-commodity level we sum the γ estimates for these two goods. The t ratios corresponding to each γ estimate are also given.

Total subsistence expenditure a head increases with GNP a head but less than proportionally. At different levels of GNP a head (1970 U.S. dollars) the average ratios of the two are: $100–500, 62 percent; $500–1,000, 56 percent; $1,000–1,500, 46 percent; $1,500–2,500, 37 percent; $2,500 and over, 25 percent. Subsistence expenditure on food follows a similar pattern but the increase with GNP is at a slightly slower rate. The ratio of food subsistence expenditure to total subsistence expenditure is about 63 percent in the GNP interval $100–500; for higher income levels it is about 50 percent. Subsistence expenditure on clothing and housing increases with GNP per capita at a faster rate than does total subsistence expenditure.

These conclusions also emerge when we perform double log regressions of per capita subsistence expenditures on per capita GNP. The ordinary least squares results are given in the left half of table 4.3. Even after introducing mixed levels of commodity aggregation there is substantial variation in the precision of the subsistence estimates (compare Sweden and Korea, for example, in table 4.2). We allow for this by carrying out weighted regressions, which are given in the right half of table 4.3. It is assumed that the variances of the errors on the regression equations are proportional to the variances of the estimates of the dependent variables; thus the appropriate weights by which the data are multiplied in the double log case are the t ratios given in table 4.2.[6]

The regression results show quite a strong relationship between subsistence expenditure and GNP per capita (R^2 values are generally above 0.85). Except for clothing, weighting leads to a reduction in standard errors of about half. The coefficients of GNP per capita are higher for the weighted regressions largely because of the rela-

5. For Greece and the United Kingdom we necessarily substitute the γ estimates for clothing and housing obtained at the four-commodity level.

6. These weights provide only an approximate measure of the relative degrees of precision; in most cases they will be biased estimates owing to the presence of serial correlation in the errors on the expenditure equations (see chapter 3). For other applications of the weighting procedure see Parks and Barten (1973) and Saxonhouse (1976).

Table 4.2. *Estimates of Annual per Capita Subsistence Expenditure at Sample Midpoints in 1970 U.S. Dollars, Mixed Aggregation*

Country	Sample midpoint	GNP a head	Per capita subsistence expenditure				t ratio[b]			
			Food	Clothing	Housing	Total[a]	Food	Clothing	Housing	Total
Korea	1962	142	69	12	16	110	87.9	38.0	29.3	95.5
Thailand	1964	148	53	7	10	86	22.0	11.5	29.8	17.4
Taiwan	1962	216	74	5	18	112	68.0	35.8	26.3	52.2
Jamaica	1964	541	171	27	59	309	30.8	6.2	8.0	11.9
South Africa	1962	596	134	39	92	356	18.3	9.3	16.6	12.9
Greece	1963	676	182	31	75	343	33.5	12.0	18.4	21.7
Ireland	1962	1,014	314	47	98	564	29.6	14.2	13.2	18.2
Italy	1962	1,207	173	38	52	324	5.0	4.8	2.2	3.0
Israel	1964	1,468	275	69	217	799	61.0	20.1	31.1	35.9
United Kingdom	1962	1,900	446	104	226	929	99.0	44.5	14.8	19.2
Australia	1961	2,192	424	141	152	977	39.3	20.7	5.1	13.2
West Germany	1962	2,203	230	66	41	362	8.9	7.3	1.4	4.4
Sweden	1962	2,962	313	117	138	628	2.9	8.3	2.1	1.7
United States	1962	3,669	501	82	305	1,084	22.0	4.7	4.8	4.3

a. Defined as sum of positive γ estimates at most appropriate level of commodity aggregation. See text for details.

b. The ratio of the γ sum estimate to the estimate of its asymptotic standard error in the base year.

72

Table 4.3. *Double-Log Regressions of per Capita Subsistence Expenditure on GNP per Capita*

Per capita subsistence expenditure	Unweighted			Weighted		
	a	b	R^2/d	a	b	R^2
Food	0.449	0.625[a]	0.884	0.264	0.714[a]	0.963
	(0.195)	(0.065)	2.11	(0.095)	(0.033)	
Clothing	−1.052	0.895	0.880	−1.335	1.012	0.893
	(0.285)	(0.096)	1.73	(0.286)	(0.101)	
Housing	−0.647	0.846	0.738	−1.522	1.204[b]	0.966
	(0.434)	(0.146)	1.66	(0.171)	(0.065)	
Total	0.477	0.714[a]	0.848	0.226	0.829[a]	0.975
	(0.260)	(0.087)	1.87	(0.113)	(0.047)	

Note: All equations are of the form $\log_{10} Y = a + b \log_{10} X$, where Y is the dependent variable listed in the first column of the table and X is GNP per capita at sample midpoint in 1970 U.S. dollars. All data are taken from table 4.2. Standard errors are given in parentheses. Data are arranged in order of increasing GNP per capita so that the Durbin-Watson d statistic affords an indication of the appropriateness of the functional form. The R^2 value for weighted regressions is defined as $1 - $ (weighted residual sum of squares/weighted total sum of squares) as given, for example, in Buse (1973).

a. Significantly less than one at 5 percent level.
b. Significantly greater than one at 5 percent level.

tively small weights given to West Germany and Sweden, two countries where the subsistence estimates are relatively low. For food and total subsistence expenditure the coefficient of GNP per capita is significantly less than one (at the 5 percent level) for both the weighted and unweighted regressions; thus less than proportional increases are implied. In the weighted regressions the income co-efficient for food is significantly less than the corresponding coefficient for total subsistence expenditure (at the 5 percent level). Subsistence expenditure on clothing appears to increase proportionally with GNP per capita. The weighted results for housing show subsistence expenditure increasing faster than GNP per capita. This is probably due in part to the fact that household equipment is a component of housing.

Since subsistence expenditures increase substantially with per capita GNP they cannot be interpreted in an absolute sense as measuring that which is necessary to survive. They must be interpreted in a relative sense as measuring that which is regarded as tolerable minimum consumption at a given level of economic development. It is likely, however, that if concepts of purchasing power parity[7] were used in converting γ estimates to comparable units, estimates of subsistence expenditures would show smaller increases over the development profile.

Elasticities of the Marginal Utility of Expenditure and Income

Under atemporal maximization of the Stone-Geary utility function, the expenditure elasticity of the marginal utility of expenditure (ω) is a function of the sum of the γ parameters and actual consumption (see equations 2.7 and 2.4). In this section we calculate estimates of ω for each country at the four levels of commodity aggregation used in the previous section. Again, for each country the preferred level of aggregation is that for which the t ratio for the γ sum is a maximum.

Sample mean values of ω are given in table 4.4.[8] The estimates

7. See, for example, Kravis et al. (1975), David (1972, 1973), and Balassa (1973, 1974).

8. For values of $\Sigma p_i \gamma_i$ near ν, $-\omega$ becomes very large. To avoid possible distortions, ω was calculated as the negative inverse of the mean value of the supernumerary ratio, $(\nu - \Sigma p_i \gamma_i)/\nu$, over the sample period. For all countries, levels of aggregation, and time periods, in only two cases did $\Sigma p_i \gamma_i$ exceed ν, and these were small in absolute magnitude (Korea and Israel at the eight-commodity level, first year of sample).

Table 4.4. *Mean ELES Estimates of* ω

Country	Per capita GNP at sample midpoint (1970 U.S. dollars)	$-\omega^a$ 8	4	2	1
Korea	142	*10.34*	6.58	5.26	3.50
Thailand	148	2.14	*5.44*	3.23	1.54
Taiwan	216	*4.16*	4.11	4.22	4.26
Jamaica	541	1.92	*3.85*	1.96	0.94
South Africa	596	*6.62*	2.20	2.05	1.47
Greece	676	1.71	3.10	*3.18*	3.10
Ireland	1,014	3.71	*3.98*	4.00	4.10
Italy	1,207	*1.75*	1.19	0.91	0.75
Israel	1,468	*5.29*	5.18	5.13	5.24
United Kingdom	1,900	1.74	3.92	4.12	*4.33*
Australia	2,192	*2.84*	1.59	2.09	1.95
West Germany	2,203	*1.42*	1.37	1.33	1.32
Sweden	2,962	*1.54*	1.12	1.01	0.88
United States	3,669	*1.85*	1.51	1.40	1.44

Note: Italicized values denote highest t ratio for the γ sum.
a. At the eight-, four-, two-, and one-commodity level of aggregation.

tend to decline in absolute value with income, but this is less pronounced at the two- and one-commodity levels of aggregation. For the most preferred level of aggregation the mean values of ω for different ranges of GNP per capita (1970 U.S. dollars) are: $100–500, —6.6; $500–1,000, —4.6; $1,000–1,500, —3.7; $1,500–2,500, —2.9; $2,500 and over, —1.7.

The relation between the expenditure elasticity of the marginal utility of expenditure and GNP per capita is further explored by fitting double-log regressions. The first four rows in table 4.5 show unweighted regression results obtained by regressing log —ω on the log of GNP per capita at each of the four levels of commodity aggregation. A cross-country pattern is most apparent at the four-commodity level, but it is not apparent at all at the one-commodity level, which is not surprising given the imprecision of the γ-sum estimates at that level (see table 4.1). The last two equations in table 4.3 relate to the preferred or mixed levels of aggregation for each country, as indicated by the italicized values in table 4.4. In figure 2 results for the four-commodity level and the mixed commodity level (unweighted) are compared. It is rather apparent that the difference between them is a moderate upward shift of the regression line when the most precise ω estimates are chosen. The strength of the relationship, as measured

Table 4.5.   *Double-Log Regressions of ω on GNP per Capita*

Commodity level of aggregation	a	b	R^2	d
8[a]	1.338 (0.420)	−0.302 (0.141)	0.276	3.11
4	1.645 (0.340)	−0.409 (0.114)	0.518	2.28
2	1.284 (0.399)	−0.304 (0.134)	0.300	2.16
1	0.747 (0.516)	−0.148 (0.173)	0.058	2.30
Mixed				
Unweighted	1.714 (0.318)	−0.399 (0.107)	0.538	2.00
Weighted	1.565 (0.285)	−0.358 (0.102)	0.508[b]	

Note: The regressions are: $\log_{10}(-\omega) = a + b \log_{10}X$, where X is GNP per capita in 1970 U.S. dollars, as given in table 4.4. In the last row, the variables are weighted by the reciprocal of the (approximate) standard error of log −ω. Standard errors of a and b are given in parentheses.

Countries enter the regression in increasing order of GNP per capita, so that the Durbin-Watson d statistic affords some indication of the appropriateness of the functional specification.

a. Jamaica is excluded because the sign pattern of the price elasticity matrix does not satisfy the utility specification of the model.

b. Defined as 1 − (weighted residual sum of squares/weighted total sum of squares about weighted mean).

by R^2, increases marginally (from 0.52 to 0.54) when the most precise estimates are used. The last row of table 4.5 presents a weighted regression for the mixed level of aggregation, where the weights are the reciprocal of the (approximate) standard error of the dependent variable, log −ω.[9] With weighting, the estimated elasticity of −ω with respect to GNP per capita is −0.36, compared with about −0.40 in the second and fifth rows. We therefore arrive at an approximate relationship between −ω and GNP per capita in 1970 U.S. dollars (X): $-\omega \simeq 36X^{-.36}$, that is, the absolute value of ω is about thirty-six times the reciprocal of GNP per capita to the power 0.36. For an economy with a GNP per capita of $100 the estimated value of ω is about −7; at $1,000, ω is about −3; and at $3,000 around −2. The absolute value of ω declines by approximately 0.36 percent for every one percent increase in GNP per capita.

9. Given by $\sigma_{\log_e} -\omega = |(\omega + 1)/t|$, where t is the ratio of $\Sigma p_i \hat{\gamma}_i$ to its standard error. The mean value of ω was used, and t was evaluated at base-year prices. Since in general the change in relative prices is small over short time periods, t is not expected to be sensitive to the choice of prices used in its evaluation.

Figure 2. Relation between ω and GNP per Capita

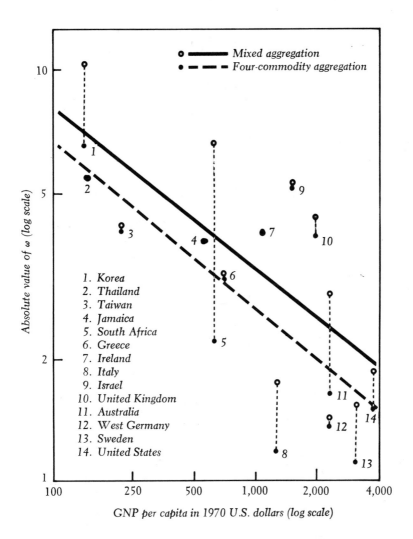

GNP *per capita in 1970 U.S. dollars (log scale)*

The above results conform with Frisch's 1959 conjecture that the expenditure elasticity of the marginal utility of expenditure is negative, declines in absolute value with GNP per capita, and lies in the interval (-10, -0.1). Within the context of ELES and LES, however, the lower bound on the absolute value of the elasticity is unity. The variation of ω with GNP per capita is estimated here with

Table 4.6. Estimates of Partial Elasticities of Substitution
at per Capita GNP Levels of $200 and $2,000

$2,000 / $200	Food	Clothing	Housing	Durables	Personal care	Transport	Recreation	Other services
Food		0.24	0.27	0.34	0.36	0.40	0.26	0.43
Clothing	0.15		0.43	0.54	0.56	0.62	0.41	0.67
Housing	0.12	0.18		0.62	0.66	0.72	0.48	0.78
Durables	0.26	0.39	0.33		0.82	0.90	0.60	0.98
Personal care	0.19	0.27	0.23	0.50		0.95	0.63	1.03
Transport	0.30	0.44	0.37	0.80	0.56		0.69	1.13
Recreation	0.24	0.35	0.29	0.63	0.44	0.71		0.75
Other services	0.22	0.32	0.27	0.58	0.41	0.65	0.52	

Note: Calculated using $\sigma_{ij} = -\omega^{-1}\eta_i\eta_j$, where the ω values are obtained from the relationship $\omega = -.36Y^{-.36}$ and the estimates of η_i are obtained from the regression equations in the first third of table 3.18. Estimates for per capita GNP of $200 are given here in the lower triangle of the body of the table, estimates for per capita GNP of $2,000 in the upper triangle.

some precision; the t ratio on the income coefficient in the last regression reported in table 4.5 is -3.5. The results at high levels of income are around the value of -2.0, the commonly accepted value for high levels of economic development.[10] Overall, at the four- and mixed-commodity levels the regression equation results are very close to those reported by de Janvry, Bieri, and Nunez (1972), who fitted regressions to estimates of ω obtained from a wide variety of demand systems studies. The pattern they found was also in close agreement with the one they observed by computing ω using a wide variety of income and price elasticity estimates for food.

In chapter 2, equation (2.5), it was shown that ϕ, the inverse of ω, was a measure of average price responsiveness.[11] Thus our findings on ω imply that the allocation of total expenditure is relatively less responsive to prices at lower levels of GNP per capita. They also imply that the partial elasticities of substitution, σ_{ij}, between goods tend to be lower at low income levels. This is because the elasticities of substitution under LES are simply the product of expenditure elasticities divided by the negative of the Frisch parameter (see table 2.2). Values of σ_{ij} at per capita GNP levels of $200 are given in the lower triangle of table 4.6, values at income levels of $2,000 are given in the upper triangle.

As discussed in chapter 2 in the section on ELES and utility, ELES permits estimation of the income elasticity of the marginal utility of income (ω^*) with the use of formula (2.8). Provided that saving is positive, ω^* must be less than ω in absolute value. We confine presentation of ω^* estimates (table 4.7) to those which correspond to the most precise ω estimates. Since ω^* is calculated from μ and ω, in table 4.7 we also give the ELES μ estimates for the preferred levels of aggregation for each country, together with their t ratios. As expected, there is a close relation between ω^* and ω estimates, with ω^* being uniformly smaller in absolute value. To measure cross-country patterns, we use (in table 4.8) double-log relationships for $-\omega^*$, as in the last two rows of table 4.5.[12] In the weighted regression the estimated elasticity of $-\omega^*$ with respect to GNP per capita is $-.34$. We therefore arrive at an approximate relationship between $-\omega^*$ and X: $-\omega^* \simeq 3^3 X^{-1/3}$, that is, the absolute value of ω^* is about twenty-seven times the reciprocal of the cubic root of GNP per capita.

10. See Brown and Deaton (1972).

11. Sato (1972) interprets $-\phi$ as an average substitution elasticity.

12. To weight $\log -\omega^*$ as $\log -\omega$ was weighted in table 4.5 requires justification. If the terms σ^2_μ and $\sigma_{\mu\omega}$ are ignored, it may be shown that $\sigma_{\log -\omega^*} \simeq \sigma_{\log -\omega}$.

Table 4.7. *Mean ELES Estimates of* ω^*

Country	Marginal propensity to consume (μ)		$-\omega^*$
	Value	t ratio	
Thailand	0.597	10.5	3.66
Korea	0.928	33.1	9.69
Taiwan	0.667	63.1	3.11
Jamaica	0.865	27.0	3.48
South Africa	0.621	7.5	4.48
Greece	0.721	45.1	2.57
Ireland	0.839	49.4	3.50
Italy	0.790	23.2	1.59
Israel	0.577	28.9	3.49
United Kingdom	0.782	35.5	2.60
West Germany	0.807	57.6	1.34
Australia	0.796	37.9	2.47
Sweden	0.810	202.5	1.44
United States	0.836	33.4	1.71

Table 4.8. *Double-Log Regressions of* ω^* *on GNP per Capita*

	a'	b'	R^2	d
Unweighted	1.530	−0.368	0.572	2.25
	(0.274)	(0.092)		
Weighted	1.432	−0.345	0.507[a]	
	(0.275)	(0.098)		

Note: The regressions are $\log_{10}(-\omega^*) = a' + b' \log_{10} X$, where X is GNP per capita in 1970 U.S. dollars, as given in table 4.4. In the last row, the variables are weighted by the reciprocal of the (approximate) standard error of $\log -\omega$. Standard errors of a' and b' are given in parentheses.

a. Defined as 1 − (weighted residual sum of squares/weighted total sum of squares about weighted mean).

For an economy with a GNP per capita of $100, ω^* is about −5.5; at $1,000, ω^* is about −2.5; and around −2 at $3,000. On average, the absolute value of ω^* declines by approximately 0.33 percent for each one percent increase in GNP.

The fitted relationships imply that the ratio ω^*/ω is always less than one but increases as GNP per capita increases. But, from (2.9), ω^*/ω is the income elasticity of total consumption expenditure, which is equal in magnitude to the sum of price elasticities of total consumption expenditure (in table 2.1 $\eta + \Sigma \eta^i = 0$). It follows, therefore, that price effects on total consumption expenditure are more important at low income levels. This phenomenon was previously observed at the eight-commodity level in the second last section of chapter 3 and is examined below in a little more detail, but from the point of view of saving rather than consumption.

Average Household Savings Behavior Across Countries

In this section we examine the ability of the model to predict the mean household savings ratio over the sample period for each country, and the responsiveness of household saving to the price of food.

As shown in column (2), table 4.9, formula (2.11) was used to calculate mean household savings ratios, with estimates of μ and ω at preferred levels of aggregation as given in the preceding section. Actual values for the mean household savings ratio are given in column (1) of the table. Predicted and actual values are reasonably close; the sample correlation coefficient between the two is 0.989. The largest proportionate difference occurs for Korea, but in this case actual household saving was very small over the sample period. The predicted values are always below the actual. Taking sample means over all countries the average household savings ratio is underestimated by about 10 percent (mean actual is 0.100, mean predicted is 0.090).

Column (3) of table 4.9 presents estimates of the elasticity of the average household savings ratio (or, equivalently, average household saving) with respect to the price of food, ξ_1. The values are obtained using formula (2.12). There is a clear tendency for the elasticity to decline in absolute value as GNP per capita increases. Average values at different levels of GNP per capita are: $100–500, −1.8; $500–1,000, −1.0; $1,000–1,500, −0.8; $1,500–2,500, −0.6; $2,500 and over, −0.3. Regressing the estimates of ξ_1 against the common logarithm of GNP per capita yields the equation presented in the footnote to table 4.9. The decline in the absolute value of ξ_1 as income increases is again apparent; the coefficient of the income term is significant at the one percent level.

At low levels of income household saving appears to be very responsive to changes in the price of food, a characteristic that is explained by the fact that subsistence consumption of food is a large component of total consumption. The estimates presented here probably represent an upper limit to the responsiveness of household saving to the price of food because they are calculated in a very partial equilibrium context, with given household income.

Table 4.9.   Mean Household Savings Ratio and Its Elasticity
with Respect to the Price of Food

Country	Mean household savings ratio		Elasticity with respect to food price (ξ_1)[a]
	Actual (1)	Predicted (2)	(3)
Korea	0.016	0.007	−2.93
Thailand	0.134	0.110	−1.30
Taiwan	0.120	0.107	−1.29
Jamaica	0.043	0.039	−1.21
South Africa	0.102	0.084	−1.08
Greece	0.117	0.108	−0.78
Ireland	0.050	0.046	−1.44
Italy	0.146	0.131	−0.28
Israel	0.139	0.121	−0.78
United Kingdom	0.065	0.058	−1.15
Australia	0.086	0.082	−0.61
West Germany	0.148	0.143	−0.22
Sweden	0.137	0.132	−0.22
United States	0.098	0.095	−0.33

a. Regressing the elasticity estimates against the log of GNP per capita in 1970 U.S. dollars (X) yields:

$$\xi_1 = -4.422 + 1.171 \log_{10}X, \qquad R^2 = 0.593$$
$$(0.835) \quad (0.280) \qquad d = 2.15$$

The estimates are likely to be most useful in situations in which
the change in the price of food does not significantly affect farmers'
incomes, as, for example, when the price of food imports changes
or when a government subsidy or tax on food is imposed in a manner
which leaves farm income unchanged.

Household Saving in Korea

During the 1953–72 period the household savings ratio in Korea
varied from −0.04 (in 1962) to 0.08 (1953). In the decade from
1963 to 1972 the range was from almost zero (1965) to 0.08 (1969).[13]
In this section the ability of ELES to predict these fairly sharp movements in household saving in Korea is examined. The prediction of
such movements is clearly a more stringent test of the model than

13. Over both the 1953–72 and 1963–72 periods household saving averaged
12 percent of gross capital formation. Since 1965 household saving has provided
an increasing share of total saving, and in 1972 represented 21 percent of gross
capital formation.

prediction of the average household savings ratio over the sample period, although we examine the latter as well.

In order to test the sensitivity of the results to sample periods and level of commodity aggregation ELES is estimated using, in turn, a five-, eight-, and twelve-commodity breakdown and two sample periods, 1953–72 and 1963–72. The eight-commodity breakdown corresponds to that used in chapter 3; the twelve-commodity breakdown is obtained by splitting up both food and housing into their three components (see table 3.1); the five-commodity level is derived from the four-commodity level used earlier in the chapter by separating fuel and light from housing.[14]

In table 4.10 we present estimates of the marginal propensity to consume (μ), and the γ sum for all levels of aggregation and both sample periods. The marginal propensity to consume is relatively insensitive to the level of commodity aggregation and sample period, although it is marginally lower at the twelve-commodity level. In the context of ELES, insensitivity to sample period provides some support for our assumption of a constant ratio of the subjective rate of discount to the rate of interest, particularly as interest rates showed substantial variability over the 1953–72 period. At values of around 0.90 the marginal propensity to consume is reasonably close to the estimate of 0.93 given in table 3.6. The γ-sum estimates are remarkably uniform at the five- and eight-commodity level for both periods. The estimates are higher at the twelve-commodity level, but the 95 percent confidence intervals for all six values of the γ sum intersect.[15] The precision of the γ-sum estimates increases with the level of aggregation.

We now proceed as in the previous section and use the estimated values of μ (table 4.10) and ω (table 4.11) to calculate the mean household savings ratio, $\hat{s}'$, for each period and level of aggregation. The estimates are compared with actual values, s', in table 4.11. The model predicts well for the 1963–72 period at the five- and eight-commodity levels, but not otherwise.

14. This follows the Korean national accounts as presented in *National Income Statistics Yearbook* (Seoul: Bank of Korea). In addition, tobacco and household operations are now included under "other."

15. Note that the γ estimates for Korea in table 3.7 are in 1965 prices. The ratio of the consumer price index in 1970 to 1965 is 1.795. If this is used as a rough conversion factor, the γ-sum estimate in table 3.7 is equivalent to 36.0 in the units of table 4.10. The stability in the estimates over sample periods is of particular interest given that real per capita income doubled over the 1953–72 period.

Table 4.10.   *The Marginal Propensity to Consume and the γ Sum, Korea*

Commodity level of aggregation	Marginal propensity to consume (μ)		γ sum	
	1953–72	*1963–72*	*1953–72*	*1963–72*
5	0.891	0.890	35.9	36.2
	(0.013)	(0.020)	(2.7)	(4.6)
8	0.891	0.892	36.0	35.6
	(0.011)	(0.013)	(1.9)	(2.4)
12	0.874	0.858	39.9	43.1
	(0.010)	(0.013)	(1.4)	(1.7)

Note: Asymptotic standard errors in parentheses. γ sum estimates are in thousands of won per capita at 1970 prices. Estimates are ML except at the twelve-commodity level of aggregation, 1963–72, where they are LS.

For the more stringent test of the ability of the model to predict movements in the household savings ratio over time, we calculate predicted values of the household savings ratio for each year by substituting the estimates of μ and the γ's into the ELES aggregate savings function (2.10):

$$\hat{s}'_t = (1 - \hat{\mu})(1 - \Sigma_j p_j \hat{\gamma}_j / y_t).$$

Since the ELES aggregate consumption function differs from the simple Keynesian function only by the inclusion of relative prices, it is of interest to compare results obtained under the two specifications. We therefore also undertake a simple regression of per capita total consumption on per capita personal disposable income (both in real terms), for both sample periods, and use these regression equations to predict the household savings ratio.

The explanatory power of the models is measured by

$$\text{Quasi } R^2 = 1 - [\Sigma_t (s'_t - \hat{s}'_t)^2 / \Sigma_t (s'_t - \bar{s}')^2],$$

and the values are given in table 4.12. The negative values of Quasi R^2 for the long period, 1953–72, imply that in predicting the household savings ratio over time ELES does worse than using the mean savings ratio. These results are clearly unacceptable. The Keynesian model yields a small positive value of Quasi R^2 for this period (the

Table 4.11. *Average Household Savings Ratio and Frisch Parameter, Korea*

Period	Actual (*s'*)	Predicted (*ŝ'*)			Frisch parameter (*ω̂*)		
		5	*8*	*12*	*5*	*8*	*12*
1953–72	0.028	0.017	0.016	0.006	−7.1	−7.5	−25.0
1963–72	0.034	0.032	0.034	0.021	−3.7	−3.6	−7.6

Note: 5, 8, 12 refer to level of commodity aggregation.

Table 4.12. *Prediction of Household Savings Ratio, Korea*

Period	Quasi R²				*d*			
	K	*5*	*8*	*12*	*K*	*5*	*8*	*12*
1953–72	0.135	−0.055	−0.115	−0.524	1.46	1.16	1.11	0.78
1963–72	0.501	0.501	0.502	0.092	2.93	2.89	2.92	1.46

Note: 5, 8, 12 refer to level of commodity aggregation under ELES. *K* refers to Keynesian consumption function. The Durbin-Watson *d* statistic is calculated from the residuals ($s'_t - \hat{s}'_t$).

marginal propensity to consume for the equation is 0.911 with a standard error of 0.023). Interpreting the Keynesian equation as a one-commodity version of ELES, the results in table 4.12 for the 1953–72 period suggest that the ability of ELES to predict the household savings ratio over time increases as the number of commodity groups is reduced. For the 1963–72 period, however, the Keynesian equation and ELES at the five- and eight-commodity levels yield almost identical results: Each explains about 50 percent of the variation in the household savings ratio. The marginal propensity to consume obtained from the Keynesian equation here is exactly the same as for ELES at the eight-commodity level: 0.892 (with standard error of 0.027).[16] The actual and predicted values for the eight-commodity classification are shown in figure 3. The graph shows that the model predicts only the general movement in the household savings ratio and fails to capture the sharp year-to-year fluctuations.[17]

Given the substantial structural changes in the Korean economy over the 1953–72 period, it is not surprising that the simple models considered here fail to explain movements in the household savings ratio over the whole twenty-year period. The introduction of relative prices within an ELES framework into the Keynesian function worsens the already poor predictive ability of that model. When the sample period is restricted to 1963–72, however, the models yield considerably better results, and the introduction of a limited number of relative prices into the Keynesian consumption function makes no difference to its predictive ability.[18]

A first step in improving the ability of ELES to forecast household saving would be to remove the well-known limitations of the Keynesian consumption function and introduce the concept of permanent income. Second, because of the high positive correlation between agricultural production and the household savings ratio in Korea, some disaggregation of consumers by economic activity would seem desirable (see chapter 5). Third, financial variables should be incorporated into the model, particularly in view of the substantial variations that have occurred in Korean monetary policy.

16. The implied estimate of the γ sum from the Keynesian function, in thousands of 1970 won per capita, is 34.9 with a standard error of 5.5 The corresponding estimate obtained using the 1953–72 sample period is 29.7 with standard error of 3.6.

17. This is also indicated by the negative serial correlation in the residuals as measured by the Durbin-Watson d statistic (see table 4.12).

18. Similar results have been obtained for the United States over the sample period, 1930–72; see Lluch and Williams (1975a).

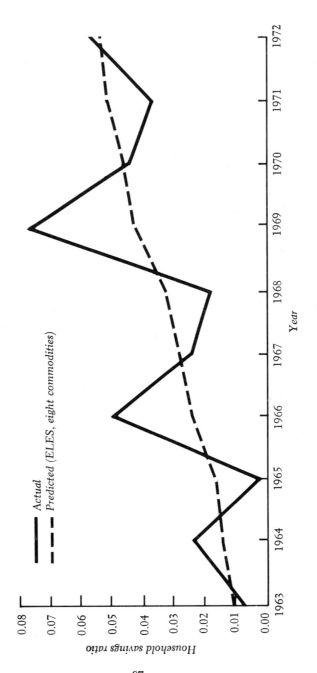

Figure 3. Household Savings Ratio, Korea, 1963–72

Actual
Predicted (ELES, eight commodities)

Household savings ratio

Year

87

Permanent Income, Household Demand, and Saving in Taiwan

All the preceding empirical results have been obtained by using current income as an explanatory variable. In this section the consequences of using alternative definitions of income are explored and the geographical coverage of our detailed analysis is expanded by the use of Taiwanese data. The low value previously obtained for the marginal propensity to consume in Taiwan (see tables 3.6 or 4.7) of 0.67 could be due to the use of a static model which uses only current income and it is of particular interest here to experiment with dynamic specifications which permit differences between the marginal propensities to consume in the short and long run. Data for the 1952–70 sample period is at the four-commodity level of aggregation used in the first section of this chapter.[19]

To facilitate explanation of our estimating equations the basic ELES equations are written as

$$(4.1) \qquad v_{it} = p_{it}\gamma_i + \beta_i^*(z_t - \sum_{j=1}^{n} p_{jt}\gamma_j) \qquad \begin{matrix} (i = 1, ..., n) \\ (t = 1, ..., T) \end{matrix}$$

and associated aggregate consumption function as

$$(4.2) \qquad v_t = (1 - \mu)\sum_j p_{jt}\gamma_j + \mu z_t$$

where z_t represents some measure of permanent income. Four definitions of z_t are considered:

$$(4.3) \qquad z_t = y_t$$

$$(4.4) \qquad z_t = y_t + \frac{\theta}{1 - \lambda L} \Delta y_t = \frac{1 - \lambda}{1 - \lambda L} y_t + \frac{(\lambda + \theta)}{1 - \lambda L} \Delta y_t$$

$$(4.5) \qquad z_t = \frac{\xi}{1 - \lambda L} y_t$$

$$(4.6) \qquad z_t = \frac{1 - \lambda}{1 - \lambda L} y_t$$

19. Data are taken from *National Accounts in Taiwan for 1951–1970*. Earlier in this chapter it was noted that estimates of the γ sum for Taiwan were insensitive to the level of commodity aggregation. The same is true for estimates of β_i and μ. For example, the value of μ in table 4.7 (seven commodities) is 0.667, at the four-commodity level for the same sample period it was 0.669.

where y_t is actual (total) income,[20] L is the lag operator, and $\Delta = 1 - L$.

The first specification, (4.3), uses current income, as in chapter 3 and the rest of chapter 4. Under the Lluch (1973a) interpretation it is therefore assumed that the present value of expected changes in labor income is zero. Definition (4.4) assumes that discounted expected changes in labor income are proportional to a geometric distributed lag on current and past changes in total income. (4.5) and (4.6) assume that permanent income is a geometric distributed lag on current and past income; (4.6) restricts the weights to sum to unity and is a special case of (4.4) ($\theta = -\lambda$).[21] (4.5) and (4.6) are introduced to enable comparison of ELES aggregate consumption functions with more conventional consumption functions that incorporate the concept of permanent income.

The estimating equations obtained by using total income for permanent income are just those obtained by substituting y_t for z_t in equation (4.1). Substitution of equations (4.4) and (4.5) into (4.1) yields, respectively:

$$(4.7) \quad v_{it} = \gamma_i p_{it} - \lambda \gamma_i p_{i(t-1)} + \beta_i^*(1-\lambda)y_t + \beta_i^*(\lambda+\theta)\Delta y_t \\ - \beta_i^* \sum_j \gamma_j p_{jt} + \lambda \beta_i^* \sum_j \gamma_j p_{j(t-1)} + \lambda v_{i(t-1)}$$

$$(4.8) \quad v_{it} = \gamma_i p_{it} - \lambda \gamma_i p_{i(t-1)} + \xi \beta_i^* y_t \\ - \beta_i^* \sum_j \gamma_j p_{jt} + \lambda \beta_i^* \sum_j \gamma_j p_{j(t-1)} + \lambda v_{i(t-1)}$$

The estimating equation using (4.6) is obtained by substituting $1 - \lambda$ for ξ in equation (4.8).

Expressions (4.7) and (4.8) are dynamic expenditure equations in which the short- and long-run elasticities of demand with respect to actual income differ, but the short- and long-run price elasticities do not.[22] The associated aggregate consumption functions may be obtained by either summing equations (4.7) and (4.8) over commodities or, more conveniently, by substituting (4.4) and (4.5) directly into equation (4.2) and rearranging.

20. To be more precise, y_t is per capita personal disposable income.
21. A negative value of θ would imply that consumers do not regard all of current income as "permanent" or they do not extrapolate past changes in income.
22. For examples of dynamic demand equations based on LES see Pollak and Wales (1969), Phlips (1972), and Taylor and Weiserbs (1972). In these models, which use total consumption rather than income, dynamism is achieved by making parameters of the Stone-Geary utility function depend on past consumption.

Since for certain values of λ, θ, and ξ the models are equivalent, we first concentrate on the estimates of these parameters. The first half of table 4.13 presents estimates of the adjustment parameters (λ, θ, ξ) and the long-run marginal propensity to consume (μ) obtained from maximum-likelihood estimation of the complete systems of demand equations such as (4.7) and (4.8).[23] In addition, derived estimates are given of the short-run marginal propensity to consume (defined as $\partial v_t / \partial y_t$). In (4.4), the estimate of θ is negative and $\lambda + \theta$ is not significantly different from zero at the 5 percent level (the t ratio is -0.4); the model is thus empirically equivalent to (4.6). In (4.5) $\xi + \lambda$ is not significantly different from unity (the t value is 1.4), and again the model reduces to (4.6). Among the dynamic formulations then, the simplest model (4.6) is preferred. In all dynamic models, however, the adjustment coefficient (λ) is small and not significantly different from zero at the 5 percent level. It follows that the differences between estimated short-run and long-run marginal propensities to consume are relatively small, as are the differences between short-run and long-run income elasticities of demand. Consumption decisions appear to be based largely on current income.

Estimates of the long-run marginal propensity to consume (μ)— or, equivalently, the marginal propensity to save—obtained from the three dynamic models are very similar to each other and to the estimate obtained using current income (4.3). Similarly, estimates of β and γ are almost the same for all four models: the β values differed only in the third decimal place, the γ-sum estimates standardized on (4.3) $= 1$ were (4.4), 1.035; (4.5), 0.929; (4.6), 1.033.[24] We therefore confine detailed results to the current income model (4.3) and the preferred dynamic model (4.6). The estimates of β and γ are given in table 4.14, together with indicators of degree of fit (R^2) and serial correlation in the residuals as measured by the Durbin-Watson d statistic.[25] Serial correlation in the errors is reduced a little

23. For an alternative approach which uses the concept of permanent income but estimates directly the ELES aggregate consumption function, see Powell (1973b). In estimation we assume that the errors on the demand systems such as (4.7) and (4.8) are classical. If, alternatively, the errors on (4.1) are assumed to be classical then the errors on (4.7) and (4.8) will be serially correlated. Calculated values of Durbin's h statistic did not reveal any significant first-order serial correlation in the residuals.

24. The standard errors on the γ estimates, however, tend to be higher under the dynamic formulations.

25. Since d is used solely in a descriptive sense, we omit discussion of its statistical properties when lagged dependent variables are present.

Table 4.13. *Estimates of Marginal Propensity to Consume and Permanent Income Parameters, Taiwan, 1952–70*

Permanent income definition	Permanent income parameter			Marginal propensity to consume	
	λ	θ	ξ	Long run (μ)	Short run
ELES models					
(4.3)	—	—	—	0.685	0.685
				(0.011)	(0.011)
(4.4)	0.115	−0.137	—	0.693	0.598
	(0.167)	(0.141)		(0.016)	(0.089)
(4.5)	0.144	—	0.920	0.636[a]	0.585
	(0.089)		(0.100)	(0.039)	(0.057)
(4.6)	0.128	—	—	0.692	0.603
	(0.088)			(0.013)	(0.067)
Conventional models					
(4.3)	—	—	—	0.685	0.685
				(0.012)	(0.012)
(4.4)	0.213	−0.381	—	0.709	0.439
	(0.166)	(0.148)		(0.017)	(0.098)
(4.6)	0.303	—	—	0.703	0.490
	(0.091)			(0.016)	(0.059)

— Parameter does not appear in model.

Note: Asymptotic standard errors in parentheses.

a. (4.5) differs from the other models in that the sum of the coefficients on actual income exceeds one. In this case the long-term marginal propensity to consume out of actual income is $\mu\xi/(1 - \lambda) = 0.684$.

by dynamic formulation, but it is not particularly severe in the static model. Since the estimates of β, γ, and μ are almost the same as those obtained for the 1955–68 period,[26] it follows that the implied estimates of elasticities, Frisch parameter, predicted average household savings ratio, and others are almost the same as those reported earlier in chapters 3 and 4.

So far we have compared the short-run and long-run responses of aggregate consumption to changes in income within the framework of ELES. It is of interest also to examine estimates obtained outside the framework of a demand system. The class of conventional aggregate consumption functions[27] most closely related to the ELES

26. Since earlier results were given in detail only at the seven-commodity level, it is necessary to add the parameter estimates of β and γ for commodities 4 to 7 to obtain comparable estimates for the category "other" at the four-commodity level.

27. See Evans (1969) and Bridge (1971) for summaries of the literature.

Table 4.14. ELES Estimates Using Current and Permanent Income, Taiwan, 1952–70

Commodity	β (4.3)	β (4.6)	γ[a] (4.3)	γ[a] (4.6)	R^2/d (4.3)	R^2/d (4.6)
Food	0.312	0.311	2,525.4	2,566.6	0.9979	0.9981
	(0.011)	(0.012)	(43.4)	(56.0)	1.29	1.48
Clothing	0.069	0.070	166.4	173.2	0.9965	0.9966
	(0.001)	(0.002)	(6.3)	(8.8)	1.40	1.59
Housing	0.252	0.251	550.4	582.5	0.9940	0.9944
	(0.008)	(0.009)	(53.3)	(42.9)	1.73	1.76
Other	0.367	0.368	438.5	480.6	0.9962	0.9968
	(0.007)	(0.008)	(36.1)	(50.4)	1.42	1.39
Sum	1.000	1.000	3,680.6	3,808.3		
			(108.2)	(148.9)		

Note: Asymptotic standard errors in parentheses.

a. Units of measurement are 1966 new Taiwan dollars per capita.

aggregate relationship (4.2) is given by

$$(4.9) \qquad v_t^* = \alpha + \mu z_t^*$$

where asterisks denote real values and the alternative definitions of z^* are given by (4.3) to (4.6) with y replaced by y^*. Substituting equations (4.3) to (4.6) into (4.9) and rearranging, we obtain

$$(4.10) \qquad v_t^* = \alpha + \mu y_t^*$$

$$(4.11) \qquad v_t^* = \alpha(1 - \lambda) + \mu(1 - \lambda)y_t^* + \mu(\lambda + \theta)\Delta y_t^* + \lambda v_{t-1}^*$$

$$(4.12) \qquad v_t^* = \alpha(1 - \lambda) + \mu \xi y_t^* + \lambda v_{t-1}^*$$

$$(4.13) \qquad v_t^* = \alpha(1 - \lambda) + \mu(1 - \lambda)y_t^* + \lambda v_{t-1}^*$$

Equation (4.10) is the simple Keynesian consumption function. The explanatory variables in equation (4.11) are equivalent to those used by Houthakker and Taylor (1970, p. 283). Equations (4.12) and (4.13) imply the same estimating equation, which may be interpreted as a habit persistence model as well as a standard model for permanent income.[28] Models (4.10) to (4.13) differ from the ELES aggregate consumption function (4.2) in that relative prices do not appear in the intercept, and past values of *real* income are used in defining permanent income. The latter difference means that the estimates of λ might be expected to be higher for ELES when they include an allowance for past inflation, which averaged 6.6 percent a year in Taiwan over the sample period.[29]

The conventional aggregate consumption functions (4.10) to (4.13) were estimated by ordinary least squares. Estimates of the underlying parameters of the models are given in the lower section of table 4.13. The dynamic models perform somewhat better than the static model (4.10), and as the coefficient of Δy^* in (4.11) has a t value of only -0.66, the simplest dynamic specification (4.13) is preferred, as it was under ELES. A comparison with ELES estimates in table 4.13 shows similar estimates of the long-term marginal propensity to consume, but the conventional models yield lower

28. In the tradition of Brown (1952) and Friedman (1957) respectively. Equations (4.10) to (4.13) have been used by Oksanen and Spencer (1973) in a comparative study of consumption functions for fifteen countries.

29. This is easiest to see using (4.5), $z_t = \xi[1-\lambda L]^{-1}y_t$, in ELES. Dividing by a general consumer price index with time subscript t yields $z_t^* = \xi[1-\lambda^* L]y_t^*$ where $\lambda^* = \lambda(1 + g)^{-1}$ and g is the annual (assumed constant) rate of inflation. If, in addition, relative prices are constant over time, the ELES aggregate consumption function then reduces exactly to (4.12) with the new interpretation of λ and with $\alpha = (1 - \mu)\Sigma\gamma_t$.

short-run propensities. The lower λ values for the ELES models do not meet the a priori expectations outlined above.

Comparison of the ability of models to predict the household savings ratio over time is limited to those models which use either current income (4.3) or the permanent income variable (4.6). When current income is used, the household savings ratio is calculated as it was in the previous section on Korea. When (4.6) is used, the predicted household savings ratio for ELES is given by

$$\hat{s}'_t = [1 - \hat{\mu}(1 - \hat{\lambda})] - (1 - \hat{\mu})\,(p'_t\hat{\gamma} - \hat{\lambda}p'_{t-1}\hat{\gamma})/y_t - \hat{\lambda}v_{t-1}/y_t$$

and for the Brown-Friedman model (4.13) by

$$\hat{s}'_t = [1 - \hat{\mu}(1 - \hat{\lambda})] - \hat{\alpha}(1 - \hat{\lambda})/y^*_t - \hat{\lambda}v_{t-1}/y^*_t.$$

As in the case of Korea, we use a measure of goodness of fit (Quasi R^2) and d values in evaluating model performance. The estimates are given in table 4.15. Unlike the results from the Korean data, all models yield high values of Quasi R^2 that exceed 0.9. For this reason we also report mean square errors, which permit greater discrimination among the specifications. The results again show that with current income ELES performs almost exactly as a simple Keynesian function; the introduction of relative prices does not help. For both ELES and the conventional models, the use of the permanent income variable (4.6) improves predictive ability. The Brown-Friedman model performs somewhat better than ELES, with a mean square error 30 percent less. The relative ability of the models to trace cyclical movements in the household savings ratio is nicely summarized by the values of the Durbin-Watson statistic: low for the static formulations, increasing to around two for the Brown-Friedman model. In figure 4 actual values of the household savings ratio are compared with predicted values obtained by using the permanent income version of ELES. The Brown-Friedman model (4.13) outperforms ELES (4.6) over the 1957–60 period but otherwise yields predictions which are similar to those in figure 4.

Since this book aims at broad characterizations of demand and savings behavior, the findings of this section are encouraging. They imply that, at least for Taiwan, the estimates of μ, β, and γ in chapter 3 and the derived measures in chapter 4 may be interpreted as measuring long-run responses of demand and saving to changes in income. In particular, the relatively low estimate obtained for the marginal propensity to consume in Taiwan of around 0.7 seems not to be due to misspecification of the model, but rather reflects underlying long-run consumer behavior. More work remains to be

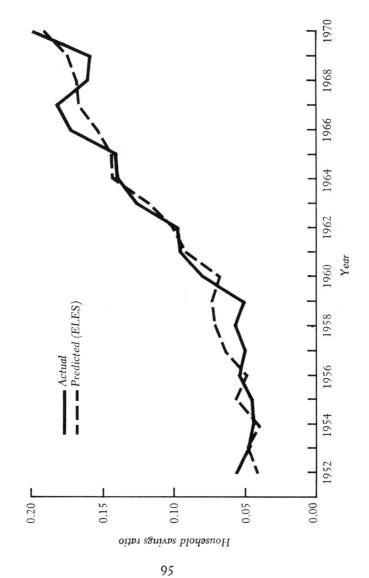

Figure 4. *Household Savings Ratio, Taiwan, 1952–70*

95

Table 4.15.   Ability of Models to Predict Household
Savings Ratio over Time, Taiwan, 1952–70

	Current income (4.3)		Permanent income (4.6)	
	ELES	Keynesian	ELES	Brown/Friedman
Quasi R^2	0.9262	0.9295	0.9535	0.9669
Mean square error[a]	0.1929	0.1843	0.1280	0.0865
d	0.98	1.00	1.43	2.16

a. Defined as $\Sigma(\hat{s}'_t - s'_t)^2/19$; entries multiplied by 10^3.

done, however, on the dynamic specification of ELES. The superior
short-run predictive ability of the Brown-Friedman aggregate consumption model, in which permanent income is expressed as a
function of current and past real income, suggests that some improvement is required in the treatment of price movements in the dynamic
specification of ELES used here. Because savings behavior in Taiwan,
as measured by the household savings ratio, moved fairly uniformly
upward over the sample period, it is not too surprising that, even
when current income was used in ELES, the model predicted general
movements in the household savings ratio over time with some
accuracy. In contrast, a much poorer fit was obtained for Korea in
the previous section, where the household savings ratio fluctuated
substantially over time. To obtain a robust model of household
saving it would seem necessary to include variables other than income
and prices and to disaggregate by type of household.

5
Household Disaggregation: Empirical Results for Korea

THE TIME-SERIES RESULTS presented in the previous two chapters are construed as measuring the patterns of household saving and demand for the average or "representative" consumer in each country. In this and subsequent chapters we look beyond the aggregate agent and explore demand and savings behavior for different categories of typical consumers, using the survey data available.

Reasons for Disaggregating

In the context of ELES disaggregation has many advantages. First, it permits an examination of the effects on demand and saving of household attributes such as location, socioeconomic class, family size, and age of head of household. This information is important for predicting the economic effects of social changes such as smaller family size or migration from rural to urban areas. Second, disaggregation enables quantification of the differential effects on *saving* and consumption of changes in relative prices. An increase in the relative price of food, for example, is likely to be most detrimental to the economic welfare of low-income urban households. Third, disaggregated results can be used to measure some of the economic effects of changes in income distribution. Fourth, disaggregation is useful for building economic models; it provides guidance as to the range of data over which a linear model may be valid, or it may indicate the desirability of using a model with constant elasticities rather than constant marginal responses. Fifth, disaggregation provides evidence as to whether the γ parameters in ELES may be interpreted in any sense as measuring subsistence consumption.

In the case of Korea, the first distinction made is between farmers on the one hand and urban wage and salary earners on the other. Urban households are then broken down into six groups according to socioeconomic class, family size, and age of household head. For the rural-urban breakdown we use annual time series (1963–72) of aggregate sample survey data; in the subdivision of urban consumers we use individual household observations from cross-section data for the first quarter of 1971.

Rural-Urban Dualism

The effect of the allocation of consumer expenditure on the growth and structure of output has recently been shown to be important in dualistic development models. Kelley, Williamson, and Cheetham (1972) (henceforth KWC), state that "the sensitivity of the economy to shifts in tastes towards urban goods may be as stimulatory to structural change in the long run as alterations in savings parameters" (p. 197). The work of KWC is particularly relevant here because they use LES in the demand side of their model. Shifts in tastes in their formulation refer to significant differences between marginal budget shares in a model composed of two sectors (rural and urban) and two commodities (food and nonfood). KWC reach their conclusions by examining the sensitivity of model solutions to changes in the values of demand and savings parameters, within ranges relevant for Asian economies. Two restrictions are, however, placed on the parameter values for LES: The marginal budget share for nonfood is higher in the urban sector than in the rural; subsistence consumption is the same in both sectors and zero for nonfood.

By fitting ELES to Korean data it is possible to explore the differences between the demands of rural and urban households and, in addition, to investigate the explicit effects of a change in taste (in the KWC sense) on savings behavior. To this effect, we use aggregate survey data on per capita expenditures and per capita personal disposable income, together with prices, to estimate ELES separately for Korean farm households and urban wage and salary earners.[1] The

1. The data are taken from two sources: *Annual Report on the Family Income and Expenditure Survey* (Bureau of Statistics, Economic Planning

period of estimation is 1963–72. A five-commodity classification of expenditure is used: food, clothing, housing, fuel and light, and other.[2] Imputed rent for owner-occupied dwellings is included in housing (and income) in the urban survey, but excluded in the rural one. Although the surveys do not cover the entire Korean rural and urban populations, the scope is probably sufficient to capture the key features of dualism in demand and savings patterns.[3] Basic characteristics of the sample are given in table 5.1, which, for purposes of comparison, also lists similar characteristics for national accounts data.

Table 5.2 contains the basic ELES estimates (β, γ, μ) for the survey data. The relative poverty of farmers over the sample period is apparent in the estimates (as in table 5.1). Their marginal budget share for food is about twice that of urban wage and salary earners; their cost of subsistence (γ sum) in 1970 prices is about 60 percent of that of urban consumers. Both these differences are significant at the one percent level. Thus the data verify the assumption in the KWC model that the marginal budget share for nonfood is higher in the urban sector than in the rural. But the assumption that subsistence consumption is the same in both sectors and zero for nonfood is not verified. The food subsistence costs for each group are significantly different at the one percent level, and about half the subsistence cost is spent on nonfood goods by both farmers and urban consumers. The implied expenditure and own-price elasticities for food for farm households are about twice those for urban dwellers. (Full sets of elasticity estimates are given in table 5.3.)

At the same time, farmers appear to be considerably more thrifty— their marginal propensity to consume is almost half that of urban consumers. Apart from the different nature of the data in rural and

---

Board, Korea) and *Report on the Results of Farm Household Economy Survey and Production Cost Survey of Agricultural Products* (Ministry of Agriculture and Forestry, Korea). Separate consumer price indexes (1970 = 1.000) for urban and farm households were obtained from *Economic Statistics Yearbook, 1973* (Bank of Korea).

2. Again our analysis is restricted to broad commodity groupings. Pak and Han (1969) give a detailed analysis of demand for various types of food in Korea. "Other" comprises tobacco, education, transport, personal care and other services.

3. Only data for wage and salary earners from the survey of urban households are considered here (income information exists only for these households). In terms of overall mean expenditure and average budget shares, other households in the survey are not very different from wage and salary earners. LES estimates of β and γ confirm this.

Table 5.1. *Basic Characteristics of Aggregate Survey Data for Urban and Farm Households and Comparison with National Accounts Data, Korea, 1963–72*

Variable	National accounts			Urban households (wage and salary earners)			Farm households		
	1963	1970	1972	1963	1970	1972	1963	1970	1972
y	15.1	63.0	93.0	13.6	66.9	92.7	14.1	42.1	73.9
v	14.9	60.2	87.7	14.6	63.6	82.8	12.1	35.1	54.2
w_1	0.584	0.539	0.550	0.551	0.406	0.413	0.603	0.459	0.481
w_2	0.103	0.112	0.114	0.061	0.105	0.092	0.065	0.084	0.073
w_3	0.086	0.066	0.060	0.142	0.182	0.185	0.035	0.042	0.057
w_4	0.043	0.047	0.041	0.061	0.058	0.053	0.092	0.079	0.067
w_5	0.184	0.236	0.236	0.185	0.249	0.258	0.206	0.336	0.321
p_1	0.389	1.000	1.347	0.374	1.000	1.347	0.386	1.000	1.337
p_2	0.353	1.000	1.127	0.373	1.000	1.156	0.411	1.000	1.130
p_3	0.467	1.000	1.135	0.420	1.000	1.171	0.375	1.000	1.148
p_4	0.290	1.000	1.218	0.412	1.000	1.191	0.416	1.000	1.216
p_5	0.373	1.000	1.258	0.390	1.000	1.227	0.353	1.000	1.314

Sources: Tables in chapter 5 are based on data from *Annual Report on the Family Income and Expenditure Survey* (Bureau of Statistics, Economic Planning Board, Korea) and *Report on the Results of Farm Household Economy Survey and Production Cost Survey of Agricultural Products* (Ministry of Agriculture and Forestry, Korea). The national accounts data and separate consumer price indexes (1970 = 1.000) for urban and farm households were obtained from *Economic Statistics Yearbook* (Bank of Korea) for the relevant years.

Note: y Personal disposable income per capita, in thousand won a year (current prices).

v Total consumption expenditure per capita, in thousand won a year (current prices).

w_i Average budget share for the ith commodity. Code: 1, food; 2, clothing; 3, housing; 4, fuel and light; 5, other.

p_i Price index of the ith commodity ($i = 1, ..., 5$; p (1970) $= 1$). For national accounts the price index is the implicit deflator.

100

Table 5.2.   *ELES Estimates, Annual Time Series of Aggregate*
Cross Sections, Korea, 1963–72

Commodity	Farm households			Urban households (wage and salary earners)[a]		
	β	γ	R^2/d	β	γ	R^2/d
Food	0.367	13.6	0.968	0.173	22.7	0.976
	(0.081)	(1.2)	1.40	(0.043)	(1.4)	0.65
	4.5	*11.4*		*4.0*	*15.7*	
Clothing	0.102	1.9	0.968	0.166	3.0	0.967
	(0.016)	(0.1)	0.99	(0.007)	(0.8)	0.80
	6.5	*13.4*		*23.9*	*3.7*	
Housing	0.110	0.7	0.940	0.254	6.3	0.995
	(0.011)	(0.2)	2.51	(0.021)	(0.8)	1.23
	10.1	*3.4*		*12.3*	*7.4*	
Fuel and light	0.077	2.0	0.977	0.052	2.4	0.981
	(0.016)	(0.1)	1.26	(0.008)	(0.2)	1.51
	4.9	*19.3*		*6.8*	*12.3*	
Other	0.344	8.5	0.985	0.355	8.5	0.997
	(0.058)	(0.7)	1.05	(0.020)	(1.4)	1.28
	5.9	*11.6*		*17.6*	*6.2*	
Sum	1.0	26.7		1.0	42.8	
		(1.7)			(4.4)	
		15.3			*9.7*	
μ	0.463			0.812		
	(0.045)			(0.037)		
	10.1			*21.8*		

Note: Subsistence (γ) is measured in thousand won per capita a year in 1970 prices. (The 1970 rate of exchange was 310 won = U.S. \$1.00.) Standard errors in parentheses; t ratios in italics. The method of estimation is maximum likelihood.

a. If imputed rent is excluded, the estimated β values for each commodity from first to fifth are 0.190, 0.203, 0.097, 0.067, 0.444; the γ values are 23.5, 3.4, 1.7, 2.4, 9.1. There are no marked changes in the t values or in R^2 and d. Also, $\mu = 0.761$ ($t = 17.9$), γ sum = 40.1 ($t = 13.8$).

urban surveys,[4] this paradox of thrift in relative poverty is probably explained in part by the consumer-producer nature of the farm household. With the high variability of income and the direct link between today's saving and tomorrow's subsistence consumption, high marginal and average savings rates are required for subsistence over time. If interest rates paid by farmers tend to be higher than those available to urban dwellers, then farmers' marginal propensity to consume will

4. About half the total income of farm households is noncash and includes, for example, imputed income from growth of cattle and trees. It is therefore not surprising that we obtain a "low" value for the propensity to consume out of changes in current income.

Table 5.3.   ELES Estimates of Total Expenditure and Price Elasticities, Farm and Urban Households, Korea, 1963–72

Commodity	Expenditure	Price				
		Food	Clothing	Housing	Fuel and light	Other
Food						
Farm	0.746	−0.457	−0.046	−0.018	−0.047	−0.179
Urban	0.391	−0.219	−0.028	−0.053	−0.019	−0.071
Clothing						
Farm	1.271	−0.537	−0.319	−0.030	−0.080	−0.305
Urban	1.719	−0.716	−0.375	−0.234	−0.081	−0.312
Housing						
Farm	2.483	−1.049	−0.151	−0.529	−0.157	−0.597
Urban	1.466	−0.610	−0.106	−0.414	−0.069	−0.266
Fuel and light						
Farm	0.993	−0.419	−0.061	−0.023	−0.251	−0.239
Urban	0.951	−0.396	−0.069	−0.130	−0.184	−0.173
Other						
Farm	1.125	−0.475	−0.069	−0.026	−0.071	−0.484
Urban	1.520	−0.633	−0.110	−0.207	−0.072	−0.498

be smaller.[5] Needless to say, the model fitted here cannot capture directly this feature of the farm household since it is derived from neoclassical demand theory, with exogenously given income and prices. The farm saving ratio predicted from this model is, however, close to the actual one over the sample period (see table 5.4).

Other elements of dualistic behavior appear in the composition of nonfood expenditure, at the margin. If imputed rent for owner-occupied housing is included in the definition of both expenditure and income of urban consumers, dualism is apparent mainly in housing and clothing, as reflected in differences in estimated marginal

5. McLaren (1976) has extended the ELES framework to incorporate decisions on production, investment, and financing for a family firm; under plausible assumptions the final form of the expenditure system is no different from ELES. Since the marginal propensity to consume (μ) in ELES is the ratio δ/ρ, it is clear that if an externally given ρ is higher for farmers than for urban consumers (as has been true historically of the dualistic Korean economy), the rural group will have a lower marginal propensity to consume than the urban, provided there is no countervailing inequality in pure time preferences (δ) between the two groups. An additional complication arises from our implicit assumption that δ moves roughly in line with changes in ρ over the sample period, for each group. To the extent that this is not true the estimates of μ are at best sample mean values.

Table 5.4. *Actual and Predicted Average Household Savings Ratios,*
Frisch Parameter, and Food-Price Elasticity of Savings Ratio,
Korea, 1963–72

Symbol	Farm households	Urban households (wage and salary earners)
s'	0.170	0.023
$\hat{s}'$	0.181	0.033
ω	−5.3	−6.8
Quasi R^2	0.885	0.767
ξ (food)	−1.0	−2.2

budget shares. If imputed rent is excluded, dualism is reflected mainly in the categories of clothing and other expenditure (see the footnote to table 5.2).

Table 5.4 presents evidence as to the success with which the system predicts the average household savings ratio and its variation over time for each of the two population groups. The sample average household savings ratio (s') for each group is given in the first row. The estimated values of the Frisch parameter (ω) in the third row are then combined with μ, using (2.11), to yield a prediction, $\hat{s}'$ (second row). The differences between s' and $\hat{s}'$ during the sample period are summarized by the goodness of fit measure (fourth row), quasi R^2.[6] The model is quite successful at predicting saving, particularly for farm households. The last row of table 5.4 presents estimates of the elasticity of the average savings ratio with respect to the price of food. The savings ratio is quite responsive to the price of food, especially in urban areas.

Although the difference between estimates of the Frisch parameter for both population groups is relatively minor, it does not conform with Frisch's original conjecture that the absolute value of ω is larger for smaller values of income. This suggests that income is not the only determinant of ω.

Cross-Section Analysis of Urban Households

For this section data on individual urban households are taken for the first quarter of 1971, and separate ELES estimates are obtained

6. Defined as quasi $R^2 = 1 - \left[\sum_t (s'_t - \hat{s}'_t)^2 / \sum_t (s'_t - \bar{s}')^2 \right]$, where $\hat{s}'_t = (1 - \hat{\mu})$ $(1 - \sum_i p_{it}\hat{\gamma}_i/y_t)$.

Table 5.5. *Selected Characteristics of Urban Households: Sample Survey, Korea, 1971, First Quarter*

| | Nine cities | | | | | | Seoul | | | | | |
| | Salary earners | | | Wage earners | | | Salary earners | | | Wage earners | | |
Characteristic	Y	O,S	O,L	Y	O,S	O,L	Y	O,S	O,L	Y	O,S	O,L
Number of households	110	86	114	101	84	99	65	55	59	42	39	27
Means												
Age of head	31.2	41.0	43.7	29.7	44.5	47.1	31.0	41.9	44.4	29.8	44.2	46.1
Family size	4.2	4.5	6.9	4.1	4.2	7.0	3.9	4.4	6.8	4.8	4.8	7.0
Income[a]	26.8	24.7	21.0	18.4	15.7	11.6	30.7	27.8	25.1	19.0	16.2	14.4
Consumption[a]	22.8	23.1	19.1	17.0	15.1	11.4	25.3	26.3	19.6	16.8	14.5	12.5
Savings ratio	0.148	0.062	0.092	0.075	0.042	0.019	0.176	0.053	0.221	0.159	0.102	0.134
Budget shares												
Food	0.359	0.358	0.352	0.441	0.454	0.439	0.341	0.325	0.309	0.416	0.456	0.396
Clothing	0.131	0.118	0.109	0.106	0.077	0.093	0.139	0.120	0.133	0.102	0.068	0.065
Housing	0.178	0.167	0.152	0.171	0.158	0.151	0.164	0.161	0.135	0.161	0.159	0.209
Fuel and light	0.072	0.063	0.056	0.065	0.065	0.068	0.071	0.063	0.058	0.071	0.067	0.064
Other	0.260	0.294	0.331	0.217	0.246	0.250	0.285	0.330	0.365	0.250	0.251	0.266

Note: Households are divided by age of head into Y (young, less than 35 years) and O (old, 35 years and over); and by family size into S (small, 5 or less) and L (large, more than 5).

a. Income (disposable) and consumption are per capita in thousand won a quarter.

for a number of representative consumers. After preliminary analysis of the data, households were subdivided in three ways: by socioeconomic class into salary earners and wage earners; by age of family head into young (Y, less than 35 years) and old (O, 35 years or more); and by family size into small (S, 5 or less) and large (L, more than 5). Initially households were subdivided by income, but the resulting estimates were unacceptable. In particular, total subsistence expenditure was generally negative, and price elasticities had the "wrong" sign. The classification by socioeconomic groups is to some extent according to permanent income rather than measured income. The dividing points for family size and age of head are necessarily somewhat arbitrary, but they are based on observed savings behavior and a need to keep a sufficient number of observations in each cell. Young families have not been subdivided by age because relatively few have over five members. The average size of all young households is smaller than that of old, small households (see table 5.5).

The adopted classification yields six groups of relatively homogeneous consumers. For each group or cell ELES is fitted to data on urban households for the same five-commodity subdivision used in the previous section. In addition, comparable estimates for Seoul households only are obtained.

All Urban Households

The basic characteristics of the sample data are given in table 5.5. The subgroups of households are arranged in order of decreasing per capita income. Notice that young households have higher per capita income than old households in each socioeconomic class.

For each subgroup ELES is fitted to data on per capita expenditures, per capita personal disposable income, and regional prices (weighted average price level across cities = 1.000 for each commodity). The relevant estimating equation is (2.25) and, as detailed in chapter 2, the method of estimation (ML) is essentially the same as in time-series analysis: Regional price differences replace price variation over time.

Price data were obtained for the nine largest cities in Korea: Seoul, Busan, Dae-gu, Incheon, Daejeon, Gwangju, Chungju, Chuncheon, Cheongju. Thus nine values of each p_i are observed; the price of a commodity is assumed to be the same for all households in a given city. The ratios of maximum to minimum prices for each commodity are: food 1.042, clothing 1.013, housing 1.046, fuel and light 1.117, other 1.044. Households in the sample residing in urban areas outside the nine cities for which price data are available have been excluded from the analysis, and to this extent the coverage is less complete than that of the aggregate data used in the previous section.

Values of the coefficient of determination (R^2) are given in table 5.6. For the individual commodity equations, R^2 lies between 0.2 and 0.4 in about a third of the cases, between 0.4 and 0.6 in about a quarter. The R^2 values lie between 0.4 and 0.7 for the aggregate consumption function. Since the units of observation are individual households, the results suggest that it is not inappropriate to fit a linear system to each of the six chosen groups of consumers. Values of the Durbin-Watson d statistic (table 5.7) confirm this. Within each group, households are arranged in order of increasing per capita income, so that the d statistic affords an indication of the appropriateness of the chosen functional form. In particular, low values of d would suggest that the linear model was inadequate. The observed range of d values is 1.26 to 2.40, however, and only four of the thirty values lie outside the range of 1.5 to 2.3.

Table 5.8 contains estimates of the basic ELES parameters (β, γ, μ), plus estimates of the Frisch parameter (ω). The estimates of the marginal budget shares (β_i) are all positive as required by the underlying utility function, except for one minor violation.[7] Only four of the thirty values of β_i are not significantly different from zero at the 5 percent level.[8] The estimated subsistence quantities, γ_i, are all positive and all significant. Total subsistence expenditure, the γ sum, is in each case less than actual mean total expenditure, and it follows that estimates of ω always have the "correct" sign.

The subgroups in table 5.8 are again arranged in order of decreasing income. Any irregularities observed in moving up or down a column may therefore be ascribed to influences other than income. The marginal budget share for food, for example, tends to rise as income falls, with the major exception of the low values found for large families. The marginal budget shares for fuel and light and clothing[9] are positively related to income; the β values for housing are irregular and less than their standard errors in two cases (salary earners, O,L, and wage earners, Y). For all commodities there is a pronounced tendency for estimates of subsistence quantities to in-

7. Housing for salary earners, O,L.
8. Food and housing for salary earners, O,L; housing for wage earners, Y; and clothing for wage earners, O,L.
9. With an irregularity for salary earners, O,S.

Table 5.6. R^2 Values: ELES, Cross-Section Data for
Urban Households, Korea, 1971, First Quarter

Type of household[a]	Food	Clothing	Housing	Fuel and light	Other	Consumption function
Salary earners						
Y	0.141	0.490	0.123	0.239	0.425	0.631
O,S	0.105	0.362	0.185	0.152	0.289	0.496
O,L	0.025	0.468	0.004	0.216	0.593	0.539
Wage earners						
Y	0.286	0.342	0.008	0.214	0.426	0.420
O,S	0.458	0.324	0.264	0.193	0.345	0.687
O,L	0.347	0.025	0.445	0.095	0.419	0.632

a. Age of household head is denoted by Y (young, less than 35 years) and O (old, 35 years and over). Household size is denoted by S (small, 5 or less) and L (large, more than 5).

Table 5.7. d Values: ELES, Cross-Section Data for
Urban Households, Korea, 1971, First Quarter

Type of household	Food	Clothing	Housing	Fuel and light	Other
Salary earners					
Y	1.68	1.99	1.99	1.98	1.26
O,S	1.35	1.69	2.08	2.08	1.78
O,L	1.59	2.27	1.91	1.85	2.04
Wage earners					
Y	1.99	2.40	2.04	1.86	2.30
O,S	1.82	1.78	2.18	2.14	2.02
O,L	1.94	1.89	1.32	1.93	2.06

a. Households are arranged within each subgroup in order of increasing per capita income. Age of household head is denoted by Y (young, less than 35 years) and O (old, 35 years and over). Household size is denoted by S (small, 5 or less) and L (large, more than 5).

crease with income. Estimates of the Frisch parameter fall in absolute value as income rises—the Frisch conjecture—except for one major deviation (wage earners, O,S). The marginal propensity to consume (μ) is influenced by both family size and age, young households having a low marginal propensity to consume and small, old households a high one.

A necessary condition for exact aggregation over consumers in ELES is that the β_i^* be constant across households for all commodities.

Table 5.8. *ELES Estimates: Cross-Section Data for Urban Households, Korea, 1971, First Quarter*

Type of household[a]	Income[b]	β					μ^o
		Food	Clothing	Housing	Fuel and light	Other	
Salary earners							
Y	26.8	0.170	0.278	0.123	0.066	0.363	0.524
		(0.038)	(0.027)	(0.031)	(0.011)	(0.040)	(0.038)
O,S	24.7	0.164	0.162	0.202	0.065	0.408	0.628
		(0.048)	(0.023)	(0.046)	(0.016)	(0.069)	(0.068)
O,L	21.0	0.062	0.242	−0.004	0.039	0.660	0.484
		(0.042)	(0.024)	(0.034)	(0.007)	(0.051)	(0.042)
Wage earners							
Y	18.4	0.369	0.218	0.059	0.040	0.313	0.571
		(0.057)	(0.030)	(0.088)	(0.007)	(0.036)	(0.066)
O,S	15.7	0.410	0.128	0.162	0.036	0.263	0.819
		(0.048)	(0.020)	(0.029)	(0.008)	(0.039)	(0.060)
O,L	11.6	0.280	0.058	0.354	0.020	0.288	0.796
		(0.037)	(0.036)	(0.040)	(0.006)	(0.034)	(0.060)

Type of household[a]	Total expenditure[b]	γ[d]					γ sum[e]	ω
		Food	Clothing	Housing	Fuel and light	Other		
Salary earners								
Y	22.8	7.46 (0.45)	1.77 (0.33)	3.51 (0.36)	1.35 (0.13)	4.33 (0.60)	18.42 (1.44)	−5.3
O,S	23.1	7.89 (0.60)	2.31 (0.39)	3.36 (0.65)	1.28 (0.20)	5.74 (1.12)	20.58 (2.54)	−9.1
O,L	19.1	6.63 (0.28)	1.64 (0.21)	2.92 (0.21)	1.01 (0.05)	5.12 (0.59)	17.32 (1.03)	−10.5
Wage earners								
Y	17.0	6.84 (0.49)	1.40 (0.24)	2.79 (0.47)	1.04 (0.05)	3.11 (0.34)	15.17 (1.33)	−9.4
O,S	15.1	5.57 (1.01)	0.74 (0.33)	1.84 (0.04)	0.87 (0.10)	2.86 (0.69)	11.87 (2.46)	−5.2
O,L	11.4	4.71 (0.47)	0.99 (0.20)	1.33 (0.52)	0.76 (0.04)	2.54 (0.44)	10.33 (1.57)	−13.5

Note: Asymptotic standard errors in parentheses. Sample sizes are 110, 86, 114, 101, 84, 99 for rows 1–6 respectively.

a. Age of household head is denoted by Y (young, less than 35 years) and O (old, 35 years and over). Household size is denoted by S (small, 5 or less) and L (large, more than 5).

b. Mean values in thousand won per capita a quarter.

c. If price information is ignored, the corresponding estimates of μ are, from top to bottom: 0.522 (0.038), 0.626 (0.069), 0.484 (0.042), 0.569 (0.067), 0.814 (0.061), and 0.793 (0.061).

d. In thousand won per capita a quarter at (weighted) average prices for all cities in 1971, first quarter. The rate of exchange at that time was 320 won = U.S. $1.00

e. If price information is ignored, the corresponding estimates of the γ sum are, from top to bottom: 18.48 (1.45), 20.58 (2.55), 17.29 (1.05), 15.20 (1.33), 12.18 (2.37), and 10.54 (1.54).

If the β_i^* are to be constant across households then the same condition must hold for the marginal budget shares.[10] Comparison of the six groups of consumers in table 5.8 shows that for any two groups the β_i values for at least one commodity are significantly different from each other at the 5 percent level. The differences imply that pooling of household data from any two or more groups would be inappropriate. To analyze the implications of structural change it would therefore seem necessary to disaggregate urban households into at least as many types as in table 5.8.

It is relatively unusual in cross-section demand analysis to have suitable data on price differentials.[11] More commonly it is necessary to assume that all consumers face identical prices at a given time. Indeed this assumption is made in all subsequent chapters. It is therefore of some interest to compare the estimates discussed above with those obtained by ignoring information on price differentials across cities. To make such a comparison we estimated ELES by least squares, assuming constant prices. The relevant model is described in the last section of chapter 2. This re-estimation produced very little change in parameter estimates or degree of fit, and therefore only the values for μ and the γ sum are reported (see the footnotes of table 5.8). The overall results suggest that ELES estimates obtained without price data will be quite reliable if price differentials across consumers are thought to be no more than 5 to 10 percent.

Estimates of total expenditure elasticities and own-price elasticities (obtained using regional price data) are given in tables 5.9 and 5.10. Total expenditure elasticities follow the patterns observed for the β_i. The own-price elasticity for food is low in absolute terms for old, large households. Demand for fuel and light appears to become more price elastic as incomes rise. Elsewhere, own-price elasticities show little pattern.

Among cross-price elasticities, those with respect to the price of food tend to dominate, and only these results are reported (table 5.11). Estimates of the elasticity of the average savings ratio with respect to food price are given in the last column of table 5.10.

---

10. The aggregation problem is discussed in more detail in the next section. For exact aggregation under LES, constancy of marginal budget shares is a necessary condition; see, for example, Goldberger (1967), pp. 70–71. The importance to aggregation of constancy of marginal budget shares has been particularly emphasized, in wider contexts, by Barten (1974) and Dixon (1975).

11. However, see Lluch (1971) where regional price indexes are used in fitting demand systems to Spanish data.

Table 5.9.   *Total Expenditure Elasticities: ELES,*
Urban Households, Korea, 1971, First Quarter

Type of household[a]	Food	Clothing	Housing	Fuel and light	Other
Salary earners					
Y	0.47	2.12	0.69	0.92	1.40
O,S	0.46	1.37	1.21	1.04	1.39
O,L	0.18	2.23	−0.02	0.69	2.00
Wage earners					
Y	0.84	2.06	0.35	0.62	1.44
O,S	0.90	1.68	1.03	0.56	1.07
O,L	0.64	0.63	2.35	0.30	1.15

a. Age of household head is denoted by Y (young, less than 35 years) and O (old, 35 years and over). Household size is denoted by S (small, 5 or less) and L (large, more than 5).

Table 5.10.   *Own-Price Elasticities and Elasticity of Average*
Savings Ratio with Respect to Food Price: ELES,
Urban Households, Korea, 1971, First Quarter

Type of household[a]	Food	Clothing	Housing	Fuel and light	Other	ξ (food)
Salary earners						
Y	−0.25	−0.57	−0.24	−0.23	−0.53	−0.90
O,S	−0.20	−0.29	−0.31	−0.17	−0.50	−1.92
O,L	−0.08	−0.40	−0.01	−0.10	−0.72	−1.77
Wage earners						
Y	−0.43	−0.39	−0.10	−0.10	−0.42	−2.13
O,S	−0.52	−0.44	−0.35	−0.15	−0.43	−1.54
O,L	−0.32	−0.12	−0.50	−0.04	−0.36	−4.35

a. Age of household head is denoted by Y (young, less than 35 years) and O (old, 35 years and over). Household size is denoted by S (small, 5 or less) and L (large, more than 5).

Income effects are noticeable, with ξ (food) decreasing in absolute size as income rises.

Seoul Households

Basic characteristics of the sample data for Seoul households are given in table 5.5. It is possible to arrange the subgroups by income exactly as for the full sample, although in each group mean per capita disposable income is higher in Seoul than in the sample as a whole. Because price information is not available it is necessary to fit ELES by least squares, that is, equation (2.26).

Table 5.11. Cross-Elasticities with Respect to Food Prices: ELES, Cross-Section Data, Urban Households, Korea, 1971, First Quarter

Type of household[a]	Total Urban				Seoul			
	Clothing	Housing	Fuel and light	Other	Clothing	Housing	Fuel and light	Other
Salary earners								
Y	−0.69	−0.23	−0.30	−0.46	−0.70	−0.19	−0.27	−0.39
O,S	−0.47	−0.41	−0.35	−0.47	−0.44	−0.43	−0.34	−0.38
O,L	−0.77	0.01	−0.24	−0.69	−0.50	−0.05	−0.18	−0.45
Wage earners								
Y	−0.83	−0.14	−0.25	−0.58	−1.07	0.14	−0.29	−0.56
O,S	−0.62	−0.38	−0.21	−0.40	−0.71	−0.14	−0.14	−0.35
O,L	−0.26	−0.97	−0.12	−0.48	−0.20	−0.41	−0.05	−0.19

a. Age of household head is denoted by Y (young, less than 35 years) and O (old, 35 years and over). Household size is denoted by S (small, 5 or less) and L (large, more than 5).

Estimates of the basic parameters (β, γ, μ) are given in table 5.12.[12] The most noticeable changes in the γ estimates are an increase for salary earners, O,S, and a decrease for wage earners, O,L, where insufficient observations (27) remain to determine the γ's with much precision.[13] The changes in the γ sum estimates relative to income destroy the tendency for the Frisch parameter (ω) to increase in absolute value as income falls. The low marginal propensities to consume for young households are still apparent.

Only five of the β values are not significant at the 5 percent level, although now two of these are negative.[14] The most noticeable change in the β estimates is an increase for clothing in all six groups, but particularly among young households. The expenditure elasticities for clothing (table 5.13) also tend to be higher, and the young-family effect is quite pronounced here.

Own-price elasticities for Seoul households are given in table 5.14. Compared with all urban households the elasticities are noticeably higher for clothing, fuel and light, and others. No pattern is discernible in the elasticity of the average savings ratio with respect to food price (last column of table 5.14).

Results at Different Levels of Consumer Disaggregation

In this section we compare results obtained using national accounts, 1963–72; time series of aggregate survey data for farm and urban households, 1963–72; and cross-section data on individual urban households for the first quarter of 1971. Results from the preceding two sections are compared with national accounts ELES estimates at the same five-commodity level used in the rest of this chapter. Differences between the national accounts and aggregate survey data must be noted when comparing estimates. In particular, per capita values for national accounts data do not always lie between the farm and urban figures, and the discrepancies show an irregular pattern over time (see table 5.1). Except that the cross-section data

12. The R^2 and d values are in general comparable to those obtained for the full sample and are not reproduced. Only two marked changes in R^2 values occur: Clothing for wage earners, O,L, increases from 0.03 to 0.28, and housing for wage earners, O,S, falls from 0.26 to 0.05.

13. The γ estimates in table 5.8 are at (weighted) average urban prices, those in table 5.12 at Seoul prices, but these price differences are unimportant when making broad comparisons. The ratio of the Seoul price level to the weighted average of all cities was 0.991.

14. Housing for salary earners, O,L (as in table 5.8) and for wage earners, Y.

Table 5.12. ELES Estimates: Cross-Section Data, Seoul Households, 1971, First Quarter

Type of household[a]	Income[b]	β					μ
		Food	Clothing	Housing	Fuel and light	Other	
Salary earners							
Y	30.7	0.157 (0.044)	0.318 (0.052)	0.101 (0.037)	0.062 (0.016)	0.362 (0.043)	0.520 (0.053)
O,S	27.8	0.148 (0.059)	0.169 (0.033)	0.222 (0.055)	0.068 (0.023)	0.394 (0.083)	0.567 (0.090)
O,L	27.6	0.067 (0.048)	0.260 (0.043)	-0.024 (0.044)	0.038 (0.008)	0.659 (0.056)	0.485 (0.057)
Wage earners							
Y	19.9	0.337 (0.103)	0.292 (0.081)	-0.062 (0.058)	0.055 (0.014)	0.378 (0.081)	0.407 (0.070)
O,S	16.2	0.452 (0.087)	0.157 (0.035)	0.073 (0.044)	0.031 (0.011)	0.288 (0.054)	0.743 (0.115)
O,L	14.4	0.258 (0.050)	0.064 (0.021)	0.419 (0.073)	0.015 (0.010)	0.245 (0.054)	0.826 (0.103)

Type of household[a]	Total expenditure[b]	γ^c Food	Clothing	Housing	Fuel and light	Other	γ sum	ω
Salary earners								
Y	25.3	7.70 (0.72)	1.66 (0.51)	3.57 (0.55)	1.43 (0.20)	5.08 (1.00)	19.43 (2.31)	−4.3
O,S	26.3	8.27 (0.75)	2.83 (0.51)	3.81 (0.90)	1.54 (0.28)	7.90 (1.42)	24.36 (3.19)	−13.6
O,L	20.8	5.52 (0.57)	1.23 (0.60)	2.79 (0.41)	0.91 (0.11)	3.94 (1.29)	14.39 (2.27)	−3.2
Wage earners								
Y	16.8	6.23 (0.66)	1.06 (0.30)	2.83 (0.20)	1.07 (0.07)	3.37 (0.53)	14.57 (1.21)	−7.7
O,S	14.5	4.46 (1.73)	0.24 (0.63)	1.95 (0.50)	0.82 (0.15)	2.26 (1.25)	9.74 (3.98)	−3.0
O,L	12.5	2.58 (2.36)	0.22 (0.51)	−1.23 (3.40)	0.67 (0.14)	1.07 (1.82)	3.31 (7.90)	−1.4

Note: Asymptotic standard errors in parentheses. Sample sizes are 65, 55, 46, 42, 39, 27 for rows 1 to 6 respectively.

a. Age of household head is denoted by Y (young, less than 35 years) and O (old, 35 years and over). Household size is denoted by S (small, 5 or less) and L (large, more than 5).

b. Mean values in thousand won per capita a quarter.

c. In thousand won per capita a quarter at Seoul prices in 1971, first quarter.

115

Table 5.13.   Total Expenditure Elasticities: ELES,
Seoul Households, 1971, First Quarter

Type of household[a]	Food	Clothing	Housing	Fuel and light	Other
Salary earners					
Y	0.46	2.29	0.62	0.88	1.27
O,S	0.45	1.41	1.38	1.07	1.20
O,L	0.23	1.87	−0.19	0.68	1.68
Wage earners					
Y	0.81	2.88	−0.39	0.77	1.51
O,S	0.99	2.30	0.46	0.47	1.15
O,L	0.65	0.99	2.00	0.23	0.92

a. Age of household head is denoted by Y (young, less than 35 years) and O (old, 35 years and over).
Household size is denoted by S (small, 5 or less) and L (large, more than 5).

Table 5.14.   Own-Price Elasticities and Elasticity of Average
Savings Ratio with Respect to Food Price: ELES,
Seoul Households, 1971, First Quarter

Type of household[a]	Food	Clothing	Housing	Fuel and light	Other	ξ (food)
Salary earners						
Y	−0.25	−0.68	−0.23	−0.25	−0.55	−0.68
O,S	−0.18	−0.26	−0.30	−0.14	−0.45	−2.43
O,L	−0.13	−0.69	0.08	−0.24	−0.84	−0.42
Wage earners						
Y	−0.41	0.56	0.12	−0.15	−0.50	−1.17
O,S	−0.63	−0.79	−0.21	−0.18	−0.56	−0.69
O,L	−0.61	−0.74	−1.28	−0.18	−0.76	−0.23

a. Age of household head is denoted by Y (young, less than 35 years) and O (old, 35 years and over).
Household size is denoted by S (small, 5 or less) and L (large, more than 5).

omit households in small towns for which price information is not
available, coverage of the sample survey is the same as that of the
urban survey used for time-series data. This permits direct comparison
of urban results from time-series and cross-section data, if changes in
income levels over time are borne in mind. The γ estimates, in particular, are subject to seasonal influences when cross-section data are
used, but these effects do not seem to be particularly pronounced
in the Korean budget data. On the basis of aggregate quarterly data
for urban wage and salary earners, the average budget shares for the
first quarter of 1971 compared with the annual values for 1971 (in

parentheses) are: food 0.407 (0.413), clothing 0.105 (0.100), housing 0.169 (0.183), fuel and light 0.067 (0.056), and other 0.252 (0.248). Quarterly estimates of average household personal disposable income in 1971, expressed in 1970 prices, are 88.6, 92.8, 92.4, and 100.0 thousand won, and of the average propensity to consume 0.93, 0.91, 0.92, and 0.93.

In considering aggregation across urban households in the 1971 cross-section survey it is assumed that all consumers face identical prices, since this implicit assumption was used above in analyzing the time series of aggregate urban survey data. In any event, allowing for price variation was found to make little difference empirically, and to allow for it here would needlessly complicate the presentation.

The deterministic part of the basic ELES estimating equation under the assumption of constant prices is obtained from equation (2.26):

$$(5.1) \qquad v_{ih} = \alpha_{ih} + \beta^*_{ih} y_h$$

where $i = 1, ..., n$ goods; $h = 1, ..., H$ households; and v_i and y are in per capita terms. If family size is denoted by $f_h (h = 1, ..., H)$, equation (5.1) may be written in aggregate per capita form by multiplying by f_h, summing over households, and dividing by the total number of individual consumers, $\sum\limits_{h} f_h$. Thus

$$(5.2) \qquad v_i = \left(\sum\limits_{h} f_h \, \alpha_{ih} / \sum\limits_{h} f_h\right) + \left(\sum\limits_{h} f_h \, \beta^*_{ih} \, y_h / \sum\limits_{h} f_h \, y_h\right) y$$

$$(5.3) \qquad = \bar{\alpha}_i + \bar{\beta}^*_i y$$

where $\bar{\alpha}_i$ and $\bar{\beta}^*_i$ are weighted mean parameter values. Only if all parameters are identical for all consumers will the parameters in (5.3) be identical with the parameters for individual households. Algebraically, if $\alpha_{ih} = \alpha_i$ and $\beta^*_{ih} = \beta^*_i$ for all i and h, then $\bar{\alpha}_i = \alpha_i$ and $\bar{\beta}^*_i = \beta^*_i$. If the second condition is not met then $\bar{\beta}^*_i$ in (5.3) depends on the distribution of income.

In the previous section it was shown that parameter estimates varied significantly across groups of urban consumers. We now proceed to aggregate these results, obtaining estimates of $\bar{\alpha}_i$ and $\bar{\beta}^*_i$ as in (5.2) and (5.3). In aggregating the six groups of consumers, f_h becomes the total number of individuals in each group (that is, average family size multiplied by number of households), y_h is mean per capita income for each group, and $h = 1, ..., 6$. The weighted values of α_i and β^*_i are used in conjunction with weighted values of mean expenditures to derive estimates of all ELES parameters[15] and

15. Note that $\mu = \sum\limits_{i} \beta^*_i = \sum\limits_{h} (f_h \mu_h y_h / \sum\limits_{h} f_h y_h)$.

Table 5.15.   *Comparison of Estimates of ELES Parameters and Elasticities Using Different Levels of Consumer Disaggregation, Korea*

Data, parameters, and elasticities	National accounts, 1963–72[a]	Aggregate survey data, 1963–72[b]		Urban[c] cross-section, 1971, first quarter[d]
		Farm	Urban[c]	
Income[e]	50.4	35.0	63.7	69.2
Marginal propensity to consume	0.890	0.463	0.812	0.598
Marginal budget shares				
Food	0.457	0.367	0.173	0.216
Clothing	0.155	0.102	0.166	0.186
Housing	0.054	0.110	0.254	0.147
Fuel and light	0.030	0.077	0.052	0.044
Other	0.304	0.344	0.355	0.406
γ (food)[f]	21.6	13.6	22.7	21.5
γ sum[f]	36.2	26.7	42.8	55.4
ω	−3.7	−5.3	−6.8	−7.4
Expenditure elasticities				
Food	0.83	0.75	0.39	0.60
Clothing	1.42	1.27	1.72	1.60
Housing	0.76	2.48	1.47	0.86
Fuel and light	0.67	0.99	0.95	0.66
Other	1.35	1.13	1.52	1.44
Own-price elasticities				
Food	−0.58	−0.46	−0.22	−0.27
Clothing	−0.48	−0.32	−0.38	−0.37
Housing	−0.25	−0.53	−0.41	−0.25
Fuel and light	−0.21	−0.25	−0.18	−0.13
Other	−0.56	−0.48	−0.50	−0.52
ξ (food)	−1.2	−1.0	−2.2	−1.7

a. *Source:* Lluch and Williams (1974).
b. For details see the section on rural-urban dualism, chapter 5.
c. Wage and salary earners.
d. Weighted mean values of urban household results in the cross-section analysis, chapter 5.
e. Per capita personal disposable income in thousand won a year converted to 1970 prices using relevant price indexes. The first three entries are sample midpoint values (1967–68).
f. In thousand won per capita a year in 1970 prices.

elasticities. These are given in the last column of table 5.15. The values turn out to be very close to simple averages of the six sets of parameter and elasticity estimates given in tables 5.8 to 5.10.

The first half of table 5.15 presents ELES parameter estimates for the three types of data considered. The points to be noted are: (a) The marginal propensity to consume is lower when cross-section data are used; (b) estimates of the marginal budget shares from the disaggregated survey data are higher than those obtained using aggregate urban data except in the case of housing; (c) the estimate of the marginal budget share for food is particularly high using national accounts; and (d) the γ estimates are extremely well behaved. Estimates of subsistence expenditure on nonfood increase uniformly with income, whereas γ (food) is constant, apart from the low value for farmers. The estimate of the Frisch parameter (ω) obtained using national accounts is relatively low in absolute terms.[16]

Total expenditure and own-price elasticities are compared in the lower half of table 5.15. National accounts estimates frequently lie outside the span of the aggregate survey estimates for farm and urban households, most markedly in the case of housing, where imputed rent is excluded from the farm data. There is much closer agreement between the time-series and cross-section results for urban wage and salary earners; again housing performs worst. Of particular interest is the apparent success in estimating price elasticities from cross-section data.

Estimates of the elasticity of the household savings ratio with respect to food price are given in the final row of table 5.15. The values are very similar for the two sets of urban data, but, perversely, they are larger in absolute value than those from the national accounts and the farm survey, where sample median incomes are lower. The distinction between farm and urban households, however, seems important for explaining movements over time in the savings ratio itself. In table 5.4 it was shown that the model explained 89 percent of the variation in the savings ratio for farm households and 77 percent of that for urban wage and salary earners. The comparable figure using national accounts data is only 50 percent.

For the reasons given in the first section of this chapter, estimates of demand and savings parameters and elasticities for disaggregated household groups are intrinsically important. The results presented in table 5.15 suggest that, when the data coverage is similar, disaggregated cross-section data yield demand parameters and elasticities which may be averaged to give results broadly consistent with time-series estimates, at least for nondurable goods and services.

16. The national accounts estimate in chapter 3 was -10.3, compared with -3.7 here, because of the difference in the time period, not in the level of commodity aggregation: eight commodities, 1963–72, $\omega = -3.6$; five commodities, 1953–72, $\omega = -7.1$.

6

Consumption and Savings
Behavior in Mexico:
A Cross-Section Analysis

THE METHODOLOGY USED for cross-section analysis of urban households in Korea is here used to analyze household demand and savings behavior in Mexico. The influences of socioeconomic factors, location, family size, and age of head are examined by subdividing into thirty-two relatively homogeneous groups the households included in the 1968 Mexican nationwide survey. ELES is fitted for each group using individual household data. Prices are assumed not to differ across households, but the results presented in chapter 5 suggest that this does not unduly distort estimates. It should be emphasized, however, that the estimates of price responsiveness given here are obtained from estimated marginal budget shares and savings behavior and are therefore heavily dependent upon the additive utility specification adopted in chapter 2.

Since the data for Mexico were able to be broken into many more representative groups of consumers than was the case for Korea, it is now possible to adopt a more formal approach in searching for systematic variation in values of ELES parameters and derived elasticities. Because the absence of national accounts data on consumption expenditures rules out any time-series estimation of demand systems for Mexico, the results presented here are of particular interest for planning purposes.

120

Data

The data analyzed in this chapter are drawn from the family income and expenditure survey of 1968 conducted by the Bank of Mexico.[1] The sample consisted of 5,608 households, of which 1,256 were in rural areas (defined as a locality with a population of less than 2,500) and 4,352 in urban areas. In 72 percent of the rural households farming was the occupation of the household head. The sample appears to be fairly representative of the urban and rural populations taken separately, but the sampling fraction is higher in the urban areas.[2] For this reason rural and urban households are analyzed separately.

The survey was conducted in March 1968, but different reference periods were used for different items of expenditure and income. The more irregular the payment or receipt, the longer the reference period. Food consumption, for example, relates to the last week of March, expenditure on durable goods is for the twelve months ending in March. All data were subsequently converted to a common period. In this chapter all monetary variables are expressed at monthly rates.

In fitting the model, consumption is divided into five commodities: food, clothing, housing, durables, and other.[3] Food includes both beverages and tobacco, with an allowance for the value of home-produced food; imputed rent enters into housing. "Other" includes transport and communication, health, and education. Net payments for motor vehicles and expenditure on television sets and radios are included in other rather than durables, which are primarily furniture, furnishings, and domestic appliances. The explanatory variable used is personal disposable income, which includes the imputed values used in the consumption figures. All data used in estimation are expressed in per capita terms.

1. For a full explanation of the data and definitions of variables used in this analysis, together with descriptive statistics, see Direccion General Coordinadora de la Programación Económica y Social, Secretaría de la Presidencia, "Estados Unidos Mexicanos—Estudio de Ingresos y Gastos de las Familias," 6 vols. (Mexico, July 1974).

2. Detailed comparisons of the sample data with known population data were carried out by Jose Luis Aburto and Gabriel Vera, Direccion General Coordinadora de la Programación Económica y Social, Secretaría de la Presidencia, Mexico.

3. The classification is based on that given in United Nations, *A System of National Accounts*, 1970.

A linear model such as the one used here is unlikely to give an adequate explanation of demand and savings behavior for all households without some subdivision of the data. Here the data set is partitioned according to household location, socioeconomic class, family size, and age of household head. The findings of chapters 5 and 8 are used to stratify by socioeconomic class rather than by current income.

The Mexican sample distinguishes nine occupational classes. These classes and the mean income in each (urban and rural separately) are grouped in table 6.1 under socioeconomic headings: workers, entrepreneurs, and technocrats. This classification was adopted after considering differences in measured income, the likely relative importance of transitory income, and the economic role of each group.

The stage in the life cycle, as indicated by the age of the household head, can be expected to affect patterns of consumption and saving. Thus households are classified by age of head into young (less than 45 years) and old (45 and over). Retired households are excluded. Similarly, in order to allow for the effect of family size a simple breakdown into small (5 members or less) and large (more than 5) families is made. Both dividing points are again somewhat arbitrary but are based on observed savings behavior and a desire to permit direct comparison with Korean results. Experiments were conducted using other dividing points (in particular, 40 years and family size of 3) but the ones initially chosen remained the preferred set. In Korea, 35 years was used to divide young and old families, but no significant breaks in demand and savings behavior at this age of household head were detected for Mexican households.

In addition to the rural-urban breakdown, urban households are further subdivided into those in Mexico City and those in other cities. In total, then, households were initially classified into thirty-six groups. Insufficient observations were available in the four cells for rural technocrats, however, and analysis is restricted to the remaining thirty-two groups.[4]

Basic characteristics of the partitioned sample data are given in table 6.2. Results in the tables are classified first by location (rural, other urban, and Mexico City), second by socioeconomic class (workers, entrepreneurs, technocrats), third by family size (large, small) and fourth by age of family head (young, old). In the case of each classification, the order of appearance of the subdivisions corresponds to their ranking by mean per capita income. Note that

4. Five urban households with negative disposable income were also omitted.

Table 6.1.   *Mean Income and Sample Size of*
Socioeconomic Classes, Mexico, 1968

	Income[b]		Sample size	
Occupation[a]	Urban	Rural	Urban	Rural
Workers				
Daily paid	191	137	329	335
Domestic servants	326	184	113	5
Unskilled	325	199	539	40
Skilled	376	230	350	30
Entrepreneurs				
Employers	587	163	191	344
Self-employed	785	224	740	351
Technocrats				
Administrative employees	819	282	909	40
Professional, technical	1,121	489	406	29
Other				
Not elsewhere classified	663	253	266	16
Head not working	690	164	509	66
Total	650	188	4,352	1,256

Source: All tables in chapter 6 are based on original data obtained in joint research with Direccion General Coordinadora de la Programación Económica y Social, Secretaría de la Presidencia, in Mexico.
a. Classification is by occupation of household head.
b. Mean per capita disposable income in pesos a month.

per capita income of small families always exceeds that of large families (all other attributes fixed), and for given family size per capita income of old families always exceeds that of young families.

Empirical Results

For each of the thirty-two subgroups, ELES (equation 2.26) is fitted by ordinary least squares to data on per capita expenditures and per capita personal disposable income. Values of the goodness of fit measure (R^2) are given in table 6.3. These tend to be substantially higher than comparable estimates for Korea. In the case of food, for example, the mean value of R^2 is 0.55, for clothing 0.39, and for housing 0.53.

Marginal Budget Shares

Estimated values of marginal budget shares and associated standard errors are given in table 6.4. The 160 β estimates are all positive as

Table 6.2. *Basic Characteristics of Household Data, Mexico, 1968*

Type of household[a]	Number of households	Means					Average budget shares				
		Age of head	Family size	Income[b]	Consumption[b]	Savings ratio	Food	Clothing	Housing	Durables	Other
Total rural[c]	1,168	44.1	6.2	191	203	−0.064	0.500	0.128	0.096	0.053	0.223
Total urban	3,572	42.3	6.0	644	592	0.081	0.332	0.115	0.191	0.067	0.296
Mexico City	1,437	41.8	5.8	906	813	0.102	0.293	0.108	0.212	0.067	0.321
Other urban	2,135	42.6	6.1	468	443	0.054	0.380	0.123	0.165	0.066	0.265
Rural households											
Workers											
L,Y	143	36.6	7.8	113	129	−0.142	0.544	0.118	0.101	0.045	0.192
L,O	91	51.7	8.2	139	144	−0.035	0.571	0.134	0.088	0.042	0.164
S,Y	112	30.4	4.1	174	194	−0.112	0.509	0.126	0.099	0.062	0.204
S,O	64	57.8	3.9	207	209	−0.010	0.561	0.093	0.109	0.044	0.193
Entrepreneurs											
L,Y	187	36.8	7.9	134	152	−0.132	0.537	0.130	0.091	0.055	0.187
L,O	197	53.4	8.0	179	187	−0.043	0.500	0.152	0.084	0.053	0.210
S,Y	141	32.8	4.1	243	249	−0.023	0.476	0.123	0.109	0.053	0.239
S,O	164	59.4	3.8	249	268	−0.076	0.484	0.118	0.094	0.049	0.255
Other urban households											
Workers											
L,Y	350	36.0	8.0	205	207	−0.013	0.479	0.111	0.147	0.056	0.208
L,O	179	52.3	8.6	254	233	0.082	0.480	0.122	0.153	0.053	0.192
S,Y	241	31.4	4.0	352	363	−0.031	0.443	0.120	0.182	0.061	0.193
S,O	112	54.0	3.8	386	402	−0.040	0.448	0.115	0.173	0.054	0.209

124

Entrepreneurs											
L,Y	144	37.0	7.9	324	322	0.006	0.399	0.109	0.150	0.071	0.271
L,O	193	54.3	8.3	422	384	0.090	0.363	0.124	0.130	0.060	0.323
S,Y	114	32.5	4.0	713	622	0.127	0.320	0.129	0.164	0.073	0.314
S,O	172	60.2	3.5	723	669	0.075	0.336	0.107	0.191	0.063	0.303
Technocrats											
L,Y	175	36.2	7.9	459	420	0.085	0.391	0.125	0.156	0.070	0.258
L,O	108	51.6	8.2	565	505	0.107	0.356	0.138	0.147	0.066	0.293
S,Y	234	31.2	3.9	756	731	0.032	0.350	0.140	0.170	0.078	0.262
S,O	113	54.9	3.8	896	816	0.089	0.333	0.119	0.178	0.070	0.299
Mexico City households											
Workers											
L,Y	179	35.3	7.9	240	258	−0.074	0.472	0.122	0.173	0.051	0.182
L,O	93	52.2	8.2	368	335	0.090	0.423	0.114	0.203	0.047	0.212
S,Y	121	31.2	4.0	424	453	−0.069	0.420	0.114	0.182	0.061	0.222
S,O	54	54.6	3.9	602	590	0.020	0.376	0.102	0.230	0.043	0.249
Entrepreneurs											
L,Y	80	37.1	7.6	642	633	0.015	0.298	0.081	0.175	0.056	0.389
L,O	86	53.1	8.0	948	795	0.161	0.300	0.132	0.225	0.055	0.288
S,Y	60	34.1	4.0	1,115	982	0.120	0.283	0.115	0.211	0.082	0.309
S,O	79	59.3	3.6	2,026	1,757	0.133	0.211	0.103	0.247	0.066	0.372
Technocrats											
L,Y	163	36.6	7.5	738	705	0.045	0.292	0.104	0.186	0.068	0.349
L,O	116	52.8	7.7	999	870	0.129	0.283	0.129	0.211	0.053	0.325
S,Y	282	31.4	3.9	1,146	1,056	0.079	0.277	0.115	0.209	0.077	0.321
S,O	124	55.7	3.8	1,783	1,405	0.212	0.262	0.083	0.229	0.072	0.354

a. Households are divided by family size into large (L, more than 5) and small (S, 5 or less), and by age of head into young (Y, less than 45 years) and old (O, 45 and over).

b. Income (disposable) and consumption are per capita in pesos a month.

c. Includes 69 technocrats.

required and are all significant at the one percent level. Two-thirds of the "*t* values" lie between 5 and 15.

An examination of the β estimates for rural households suggests that the marginal budget share for food declines with rising income and is higher for old households. Regressing the estimated values of β (food) on income and a dummy variable for old households (DO) yields the equation for the first line of table 6.5.[5] Both effects are significant at the 5 percent level. The point estimates imply that among rural households the marginal budget share for food falls by 0.014 for every 10 peso increase in per capita income and, other things being equal, has a value that is 0.103 higher for old households than for young. The income effect on the marginal share of other is estimated to be equal in magnitude but opposite in sign to that for food, but the coefficient is significant only at the 10 percent level. Apart from some tendency for the marginal share of housing

Table 6.3. R^2 *Values, ELES, Mexico, 1968*

Type of household[a]	*Food*	*Clothing*	*Housing*	*Durables*	*Other*	*Consumption function*
Rural households						
Workers						
L,Y	0.644	0.376	0.400	0.428	0.235	0.631
L,O	0.571	0.132	0.466	0.305	0.347	0.672
S,Y	0.540	0.358	0.436	0.207	0.344	0.646
S,O	0.468	0.256	0.220	0.179	0.234	0.495
Entrepreneurs						
L,Y	0.576	0.412	0.514	0.349	0.322	·0.694
L,O	0.647	0.524	0.366	0.391	0.202	0.738
S,Y	0.538	0.473	0.449	0.624	0.823	0.914
S,O	0.787	0.420	0.661	0.602	0.687	0.860
Other urban households						
Workers						
L,Y	0.588	0.471	0.600	0.371	0.520	0.811
L,O	0.518	0.408	0.486	0.340	0.516	0.752
S,Y	0.514	0.471	0.058	0.220	0.351	0.589
S,O	0.611	0.575	0.771	0.364	0.701	0.840
Entrepreneurs						
L,Y	0.482	0.447	0.669	0.627	0.620	0.822
L,O	0.450	0.431	0.539	0.377	0.621	0.731
S,Y	0.311	0.496	0.743	0.462	0.797	0.864
S,O	0.575	0.499	0.727	0.721	0.386	0.757

5. Other functional forms were tried, but for all rural β estimates the linear form performed best.

Table 6.3.   (*continued*)

Type of household[a]	Food	Clothing	Housing	Durables	Other	Consumption function
Other urban households (*continued*)						
Technocrats						
L,Y	0.534	0.218	0.574	0.566	0.723	0.823
L,O	0.463	0.394	0.471	0.266	0.365	0.602
S,Y	0.586	0.419	0.756	0.225	0.649	0.830
S,O	0.545	0.667	0.626	0.560	0.625	0.854
Mexico City households						
Workers						
L,Y	0.478	0.158	0.342	0.159	0.252	0.552
L,O	0.566	0.274	0.484	0.094	0.361	0.730
S,Y	0.562	0.267	0.467	0.209	0.258	0.694
S,O	0.309	0.166	0.436	0.280	0.202	0.494
Entrepreneurs						
L,Y	0.539	0.502	0.705	0.696	0.536	0.694
L,O	0.500	0.425	0.600	0.565	0.602	0.804
S,Y	0.558	0.632	0.619	0.644	0.555	0.774
S,O	0.515	0.374	0.746	0.626	0.634	0.819
Technocrats						
L,Y	0.647	0.600	0.406	0.729	0.559	0.728
L,O	0.629	0.269	0.612	0.588	0.621	0.747
S,Y	0.480	0.353	0.650	0.387	0.643	0.785
S,O	0.352	0.091	0.434	0.155	0.386	0.432

a. Household size is denoted by L (large, more than 5) and S (small, 5 or less). Age of household head is denoted by Y (young, less than 45 years) and O (old, 45 and over).

to fall slightly with increased income, no other patterns are apparent in the rural β estimates.

With urban households a more systematic analysis of the β estimates is possible. The twenty-four estimates of each parameter were used in the following regressions:

$$\beta_i = a_0 + a_1 \log_{10} y + a_2 \text{DL} + a_3 \text{DO} + a_4 \text{DE} + a_5 \text{DT} + a_6 \text{DMC}$$
$$(i = 1, ..., 5)$$

where y is per capita income, and DL, DO, DE, DT, and DMC are dummy variables representing family characteristics: large, old, entrepreneur, technocrat, and Mexico City respectively.[6] In searching for the dominant influences greater weight is given to avoiding bias in the estimates of a_i coefficients than to efficiency in estimation.

6. Linear and double-log equations were also used. The linear model gave clearly inferior results; the semi-log was marginally preferred to the double-log formulation, but the differences were not great.

Table 6.4. Estimated Values of Marginal Budget Shares (β_i) and Marginal Propensity to Consume (μ), ELES, Mexico, 1968

Type of household[a]	Sample size	Income[b]	β					μ
			Food	Clothing	Housing	Durables	Other	
Rural households								
Workers								
L,Y	143	113	0.364 (0.025)	0.122 (0.015)	0.084 (0.008)	0.055 (0.006)	0.375 (0.038)	1.038 (0.067)
L,O	91	139	0.490 (0.030)	0.098 (0.023)	0.110 (0.013)	0.040 (0.006)	0.262 (0.032)	0.656 (0.049)
S,Y	112	174	0.354 (0.023)	0.147 (0.017)	0.087 (0.009)	0.083 (0.015)	0.329 (0.030)	1.000 (0.071)
S,O	64	207	0.429 (0.043)	0.108 (0.023)	0.098 (0.018)	0.043 (0.011)	0.321 (0.048)	0.752 (0.097)
Entrepreneurs								
L,Y	187	134	0.378 (0.016)	0.160 (0.013)	0.107 (0.007)	0.100 (0.010)	0.255 (0.021)	0.872 (0.043)
L,O	197	179	0.362 (0.019)	0.228 (0.014)	0.074 (0.007)	0.106 (0.009)	0.230 (0.027)	0.766 (0.033)
S,Y	141	234	0.212 (0.014)	0.104 (0.008)	0.090 (0.008)	0.058 (0.004)	0.536 (0.021)	0.846 (0.022)
S,O	164	249	0.286 (0.010)	0.113 (0.010)	0.065 (0.004)	0.084 (0.005)	0.452 (0.014)	1.198 (0.038)

Other urban households

Workers

L,Y	350	205	0.258 (0.010)	0.140 (0.008)	0.131 (0.006)	0.068 (0.005)	0.403 (0.015)	0.896 (0.023)
L,O	179	254	0.344 (0.017)	0.155 (0.012)	0.143 (0.010)	0.070 (0.007)	0.290 (0.018)	0.672 (0.029)
S,Y	241	352	0.293 (0.020)	0.194 (0.014)	0.155 (0.035)	0.073 (0.008)	0.285 (0.023)	0.774 (0.042)
S,O	112	386	0.202 (0.014)	0.119 (0.009)	0.179 (0.008)	0.041 (0.005)	0.460 (0.015)	1.084 (0.045)

Entrepreneurs

L,Y	144	324	0.207 (0.014)	0.106 (0.009)	0.154 (0.008)	0.115 (0.005)	0.418 (0.015)	0.785 (0.045)
L,O	193	422	0.176 (0.011)	0.116 (0.008)	0.115 (0.007)	0.076 (0.006)	0.518 (0.017)	0.585 (0.026)
S,Y	114	713	0.096 (0.012)	0.103 (0.008)	0.160 (0.010)	0.074 (0.006)	0.568 (0.017)	0.688 (0.026)
S,O	172	723	0.178 (0.011)	0.115 (0.008)	0.208 (0.011)	0.124 (0.008)	0.375 (0.023)	0.617 (0.027)

Technocrats

L,Y	175	459	0.236 (0.013)	0.098 (0.013)	0.142 (0.009)	0.112 (0.008)	0.411 (0.016)	0.677 (0.024)
L,O	108	565	0.201 (0.021)	0.140 (0.016)	0.143 (0.014)	0.077 (0.010)	0.439 (0.031)	0.586 (0.046)
S,Y	234	756	0.207 (0.010)	0.154 (0.010)	0.179 (0.008)	0.069 (0.007)	0.391 (0.014)	0.850 (0.025)
S,O	113	896	0.148 (0.012)	0.199 (0.013)	0.137 (0.010)	0.086 (0.007)	0.429 (0.019)	0.842 (0.033)

(Table continues on the following page.)

Table 6.4. (continued)

Type of household[a]	Sample size	Income[b]	β					μ
			Food	Clothing	Housing	Durables	Other	
Mexico City households								
Workers								
L,Y	179	240	0.341 (0.020)	0.141 (0.019)	0.239 (0.024)	0.062 (0.010)	0.217 (0.020)	0.747 (0.051)
L,O	93	368	0.320 (0.027)	0.133 (0.020)	0.255 (0.026)	0.035 (0.011)	0.257 (0.028)	0.657 (0.042)
S,Y	121	424	0.308 (0.024)	0.155 (0.021)	0.183 (0.018)	0.100 (0.016)	0.254 (0.030)	0.835 (0.051)
S,O	54	602	0.214 (0.034)	0.111 (0.032)	0.250 (0.039)	0.062 (0.014)	0.363 (0.069)	0.556 (0.078)
Entrepreneurs								
L,Y	80	642	0.105 (0.011)	0.053 (0.006)	0.130 (0.012)	0.060 (0.004)	0.652 (0.028)	0.846 (0.064)
L,O	86	948	0.138 (0.013)	0.156 (0.018)	0.209 (0.017)	0.067 (0.005)	0.430 (0.029)	0.612 (0.033)
S,Y	60	1,115	0.156 (0.016)	0.154 (0.015)	0.186 (0.016)	0.131 (0.011)	0.373 (0.025)	0.674 (0.048)
S,O	79	2,026	0.078 (0.009)	0.106 (0.016)	0.224 (0.012)	0.075 (0.007)	0.518 (0.025)	0.859 (0.046)

Technocrats

L,Y	163	738	0.091 (0.006)	0.077 (0.004)	0.095 (0.011)	0.079 (0.003)	0.659 (0.018)	1.071 (0.052)
L,O	116	999	0.140 (0.010)	0.116 (0.014)	0.189 (0.015)	0.079 (0.005)	0.476 (0.018)	0.798 (0.044)
S,Y	282	1,146	0.111 (0.006)	0.102 (0.007)	0.194 (0.009)	0.100 (0.006)	0.492 (0.014)	0.756 (0.024)
S,O	124	1,783	0.098 (0.011)	0.031 (0.008)	0.190 (0.016)	0.068 (0.009)	0.613 (0.021)	0.507 (0.053)

Note: Asymptotic standard errors in parentheses.

a. Household size is denoted by L (large, more than 5) and S (small, 5 or less). Age of household head is denoted by Y (young, less than 45 years) and O (old, 45 and over).

b. Mean personal disposable income per capita in pesos a month. The 1968 rate of exchange was 12.5 pesos = U.S. $1.00.

Table 6.5. Regressions of Estimated Values of Marginal Budget Shares (β_i) and the Marginal Propensity to Consume (μ) on Household Characteristics, Mexico, 1968

Dependent variable	Constant	y/100 (rural) and log y (urban)	DL	DO	DE	DT	DMC	R^2
Rural households[a]								
β (food)	0.5568[b] (0.0619)	-0.1384[b] (0.0348)	—	0.1028[b] (0.0328)	—	—	—	0.801
β (housing)	0.1164 (0.0203)	-0.0151 (0.0109)	—	—	—	—	—	0.240
β (other)	0.0975 (0.1195)	0.1379 (0.0643)	—	—	—	—	—	0.434
Urban households[c]								
β (food)	0.9091[b] (0.1075)	-0.2578[b] (0.0386)	—	—	—	—	—	0.670
β (housing)	0.3522[b] (0.0955)	-0.0729[b] (0.0348)	-0.0425[b] (0.0154)	0.0337[b] (0.0137)	—	—	0.0581[b] (0.0152)	0.535
β (durables)	0.3636[b] (0.1160)	-0.1156[b] (0.0457)	-0.0364[b] (0.0135)	—	0.0665[b] (0.0191)	—	0.0207 (0.0131)	0.452
β (other)	-0.8034[b] (0.2804)	0.4469[b] (0.1022)	0.1114[b] (0.0455)	-0.0524 (0.0402)	—	—	-0.0751 (0.0446)	0.508
μ	-0.2193 (1.4120)	0.4286 (0.5711)	0.0938 (0.1510)	-0.1559 (0.0956)	-0.2185 (0.2132)	-0.1893 (0.2425)	-0.1089 (0.1443)	0.195

— Variable not included.
Note: Standard errors are given in parentheses. D denotes a dummy variable for L (large households of more than 5 members), O (old heads of household, 45 years and over), E (entrepreneurs), T (technocrats), and MC (households in Mexico City). Number of observations is always 8. With y/100 as explanatory variable, β

a. Number of observations is always 24. With all explanatory variables included,
b. The coefficient is significantly different from zero at the 5 percent level.
c. Number of observations is always 24. With all explanatory variables included, β (clothing) yielded R^2 = 0.259 with the largest *t* value being only 0.7.

(clothing) yielded R^2 = 0.042, β (durables) yielded R^2 = 0.001, and for μ, R^2 = 0.055.

132

For this reason an explanatory variable is dropped only when its coefficient is *both* small and exceeded in absolute value by its standard error, so that the omission of variables has little effect on the point estimates of the remaining a_i.

The equations chosen in this manner yield the regression results for urban households shown in table 6.5.[7] The marginal budget shares for food, housing, and durables decline significantly with increased income, while that for other increases. The marginal budget shares for housing and durables are significantly lower for large families, suggesting economies of scale, whereas the marginal share for other is significantly higher for large families. Socioeconomic class has no influence on the β values except for durables, where the marginal budget share is significantly lower for workers.[8] The β value for housing is significantly higher for old households and households in Mexico City. Thus even after allowances are made for location, socioeconomic class, and household composition, the marginal budget shares for urban households move significantly with income (except for clothing). The only other regular influence is family size.

There is little overlap in mean incomes between the rural and urban cells: The largest mean per capita income for a rural cell is 250 pesos a month; only two urban cells have a mean income below this. It is therefore difficult to isolate rural-urban effects from the effects of income alone. Nevertheless, for food there is no evidence of a specific rural effect on the marginal budget share. Evaluating the regression equations for food at an income level of 250 pesos per capita a month yields rural estimates of β which span the corresponding urban estimate: rural $\hat{\beta}_1 = .21$ (young), .31 (old); urban $\hat{\beta}_1 = .29$. The estimated regression lines are drawn in figure 5.

In the case of housing, however, evaluating the regression equation of table 6.5 at an income of 250 pesos yields a rural estimate of 0.09, which is below the range of estimates for other urban households of differing family composition at that income level (0.13–0.21). For other expenditure, the comparable figures are rural, 0.44, and urban, 0.22–0.38. The β estimates for clothing are irregular for both rural and urban households. The mean values are 0.14 for rural and other urban and 0.11 for Mexico City.

---

7. For a given commodity there is relatively little variation in the precision of the β estimates. For this reason standards errors are ignored and estimation is by (unweighted) ordinary least squares (OLS).

8. The coefficients of DE and DT were the same to three decimal places and the variables have been combined in the reported results.

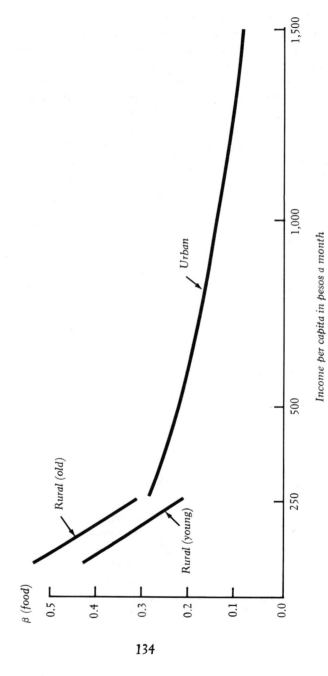

Figure 5.   Regression Lines for the Marginal Budget Shares (β) for Food

134

Marginal Propensity to Consume

In Lluch's (1973a) model the marginal propensity to consume is the ratio of the subjective rate of discount (δ) to the rate of interest (ρ). Thus a marginal propensity to consume of greater than one implies that δ exceeds ρ and optimal consumption paths decline through (planning) time (see chapter 2, on ELES and saving). Here twenty-seven of the thirty-two point estimates of μ (table 6.4) are less than unity, and only one is significantly greater at the 5 percent level (rural entrepreneurs, S,O). All μ estimates are significantly different from zero at the one percent level.

The estimated values of μ for rural households are irregular; the range is 0.66 to 1.20 and the mean value is 0.89. Similarly, little pattern is evident for urban estimates of μ after regressing on the explanatory variables used for the β estimates (see last row, table 6.5). If differences in the relative importance of transitory income are taken into consideration μ would be expected to be lower for entrepreneurs, and although this occurs the effect is not particularly pronounced. There is some tendency for the (urban) marginal propensity to consume to be lower for old households. The mean values are 0.75 for other urban and 0.74 for Mexico City, both well below the rural mean.

It is interesting to note, however, that systematic influences are more evident for the average propensity to save (APS). The preferred equations are:

$$\text{APS (rural)} = -\ 0.5253 + \underset{(0.1250)}{0.1922} \ \log y + \underset{(0.0291)}{0.0468} \ \text{DO},$$
$$\underset{(0.2758)}{}$$
$$R^2 = 0.594$$

$$\text{APS (urban)} = -\ 0.0678 + \underset{(0.0030)}{0.0070} \ (y/100) + \underset{(0.0208)}{0.0255} \ \text{DL}$$
$$\underset{(0.0231)}{}$$
$$+ \underset{(0.0186)}{0.0520} \ \text{DO} + \underset{(0.0242)}{0.0607} \ \text{DET}, \ R^2 = 0.727$$

where the dummy variables DO and DL are as defined in table 6.5, and DET is a dummy variable which is one for a household whose head is an entrepreneur or a technocrat, but which otherwise is zero. In both areas the APS increases with income and age. For urban households the coefficients for entrepreneurs and technocrats were virtually identical when included separately.

Table 6.6. *Estimated Values of Subsistence Parameters (γ_i^*) and Frisch Parameters (ω), ELES, Mexico, 1968*

Type of household[a]	Total consumption expenditure[b]	γ^{*c} Food	Clothing	Housing	Durables	Other	γ^* sum[c]	ω
Rural households								
Workers								
L,Y	129	−88 (279)	−38 (95)	−24 (64)	−18 (42)	−138 (270)	−306 (750)	−0.3
L,O	144	87 (8)	20 (3)	14 (2)	6 (1)	26 (5)	154 (15)	15.5
S,Y[d]	194							
S,O	209	120 (22)	20 (6)	23 (6)	10 (3)	42 (20)	215 (54)	35.1
Entrepreneurs								
L,Y	152	127 (22)	39 (9)	27 (6)	21 (6)	59 (16)	272 (59)	1.3
L,O	187	102 (8)	34 (6)	18 (2)	13 (3)	45 (8)	212 (25)	7.4
S,Y	249	125 (13)	34 (6)	30 (6)	15 (3)	76 (26)	279 (52)	8.2
S,O	268	97 (19)	19 (8)	18 (5)	3 (5)	16 (26)	153 (60)	−2.3

Other urban households

Workers

L,Y	207	105 (10)	26 (6)	33 (5)	13 (3)	52 (17)	230 (41)	9.3
L,O	233	97 (7)	22 (3)	30 (3)	9 (1)	32 (6)	191 (18)	−5.5
S,Y	363	172 (14)	51 (9)	72 (14)	25 (4)	81 (15)	401 (52)	9.8
S,O	402	139 (47)	22 (28)	34 (42)	13 (10)	−9 (102)	200 (227)	−2.0

Entrepreneurs

L,Y	322	127 (13)	34 (6)	47 (8)	22 (5)	85 (24)	315 (53)	−49.3
L,O	384	130 (8)	41 (5)	44 (5)	19 (4)	96 (21)	331 (37)	−7.2
S,Y	622	180 (15)	60 (13)	70 (13)	30 (10)	82 (56)	421 (96)	−3.1
S,O	669	209 (15)	61 (11)	110 (15)	31 (8)	170 (45)	582 (84)	−7.7

Technocrats

L,Y	420	145 (9)	45 (6)	54 (5)	20 (4)	75 (13)	338 (33)	−5.1
L,O	505	163 (11)	58 (9)	62 (8)	27 (6)	111 (31)	420 (59)	−5.9
S,Y	731	227 (23)	81 (19)	100 (17)	48 (9)	138 (44)	592 (109)	−5.3
S,O	816	209 (30)	13 (38)	87 (27)	21 (17)	62 (95)	392 (200)	−1.9

(Table continues on the following page.)

Table 6.6. (continued)

Type of household[a]	Total consumption expenditure[b]	γ*[c]					γ* sum[c]	3
		Food	Clothing	Housing	Durables	Other		
Mexico City households								
Workers								
L,Y	258	140	39	57	17	58	311	4.9
		(11)	(6)	(8)	(2)	(9)	(34)	
L,O	335	122	30	52	14	55	272	−5.3
		(10)	(6)	(8)	(2)	(10)	(31)	
S,Y	453	235	75	109	43	138	600	3.1
		(29)	(17)	(17)	(11)	(30)	(100)	
S,O	590	218	59	132	24	141	574	−38.4
		(18)	(11)	(17)	(5)	(37)	(75)	
Entrepreneurs								
L,Y	633	184	49	104	33	212	581	−12.3
		(38)	(19)	(46)	(22)	(267)	(389)	
L,O	795	206	68	129	28	125	554	−3.3
		(15)	(19)	(20)	(7)	(44)	(91)	
S,Y	982	235	70	156	45	201	707	−3.6
		(29)	(25)	(33)	(23)	(76)	(173)	
S,O	1,757	243	7	66	−8	−197	111	−1.1
		(71)	(103)	(214)	(70)	(535)	(974)	

138

Technocrats

L,Y	705	251	112	179	88	576	1,206	1.4
		(74)	(62)	(83)	(64)	(502)	(783)	
L,O	870	175	53	87	6	40	361	-1.7
		(34)	(38)	(45)	(20)	(128)	(258)	
S,Y	1,056	261	93	166	53	201	774	-3.8
		(14)	(15)	(21)	(14)	(62)	(120)	
S,O	1,405	330	104	248	74	259	1,015	-3.6
		(24)	(13)	(45)	(26)	(165)	(260)	

Note: Asymptotic standard errors in parentheses.

a. Household size is denoted by L (large, more than 5), and S (small, 5 or less). Age of household head is denoted by Y (young, less than 45 years) and O (old, 45 and over).

b. Mean total consumption expenditure per capita in pesos a month. (In 1968, 12.5 pesos = U.S. $1.00.)

c. In pesos per capita a month. Sum may not add exactly due to rounding.

d. γ^* values unobtainable because $\mu = 1.000$. Estimates treated as nonsignificant.

139

Table 6.7. *Weighted Regressions of Estimated Values of* γ^* *on Household Characteristics, Urban Mexico, 1968*

Commodity	Constant	Log y	DL	DO	DE	DT	DMC	R²
Food	1.714	0.1899	−0.1342ᵃ	—	0.0439	0.0764	0.0820ᵃ	0.935
	(0.190)	(0.1140)	(0.0297)		(0.0437)	(0.0488)	(0.0306)	
Clothing	1.634ᵃ	—	−0.2153ᵃ	—	0.1666ᵃ	0.2600ᵃ	0.1319ᵃ	0.907
	(0.037)		(0.0291)		(0.0358)	(0.0320)	(0.0307)	
Housing	0.778	0.3890ᵃ	−0.1966ᵃ	—	0.0907		0.2219ᵃ	0.948
	(0.441)	(0.1731)	(0.0469)		(0.0656)		(0.0453)	
Durables	1.350ᵃ	—	−0.2710ᵃ	−0.0726ᵃ	0.2446ᵃ	0.3134ᵃ	0.1522ᵃ	0.904
	(0.037)		(0.0336)	(0.0335)	(0.0419)	(0.0409)	(0.0344)	
Other	1.888ᵃ	—	−0.3005ᵃ	—	0.3252ᵃ		0.1898ᵃ	0.874
	(0.043)		(0.0379)		(0.0400)		(0.0395)	
Total	2.558ᵃ	—	−0.2416ᵃ	—	0.1931ᵃ	0.2272ᵃ	0.1705ᵃ	0.920
	(0.029)		(0.0248)		(0.0297)	(0.0291)	(0.0257)	

— Variable not included.

Note: The dependent variable is logγ^*_i; coefficients of dummy variables, when converted to natural logarithms, that is, multiplied by 2.303, measure proportionate effects on γ^*_i. Standard errors are given in parentheses. D denotes a dummy variable for L (large households of more than 5 members), O (old heads of household, 45 years and over), E (entrepreneurs), T (technocrats), and MC (households in Mexico City). Number of observations is always 24. R² is a weighted goodness of fit measure as given, for example, in Buse (1973).

a. The coefficient is significantly different from zero at the 5 percent level.

Subsistence Parameters

Estimated values of the "subsistence" parameters and their standard errors are given in table 6.6. The estimates are determined with much less precision than are the β parameters. A problem arises when the marginal propensity to consume is close to unity for, as explained in chapter 2, if $\mu = 1$ ELES collapses to LES and it is not possible to estimate the individual γ_i^*. Of the 160 γ^* estimates, 34 are not significantly different from zero at the 5 percent level, 17 of these being associated with μ estimates close to one (table 6.6, rural workers, L,Y and S,Y; other urban workers, S,O; and Mexico City technocrats, L,Y). The γ^* estimates for food are determined with greatest precision, being insignificant in only the two cases where $\mu = 1.0$ (rural workers, L,Y and S,Y). If these two cells are ignored, there are only three negative (but insignificant) values of γ^*; these occur for durables and other (both are negative for Mexico City entrepreneurs, S,O, and other is negative also for urban workers, S,O). Thus the γ^* estimates are indeed behaving as subsistence parameters.

A necessary condition for the utility function to exist is that the sum of the subsistence expenditures, the γ^* sum, be less than total consumption expenditure. This condition tends to be violated for rural households and low-income urban households (see table 6.6), although in only one case (rural entrepreneurs, L,Y) is the estimate of the γ^* sum significantly greater than $\bar{v}$ at the 5 percent level.

There are insufficient usable γ^* estimates for rural households to permit detailed analysis. There is some tendency for γ^* (other) and the γ^* sum to increase with income; the γ^* estimates for food are relatively stable. Mean values in pesos per capita a month (excluding rural workers, L,Y and S,Y) are: 110 (food), 24 (clothing), 22 (housing), 11 (durables), 44 (other), and 214 (total).

The γ^* estimates for urban households have been regressed on the same set of explanatory variables that was used in analyzing the β estimates. In this case, however, because the precision of the estimates varies substantially, weighted regressions were performed, the weights being the inverse of the standard error of the dependent variable. A double-log specification proved marginally superior to a semi-log model, and the estimated regressions are given in table 6.7.[9]

9. The appropriate weighting factor in the double-log case is the parameter estimate divided by its standard error, that is, the "t value." The three negative γ^* values were put equal to unity, but in view of their very large standard errors they have little influence on the regression coefficients. Total subsistence expenditure is calculated as the sum of positive γ^* estimates.

Except in the case of housing and, to a lesser extent, food, the influence of income is shown to be unimportant and highly insignificant.[10] Households living in Mexico City have significantly higher levels of subsistence expenditure for all goods (ranging from 19 percent for food to 51 percent for housing), partly because of higher prices there. The γ^* estimates are always larger for those in the socioeconomic classes of entrepreneur or technocrat.[11] The results strongly support the notion that γ^* estimates are a measure of an acceptable minimum standard for households identifying with a given socioeconomic group. The γ^* estimates also exhibit the effect of economies

Table 6.8.   *Total Expenditure Elasticities, ELES, Mexico, 1968*

Type of household[a]	Food	Clothing	Housing	Durables	Other	η[b]
Rural households						
Workers						
L,Y	0.67	1.03	0.83	1.21	1.95	0.91
L,O	0.86	0.73	1.25	0.96	1.59	0.63
S,Y	0.70	1.17	0.88	1.34	1.61	0.90
S,O	0.77	1.16	0.90	0.98	1.67	0.99
Entrepreneurs						
L,Y	0.70	1.23	1.18	1.83	1.36	0.77
L,O	0.72	1.50	0.87	1.99	1.10	0.73
S,Y	0.45	0.85	0.82	1.08	2.24	0.83
S,O	0.59	0.96	0.69	1.74	1.77	1.11
Other urban households						
Workers						
L,Y	0.54	1.26	0.90	1.22	1.94	0.88
L,O	0.72	1.27	0.93	1.31	1.51	0.73
S,Y	0.66	1.61	0.85	1.19	1.48	0.75
S,O	0.45	1.03	1.03	0.75	2.20	1.04
Entrepreneurs						
L,Y	0.52	0.97	1.03	1.62	1.54	0.78
L,O	0.48	0.94	0.89	1.25	1.60	0.64
S,Y	0.30	0.80	0.97	1.10	1.81	0.79
S,O	0.53	1.08	1.09	1.97	1.24	0.67

10. When log y is added back into the reported equations in table 6.7 it has the following coefficients and t values: clothing -0.05 ($t = -0.25$), durables 0.05 ($t = 0.13$), other -0.10 ($t = -0.38$), and total 0.03 ($t = 0.16$).

11. The coefficients of DT always exceed those of DE, but the difference is significant only for clothing, where it is 0.0934 with a t value of 2.73. The corresponding t values for food, durables, and total are 1.50, 1.45, and 1.06 respectively.

Table 6.8.   (continued)

Type of household[a]	Food	Clothing	Housing	Durables	Other	η[b]
Other urban households (continued)						
Technocrats						
L,Y	0.61	0.78	0.91	1.61	1.60	0.74
L,O	0.56	1.02	0.97	1.17	1.50	0.66
S,Y	0.59	1.10	1.05	0.88	1.50	0.88
S,O	0.45	1.67	0.77	1.22	1.44	0.92
Mexico City households						
Workers						
L,Y	0.72	1.16	1.38	1.21	1.19	0.70
L,O	0.76	1.17	1.25	0.75	1.21	0.72
S,Y	0.73	1.36	1.00	1.62	1.14	0.78
S,O	0.57	1.09	1.08	1.46	1.46	0.57
Entrepreneurs						
L,Y	0.35	0.65	0.74	1.07	1.68	0.86
L,O	0.46	1.18	0.93	1.22	1.50	0.73
S,Y	0.55	1.34	0.88	1.59	1.21	0.77
S,O	0.37	1.03	0.91	1.14	1.39	0.99
Technocrats						
L,Y	0.31	0.73	0.51	1.17	1.89	1.12
L,O	0.50	0.90	0.90	1.48	1.47	0.92
S,Y	0.40	0.89	0.93	1.30	1.53	0.82
S,O	0.37	0.38	0.83	0.95	1.73	0.64

a. Household size is denoted by L (large, more than 5) and S (small, 5 or less). Age of household head is denoted by Y (young, less than 45 years) and O (old, 45 and over).

b. Elasticity of total consumption expenditure with respect to income. Total income elasticities are obtained by multiplying total expenditure elasticities by the row value of η.

of scale: Large households always have lower per capita subsistence expenditure than small households (for the total, 56 percent lower). The age of households is important only for durables, where it exerts a small but significant negative effect.

Frisch Parameter

Estimates of the expenditure elasticity of the marginal utility of total expenditure (ω) are given in the last column of table 6.6. It follows from the definition of ω (2.7) that estimates have the incorrect (positive) sign whenever estimates of total subsistence expenditure exceed actual consumption expenditure. Positive values of the Frisch parameter occur for those cells (predominantly rural households) in which mean per capita income is less than 245 pesos a month; above this level all but three of the twenty-three ω esti-

Table 6.9. *Regressions of Estimated Values of Total Expenditure Elasticities on Household Characteristics, Mexico, 1968*

Commodity	Constant	y/100 (rural) and log y (urban)	DL	DO	DET	DMC	R^2
Rural households[a]							
Food	0.959[b] (0.084)	−0.1991[b] (0.0475)	—	0.1608[b] (0.0450)	—	—	0.826
Housing	1.351[b] (0.221)	−0.2348 (0.1189)	—	—	—	—	0.394
Other	1.232[b] (0.493)	0.2390 (0.2650)	—	—	—	—	0.119
Urban households[c]							
Food	1.817[b] (0.312)	−0.4792[b] (0.1138)	−0.0698 (0.0505)	0.0539 (0.0448)	—	0.0832 (0.0497)	0.503
Clothing	1.368[b] (0.118)	—	−0.1110 (0.1056)	—	−0.2773[b] (0.1120)	−0.1385 (0.1056)	0.310
Housing	3.789 (1.268)	−1.113[b] (0.513)	−0.2726 (0.1375)	0.1756 (0.0888)	0.2575 (0.2030)	0.2491 (0.1316)	0.383
Durables	5.891 (2.530)	−1.886 (1.023)	−0.4544 (0.2743)	0.1686 (0.1771)	0.8081 (0.4050)	0.4075 (0.2624)	0.195
Other	−1.967 (2.131)	1.439 (0.862)	0.3885 (0.2310)	−0.2027 (0.1492)	−0.5190 (0.3411)	−0.4889[b] (0.2210)	0.235

— Variable not included.

Note: Standard errors are given in parentheses. D denotes a dummy variable for L (large households of more than 5 members), O (old heads of household, 45 years and over), ET (entrepreneurs and technocrats), and MC (households in Mexico City).

a. Number of observations is always 8. With y/100 as explanatory variable, the value of R^2 for clothing was 0.017 and for durables 0.001.
b. Coefficient is significantly different from zero at the 5 percent level.
c. Number of observations is always 24.

144

mates are negative. There is some tendency for the urban estimates of the Frisch parameters to fall in absolute value as income rises, with a pronounced break at per capita incomes around 800 pesos a month. Above this level the median value is -3.3, below this (but above 245) the median value is -5.3. Since ω^{-1} is a measure of price responsiveness (see chapter 2), the results imply that households are more responsive to relative price changes at higher income levels.

Total Expenditure Elasticities

Estimates of total expenditure elasticities (η_i), calculated as in table 2.2, are given in table 6.8. The elasticities for food are, as expected, the lowest. For rural households they range from 0.45 to 0.86; for urban households the values are lower, ranging from 0.30 to 0.76. The total expenditure elasticities for clothing are clustered around one: The means are 1.1 for rural and other urban, 1.0 for Mexico City. All total expenditure elasticities for other exceed unity, as do three-quarters of the values for durables.

The results of the regression equations corresponding to those estimated for the β_i are reported in table 6.9. The regularities for rural households are few and similar to those observed for marginal budget shares. The total expenditure elasticity for food decreases significantly with larger income and is higher for old families; there is a tendency for the housing expenditure elasticity to decrease with larger income (significant at the 10 percent level).

For urban households the total expenditure elasticity for clothing shows more systematic variation than the corresponding β estimate, but for all other commodities the R^2 values are considerably lower and the income effect weaker when elasticities are the dependent variable. Socioeconomic effects, however, appear to be more important. The η_i estimates for clothing and other are higher for workers than for entrepreneurs and technocrats, those for housing and durables are lower.[12] The strongest result obtained is the decline in the total expenditure elasticity for food as income rises. The point estimates imply, for example, that for small, young households in Mexico City the food expenditure elasticity falls with per capita monthly income as follows: 0.65 at 400 pesos, 0.46 at 1,000 pesos, 0.38 at 1,500 pesos.

12. For all commodities there was remarkably little difference between the coefficients of DE and DT. In the results reported in table 6.9 a single dummy variable, DET, has been used, where DET = DE + DT.

Price Elasticities

Own-price elasticities (η_{ii}) are given in table 6.10. For urban house-holds 90 percent of the estimates are negative as required by the underlying utility function. Mean values are given in table 6.15. The results are much less satisfactory for rural households. First, the two cells (rural workers, L,Y and S,Y) which give unacceptable estimates of γ^* have to be excluded. Second, of the remaining thirty estimates, a third are positive. Only in the case of food are the reported rural price elasticities all negative—the mean value is −0.31. Since all β_i estimates are positive, own-price elasticities are positive only where estimates of subsistence expenditure on a commodity exceed actual expenditure (see formula for η_{ii} in table 2.2). Thus positive price elasticities occur most frequently in those cells for which ω is positive in table 6.6. The positive estimates of own-price elasticities among the urban results are concentrated in two cells for Mexico City (workers, S,Y, and technocrats, L,Y) where the γ^* estimates are

Table 6.10.   Own-Price Elasticities, ELES, Mexico, 1968

Type of household[a]	Food	Clothing	Housing	Durables	Other
Rural households					
Workers					
L,Y	—	—	—	—	—
L,O	−0.46	−0.06	−0.04	0.02	−0.19
S,Y	—	—	—	—	—
S,O	−0.42	−0.08	−0.08	−0.02	−0.29
Entrepreneurs					
L,Y	−0.03	0.66	0.73	1.21	0.55
L,O	−0.30	−0.07	0.04	0.13	−0.12
S,Y	−0.17	−0.01	0.00	0.07	−0.41
S,O	−0.47	−0.48	−0.34	−0.77	0.87
Other urban households					
Workers					
L,Y	−0.22	−0.02	−0.05	0.05	−0.28
L,O	−0.43	−0.35	−0.29	−0.29	−0.49
S,Y	−0.25	−0.06	−0.08	0.04	−0.18
S,O	−0.38	−0.57	−0.60	−0.40	−1.06
Entrepreneurs					
L,Y	−0.22	−0.12	−0.17	−0.14	−0.44
L,O	−0.23	−0.23	−0.23	−0.24	−0.63
S,Y	−0.18	−0.33	−0.42	−0.38	−0.82
S,O	−0.23	−0.24	−0.32	−0.35	−0.48

Table 6.10. (continued)

Type of household[a]	Food	Clothing	Housing	Durables	Other
Other urban households (continued)					
Technocrats					
L,Y	−0.33	−0.24	−0.29	−0.39	−0.59
L,O	−0.28	−0.29	−0.28	−0.26	−0.58
S,Y	−0.30	−0.33	−0.34	−0.23	−0.56
S,O	−0.35	−0.90	−0.48	−0.67	−0.86
Mexico City households					
Workers					
L,Y	−0.24	0.06	−0.02	0.17	−0.03
L,O	−0.42	−0.32	−0.43	−0.17	−0.43
S,Y	−0.14	0.22	0.08	0.37	0.02
S,O	−0.23	−0.14	−0.27	−0.10	−0.39
Entrepreneurs					
L,Y	−0.13	−0.10	−0.18	−0.14	−0.70
L,O	−0.26	−0.46	−0.43	−0.41	−0.69
S,Y	−0.29	−0.47	−0.39	−0.52	−0.59
S,O	−0.40	−0.97	−0.88	−1.06	−1.15
Technocrats					
L,Y	0.11	0.41	0.23	0.68	−0.20
L,O	−0.39	−0.58	−0.62	−0.88	−0.93
S,Y	−0.21	−0.32	−0.39	−0.41	−0.70
S,O	−0.19	−0.13	−0.38	−0.31	−0.80

— Model failed to yield meaningful estimates.

a. Household size denoted by L (large, more than 5) and S (small, 5 or less). Age of household head is denoted by Y (young, less than 45 years) and O (old, 45 and over).

"too high." Note, however, that positive values are not particularly associated with badly determined γ^* estimates.

Table 6.11 contains the results obtained from regressing the negative own-price elasticities (for urban areas only) on the logarithm of income and dummy variables.[13] A uniform pattern emerges: Own-price elasticities increase in absolute value with higher income and larger family size; they are higher in absolute value for workers than for entrepreneurs and technocrats and lower for residents of Mexico City than for other urban households.

Of the cross-price effects those for food tend to be most important.

13. These results are to be interpreted with due care because the γ^* estimates vary substantially in precision, and no allowance for this variation has been attempted. Since η_{ii} depends on both β_i and γ_i^*, precision will in general be higher than that for γ_i^*.

Table 6.11. Regressions of Price Elasticities on Household Characteristics, Urban Mexico, 1968

Commodity	Constant	log y	DL	DO	DET	DMC	R^2	Number of observations
Own price								
Food	1.244	−0.6051[a]	−0.1652[a]	—	0.2515[a]	0.1580[a]	0.444	23
	(0.428)	(0.1687)	(0.0500)		(0.0709)	(0.0489)		
Clothing	4.054[a]	−1.695[a]	−0.2720	—	0.4309	0.3911	0.431	21
	(1.540)	(0.600)	(0.1684)		(0.2213)	(0.1849)		
Housing	3.100[a]	−1.327[a]	−0.2023	—	0.3526[a]	0.2248[a]	0.625	22
	(0.868)	(0.339)	(0.1030)		(0.1358)	(0.1007)		
Durables	4.250[a]	−1.747[a]	−0.3037	—	0.3738	0.3496	0.532	19
	(1.430)	(0.555)	(0.1580)		(0.2081)	(0.1708)		
Other	3.732[a]	−1.658[a]	−0.2454	—	0.3380	0.3876[a]	0.560	23
	(1.311)	(0.512)	(0.1556)		(0.2038)	(0.1500)		
Food cross-price								
Clothing	−1.597[a]	0.3870[a]	0.0830	0.0440	0.1395	—	0.759	24
	(0.394)	(0.1516)	(0.0533)	(0.0433)	(0.0703)			
Housing	−2.584[a]	0.8482[a]	0.1532[a]	−0.0405	−0.1057	−0.1611[a]	0.809	24
	(0.574)	(0.2319)	(0.0622)	(0.0402)	(0.0918)	(0.0595)		
Durables	−3.256[a]	1.072[a]	0.2037[a]	—	−0.2336	−0.1813[a]	0.581	24
	(0.737)	(0.290)	(0.0859)		(0.1212)	(0.0829)		
Other	−0.746[a]	—	−0.0935[a]	0.1217[a]	0.2224[a]	0.1393[a]	0.760	24
	(0.047)		(0.0380)	(0.0380)	(0.0403)	(0.0380)		

— Variable not included.

Note: Standard errors are given in parentheses. D denotes a dummy variable for L (large households of more than 5 members), O (old heads of household, 45 years and over), ET (entrepreneurs and technocrats), and MC (households in Mexico City).

a. The coefficient is significantly different from zero at the 5 percent level.

The food cross-price elasticities (η_{i1}), calculated as in table 2.2, are listed in table 6.12 and mean values in table 6.15. All estimates are negative (again those for rural workers, L,Y and S,Y, are ignored), and the mean values for rural households are approximately double the mean urban estimates, for all commodities. The regression equations for urban households in table 6.11[14] show a strong tendency for the food cross-price elasticity to decline in absolute size as income increases. Family size and location are also important causal factors. Patterns in the total cross-price effects of nonfood items can be approximately obtained from the regression results for η_i, η_{ii}, and η_{i1} (tables 6.9 and 6.11) by using both homogeneity ($\eta_i + \Sigma_j \eta_{ij} = 0$) and the property of least squares regression that if dependent variables sum to zero then the estimated coefficients on each of the explanatory variables will do likewise across equations.[15]

Estimates of the elasticity of the average savings ratio with respect to the price of food are given in table 6.13 for urban areas (calculated from equation 2.12). Five of the twenty-four estimates have an incorrect positive sign; in four of these cases mean saving is negative, in the fifth μ exceeds one (Mexico City technocrats, L,Y). Rural results are not presented because mean saving is always negative. As with the Frisch parameter there is a break in the urban values at a per capita income level of 800 pesos a month. Above this level the range of values of ξ (food) is -0.70 to -0.13 with a median value of -0.43, below this (but above 240 pesos) the median value is -1.26. Thus there is evidence that saving is more responsive to the price of food at lower income levels.

An Overview of Findings

Fitting the extended linear expenditure system to data for homogeneous groups of households in Mexico has uncovered important

---

14. Estimation is by OLS. In general the estimates of η_{i1} will be determined reasonably precisely since they are functions only of γ_1^* and μ (plus data), two well-determined parameters.

15. This is an exact property only if explanatory variables are identical in each equation. Since explanatory variables are omitted only when their influence is both quantitatively small and statistically insignificant, the residual method outlined in the text will give a good approximation. The other departure from exactness is that in some regressions we drop own-price elasticities with the "wrong" sign.

systematic variations in demand behavior. Key findings for urban households are:

1. Marginal budget shares are influenced primarily by income and family size. Even after allowance is made for socioeconomic class, the marginal budget shares for food, housing, and durables fall significantly with higher income, and those for other increase.

2. Per capita subsistence expenditure (γ^* estimates) for all commodities is significantly lower for large families, lower for the socioeconomic group labeled workers, and higher for residents of Mexico City. When these factors are allowed for, income differences are an unimportant cause of variations in estimates of subsistence expenditures except for housing and, to a lesser extent, food. Thus the γ^* estimates may be interpreted as measuring an acceptable minimum standard as perceived by households in a given socioeconomic group.

Table 6.12.   *Food Cross-Price Elasticities, Mexico, 1968*

Type of household[a]	Clothing	Housing	Durables	Other
Rural households				
Workers				
L,Y	—	—	—	—
L,O	−0.44	−0.75	−0.58	−0.96
S,Y	—	—	—	—
S,O	−0.66	−0.52	−0.56	−0.95
Entrepreneurs				
L,Y	−1.03	−0.99	−1.53	−1.14
L,O	−0.82	−0.48	−1.09	−0.60
S,Y	−0.43	−0.41	−0.54	−1.13
S,O	−0.35	−0.25	−0.63	−0.64
Other urban households				
Workers				
L,Y	−0.64	−0.45	−0.62	−0.98
L,O	−0.53	−0.39	−0.55	−0.63
S,Y	−0.76	−0.40	−0.56	−0.70
S,O	−0.36	−0.36	−0.26	−0.76
Entrepreneurs				
L,Y	−0.38	−0.41	−0.64	−0.61
L,O	−0.32	−0.30	−0.42	−0.54
S,Y	−0.23	−0.28	−0.29	−0.52
S,O	−0.34	−0.34	−0.62	−0.39

Table 6.12. *(continued)*

Type of household[a]	Clothing	Housing	Durables	Other
Other urban households (continued)				
Technocrats				
L,Y	−0.27	−0.31	−0.56	−0.55
L,O	−0.33	−0.31	−0.38	−0.48
S,Y	−0.34	−0.33	−0.27	−0.46
S,O	−0.43	−0.20	−0.31	−0.37
Mexico City households				
Workers				
L,Y	−0.63	−0.75	−0.66	−0.65
L,O	−0.42	−0.46	−0.27	−0.44
S,Y	−0.71	−0.52	−0.84	−0.59
S,O	−0.40	−0.40	−0.54	−0.54
Entrepreneurs				
L,Y	−0.19	−0.22	−0.31	−0.49
L,O	−0.31	−0.24	−0.32	−0.39
S,Y	−0.32	−0.21	−0.38	−0.29
S,O	−0.14	−0.13	−0.16	−0.19
Technocrats				
L,Y	−0.26	−0.18	−0.42	−0.67
L,O	−0.18	−0.18	−0.30	−0.30
S,Y	−0.22	−0.23	−0.32	−0.38
S,O	−0.09	−0.20	−0.22	−0.41

a. Household size is denoted by L (large, more than 5) and S (small, 5 or less). Age of household head is denoted by Y (young, less than 45 years) and O (old, 45 and over).

3. Total expenditure elasticities show less systematic variation than the corresponding β estimates, except for clothing. This earlier conclusion is reinforced by comparing the coefficients of variation presented in table 6.14.

4. Own-price elasticities appear to increase in absolute value with higher income, to be higher in absolute value for small families and workers, and lower for households in Mexico City.

5. The effect of a change in the price of food on the demand for other commodities is much stronger at low income levels.

6. The Frisch parameter and the elasticity of the average savings ratio with respect to the price of food are both lower in absolute value for per capita incomes over about 800 pesos a month.

There is still some doubt, however, as to the precision with which the effects of socioeconomic class, location, and income have been isolated in examining patterns in marginal budget shares and in

Table 6.13.   *Elasticity of Average Savings Ratio with Respect to Food Price, Urban Mexico, 1968*

Type of household	L,Y	L,O	S,Y	S,O
Other urban				
Workers	4.37	−1.54	3.58	−0.75
Entrepreneurs	−15.31	−1.42	−0.62	−1.49
Technocrats	−1.20	−1.12	−1.39	−0.41
Mexico City				
Workers	1.99	−1.26	1.34	−7.90
Entrepreneurs	−3.01	−0.52	−0.57	−0.13
Technocrats	0.54	−0.27	−0.70	−0.43

Note: Household size is denoted by L (large, more than 5) and S (small, 5 or less). Age of household head is denoted by Y (young, less than 45 years) and O (old, 45 and over).

Table 6.14.   *Coefficient of Variation for Marginal Budget Shares (β_i) and Expenditure Elasticities (η_i), Mexico, 1968*

(*Percent*)

Parameters and elasticities	Food	Clothing	Housing	Durables	Other
Rural households					
β_i	22	30	16	34	29
η_i	17	21	19	27	20
Urban households					
β_i	42	31	24	30	28
η_i	25	27	17	23	16

Note: The coefficient of variation is defined as the standard deviation of individual cell estimates as reported in tables 6.4 and 6.8 divided by mean value multiplied by 100.

expenditure and price elasticities. There is a strong tendency in these regressions for the coefficients of the dummy variables for entrepreneur-technocrat and Mexico City to be opposite in sign to that of the income variable. Since households with the highest incomes fall in these categories, any functional misspecification of the role of income as a determinant of elasticities and marginal budget shares would automatically be reflected in the estimated values of the location and socioeconomic dummies. Thus these estimated regressions might be expected to perform poorly for predicting the consequences of any major changes in the distribution of income by location and socioeconomic class. Although experimentation with functional form was admittedly limited, it failed to diminish the influence of the nonincome attributes. The reported results seem fairly robust as a description of the existing set of data, but the doubt about their wider applicability remains. The regression coefficients for urban households in tables 6.5, 6.9, and 6.11 would seem to represent upper bounds on the magnitude of responses.

For rural households the strongest results are obtained for food. Both the marginal budget share and total expenditure elasticity fall significantly with rising income and are significantly higher for old households. There is no evidence of a specific rural effect, because the differences between these urban and rural results can be explained by disparity of income. Similarly, the mean estimate of subsistence expenditure for food in rural areas lies within the relevant bounds implied by the urban estimates. Total expenditure elasticities again show less variation than the corresponding marginal budget shares (see table 6.14).

Although we emphasize the importance of disaggregation and have found significant differences in demand and savings behavior across consumers, it is of some interest to collapse all our results into simple average values of elasticities for rural and urban households. These are presented in table 6.15. Mean total expenditure elasticities for rural and urban households are remarkably similar. The biggest difference occurs for food (0.68 rural, 0.52 urban); overall averages for the other commodities are clothing 1.1, housing 0.95, durables 1.3, other 1.6. The food cross-price elasticity in rural areas is about double that for urban households for all commodities. The model failed to yield reliable estimates of rural own-price elasticities except for food, where the mean value is −0.31 (urban −0.27). For urban households we can calculate total nonfood cross-price effects by using the homogeneity property of the system, namely, that for each good the sum of all price elasticities is equal (apart from a change of sign) to the total expenditure elasticity. At mean values, total expenditure elasticities break down evenly between own-price effect, food cross-price effect, and all other cross-price effects. For food, the mean own-price elasticity is about half the total expenditure elasticity. Again we emphasize that average values are only of limited interest. The relative importance of different price effects differs substantially across groups of consumers.

Estimates of the demand parameters imply that, if disaggregated data are to be pooled, the model must be modified to allow for the effect of family size; a shift variable should be introduced to permit the subsistence parameters to take different values for two socioeconomic groups, workers and nonworkers; and the marginal budget

Table 6.15.   Unweighted Mean Values of Elasticities, Mexico, 1968

Elasticity	Food	Clothing	Housing	Durables	Other
Total expenditure					
Rural	0.68	1.08	0.93	1.39	1.66
Urban	0.52	1.06	0.95	1.26	1.53
Own price[a]					
Rural	−0.31	—	—	—	—
Urban	−0.27	−0.34	−0.34	−0.39	−0.59
Food price					
Rural	—	−0.62	−0.57	−0.82	−0.90
Urban	—	−0.37	−0.32	−0.43	−0.51

— Insufficient plausible values to average.
Note: This table presents simple averages of values in tables 6.8, 6.10, and 6.12.
a. Average of negative values only.

shares must be allowed to vary with income. Specific allowance for rural-urban differences has a lower priority. On the savings side no strong intraregional regularities are apparent in estimates of the marginal propensity to consume. The mean value for rural households is 0.89 and for urban households 0.75. This statistically significant interregional difference implies that if urban and rural data are to be pooled, μ should be allowed to take two different values in ELES.

7

An Analysis of ECIEL Household Budget Data for Bogotá, Caracas, Guayaquil, and Lima

Howard Howe and Philip Musgrove

THIS CHAPTER INVESTIGATES PATTERNS of household consumption among different income classes in the principal city of four developing countries: Colombia, Ecuador, Peru, and Venezuela. The ELES is estimated separately for each city and, within each city, by socioeconomic stratum and by age of household head. The data consist of 4,117 observations from household budget surveys carried out in these cities between 1966 and 1969 as part of the ECIEL program's study of urban household income and consumption.[1] Estimation of

1. The authors wish to acknowledge their debt to their colleagues in the ECIEL program (Estudios Conjuntos sobre Integración Económica Latinoamericana, joint studies on Latin American economic integration), who collaborated in the study from which this analysis is derived. The member institutes of the ECIEL program whose data are used are: Centro de Estudios sobre Desarrollo Económico, Universidad de los Andes, Bogotá, Colombia; Banco Central de Venezuela, Caracas; Instituto Nacional de Estadística, Quito, Ecuador; and Pontificia Universidad Católica del Perú, Lima.

The authors are also grateful to Constantino Lluch, Alan Powell, and Ross Williams for encouragement and help in specifying and estimating the model; to Jorge Spencer and Jorge Lamas of the ECIEL staff for organizing the data and

ELES complements a variety of other analyses performed with these data and with those of six other Latin American cities surveyed at the same time. This prior body of work was drawn on in specifying the models and interpreting the results presented here.[2]

Methodology

The estimating procedure conforms generally to that described in chapter 2 for cross-section estimation in the absence of price data. Maximum likelihood estimates of μ, β_i, and γ_i^* are obtained from OLS reduced-form parameters as described by (2.29) and (2.30). Certain modifications should be noted, however:

1. Expenditures and income are totals for the household, not per capita values.

2. To compensate in part for this, subsistence expenditure (γ_i^*) is assumed to be different for small households (four members or fewer) and large ones (five members or more), but μ and β_i are assumed not to differ by household size. The structural ELES equation corresponding to (2.25) is written

$$(7.1) \qquad v_{ih} = \sum_{f=1}^{2} \gamma_{if}^* z_{fh} + \mu \beta_i \left(y_h - \sum_{f=1}^{2} \sum_{k} \gamma_{kf}^* z_{fh} \right) + e_{ih}$$

where z_{fh} are dummy variables representing the two household sizes.

3. The error term is assumed, on the basis of tests for Bogotá by Howe (1974), to be heteroscedastic with a variance proportional to the square of income. To restore homoscedasticity, the reduced-form equations are normalized on income for estimation. Equation (7.2)

performing the calculations; and to Robert Ferber and two anonymous referees for comments on a previous draft.

ECIEL acknowledges the financial support of the Development Research Center of the World Bank for this study. The work was conducted at the Brookings Institution. The views expressed are those of the authors and not of their respective institutions.

2. Musgrove (1977) describes the surveys in detail, discusses the procedures for data cleaning and analysis, and presents a wide selection of empirical results for ten cities in five countries. Another major investigation using ECIEL data is the estimation of LES, ELES, and QES (quadratic expenditure system) by Howe (1974) for Bogotá and three other Colombian cities. Meyer (1973) estimated linear Engel curves for Bogotá, Lima, and Caracas. For studies of other household budget data from South America see Belandria (1971) on Venezuela and Betancourt (1973 and chapter 8 of this volume) on Chile.

is the modification of (2.26) where the intercept differs between large and small households and the data are divided by income before estimation:

$$(7.2) \qquad v_{ih}/y_h = \sum_{f=1}^{2} \alpha_{if}(z_{fh}/y_h) + \beta_i^* + w_{ih}.$$

The resulting Engel curves pass through the means of v_{ih}/y_h, so the value of v_i corresponding to mean income $\bar{y}$ is not equal to $\bar{v}_i$.

4. Therefore uncompensated income elasticities $(\tilde{\eta}_i)$ are evaluated at mean income and mean household size (with the γ_i^* for each size class weighted by the relative frequency of households of that size), whereas uncompensated price elasticities $(\tilde{\eta}_{ii}$ and $\tilde{\eta}_{ij})$ are evaluated at mean size and mean expenditure in the category $\bar{v}_i$.

5. The covariances across equations are ignored when deriving the variances of the parameter estimates. As indicated in chapter 2, this is equivalent to assuming a diagonal Σ_{β^*,β^*}.

Despite these methodological differences it is possible to compare the results with those in other chapters, except of course that the subsistence parameters cannot be compared with per capita values unless they are divided by mean household size. Estimates of μ and β_i are not affected, but their variances are computed differently because of points 3 and 5.

The Data

Household budget data for the largest city in each of the four countries in the ECIEL study are analyzed: Bogotá, Colombia; Guayaquil, Ecuador; Lima, Peru; Caracas, Venezuela. These four countries are at comparable levels of development and all are members of the Andean Pact. The four cities cover a fairly wide range of per capita annual income (from $632 in Guayaquil to $1,112 in Caracas in 1968 U.S. dollars) and of income concentration (Gini coefficients from 0.429 in Caracas to 0.489 in Guayaquil).

Description

In the Caracas survey each family was interviewed in the course of one month, whereas in the other three cities interviews were distributed in four waves throughout twelve months or more. No family was interviewed twice in Caracas or Lima, but in Bogotá and

Table 7.1.   *Sample Size of Households in Bogotá, Caracas, Guayaquil, and Lima*

City and age class[a]	Socioeconomic stratum			Total
	Low	Middle	High	
Bogotá (February 1967–May 1968)				
Young	235	213	76	797
Old	149	81	43	
Caracas (October–November 1966)				
Young	137	357	153	929
Old	46	190	46	
Guayaquil (June 1967–November 1968)				
Young	219	352	76	1,050
Old	144	207	52	
Lima (February 1968–February 1969)				
Young	275	277	174	1,341
Old	176	237	202	

Source: Except as noted (table 7.14) the data for all tables in this chapter come from original calculations undertaken for this study. See note 1 in text.
   a. Households are classified according to the age of their head. Those aged 45 years and less are "young"; over 45 are "old."

Guayaquil some households were interviewed between two and four times. The sample size, shown in table 7.1, refers to observations rather than to independent households; in estimating ELES no account was taken of the fact that some families were interviewed more than once. The full samples range from 797 to 1,341 observations, or from 43 to 357 after classification by stratum and age.

All financial data were adjusted to a quarterly period of reference. Weighted regressions were estimated for the reduced-form expenditure functions. The weights make each quarterly survey representative of the population and correct the bias from three sources: differences among sample sizes in each quarter, deliberate nonproportionality among socioeconomic strata, and accidental nonproportionality with respect to such characteristics as family size, age of the head of household, and current income or employment situation. In Caracas, Bogotá, and Guayaquil the survey period seems to have been relatively normal with a representative degree of unemployment, rate of growth of output, and rapidity of price changes. In Lima the survey period began only five months after a major currency devaluation, and incomes and expenditures had not yet returned to normal.

Stratification

The six strata into which each sample was divided for estimation are defined by two independent criteria: the socioeconomic level of the household and the age of the head. Except in Caracas, the first stratification was part of the sample design, and the second was adopted only after the data were collected. Inasmuch as the socio-economic strata are meant to separate households by their permanent income rather than by their tastes or needs or by the prices they face, the strata differ somewhat from the groupings used in chapters 6 (Mexico) and 8 (Chile). The simultaneous classification of households by age more nearly resembles the way families are classified in the other chapters.

Neighborhoods were assigned to a high, middle, or low stratum on the basis of the external characteristics of dwellings, and sampling was proportional within each stratum. The samples were nonproportional (the sampling fraction differed among strata) in Bogotá, Guayaquil, and Lima. In Caracas the sample was proportional, but one stratum accounted for a very large share, and the strata correspond somewhat less well to the levels of permanent income. The low-income stratum was therefore defined as in the original sampling design according to place of residence (slums and marginal settlements), but the high and middle strata were separated according to the occupation of the household head. Professional, technical, and administrative jobs constitute the high-income classification, and all others are considered middle income.

The age of the household head appears to influence expenditure independently of income level. Because this effect is nonlinear, it was decided to partition each sample at age 45.[3] Households whose head is 45 or younger are called "young," and all others are "old." The old households include some whose heads are retired and whose saving behavior may differ from that of employed heads of the same age.

Choice of Variables

Any variable which is presumed to affect expenditures can be used to stratify the sample or included in the reduced-form equations. Two variables—current income and household size—are included in the equations.

3. The results make it appear that three age classes would have been more satisfactory, but some of the samples would then have been extremely small.

Income. Total current income of all household members includes imputed rent of owned dwellings and income in kind received from employers or produced at home. It also includes transitory elements such as year-end bonuses, lottery winnings, and capital gains. Apart from the possibility of large errors in reporting current income, the chief drawback to using this variable is that the households have already been stratified by a proxy for the level of permanent income. There may then be a great deal of transistory variation in the observed incomes, which may bias the expenditure-income relations more than the sample as a whole.

Household size. Because the smallest strata leave relatively few degrees of freedom, and because of the difficulty of specifying exactly how expenditures vary with household size at a given income level, a simple binary distinction was made. Households of four or fewer members are "small" and all others are "large."[4] No account was taken of the age and sex of household members, so the size is not based on the number of adult members only. For some households, the number will include members who were absent for part of the period of reference and therefore contributed to determining some expenditures (shelter and durables, for example) but not others (such as food).[5]

Expenditures. The five expenditure categories are: (a) food, beverages, and tobacco, excluding food purchased in restaurants; (b) clothing and personal accessories; (c) housing and related services, including paid or imputed rent, but not mortgage payments; services such as fuel, water, and electricity; maintenance and repairs; insurance and taxes; paper products; washing and cleaning supplies; and garden supplies; (d) durable goods, including payments made

4. One-member households are included in Bogotá and Guayaquil but not in Lima or Caracas. Except for the impossibility of estimating economies of scale, the best approach would be to estimate a separate γ^* for members of different ages, as was done by Howe (1974).

5. The typical composition of households of a given size may vary among cities, and among income levels and age classes in each city. In Bogotá households were defined as excluding supplementary members—those who share part but not all of their incomes and expenditures with the unit—whereas in the other cities the definition includes these members. Since supplementary members are usually adults, households in Bogotá will appear to contain a higher proportion of children and will, on the average, be smaller. In every city children are more common, for a given household size, in young than in old households. Finally, high-income households, except in Bogotá, will often include domestic servants.

for vehicles as well as for furniture and household effects, and semidurable goods such as household textiles (as in most household survey data, expenditures may be a poor measure of the consumption—that is, depreciation—of durables); (e) all other expenditures, including education, transportation and communication, personal care, medical care, entertainment, direct taxes, gifts and transfers, and a variety of nonconsumption expenditures.

Mean income, expenditures, and household sizes. The mean values of income and of each of the expenditure classes, for each stratum and city, are shown in national currency in table 7.2. Annual income per capita is also shown in 1968 U.S. dollars. Average budget shares and average income shares or spending propensities can be derived from these means. Also shown are the mean household sizes, in number of members, and the mean saving ratios.

Empirical Results: ELES Parameter Estimates

The parameters of the system (μ, β and γ^*) are discussed in this section, and subsistence expenditures are compared with observed mean income and total expenditure. Discussion of income elasticities and price elasticities derived from the parameters is left to the following section.

The Marginal Propensity to Consume

The parameter μ should lie between zero and one, being fairly close to one. It can be expected to stay constant or decline as income rises, but it is not clear how μ behaves with age, independently of income. The twenty-eight values of $\hat{\mu}$ are assembled in table 7.3 by income stratum and age. The cities with the highest income (Caracas and Lima) have the lowest overall marginal propensities, but these are barely distinguishable from the estimate for Guayaquil, where income is at about the level of Bogotá.[6]

When the $\hat{\mu}$ are analyzed by stratum, the results are less satisfactory. Only in Bogotá does $\hat{\mu}$ decline with rising income in each age group, and only there does $\hat{\mu}$ (young) consistently exceed $\hat{\mu}$ (old),

6. For some categories the Caracas data have a shorter reference period than do those for other cities. The μ for Caracas is therefore probably underestimated to a slightly greater degree than in other cities since transitory variation is more important in the short run.

Table 7.2. *Mean Quarterly Income and Expenditure, Mean Household Size, and Average Savings Ratio in Four South American Cities*

Item	Low		Middle		High		Total
	Young	*Old*	*Young*	*Old*	*Young*	*Old*	*Total*
Bogotá (tens of pesos)							
Income	608.2	659.8	869.3	1,311.1	2,844.3	4,744.7	945.1
Expenditure	647.2	650.2	867.1	1,134.7	2,483.7	4,199.0	911.6
Food	252.9	259.1	318.4	330.7	580.3	802.1	304.7
Clothing	59.5	48.0	71.8	87.7	234.9	412.0	78.6
Housing	160.6	197.8	249.4	321.0	737.6	1,233.5	256.5
Durables	26.7	7.9	26.1	26.2	138.4	136.9	32.1
Other	147.6	137.5	191.5	369.2	792.5	1,614.5	239.8
Size (persons)	6.02	5.55	6.70	6.53	5.81	6.92	6.13
Average savings ratio	−0.0641	0.0145	0.0025	0.1345	0.1268	0.1150	0.0354
Caracas (bolívars)							
Income	2,764.1	3,396.2	5,550.1	7,473.9	10,863.0	14,500.0	6,728.6
Expenditure	2,359.6	3,119.9	5,581.9	6,494.6	9,951.9	12,532.0	6,219.6
Food	1,066.5	1,347.1	1,546.3	1,688.2	1,988.0	2,293.8	1,602.3
Clothing	189.4	268.5	415.6	400.1	700.2	445.0	419.16
Housing	502.4	736.3	1,753.2	2,270.8	3,349.5	4,936.4	2,038.4
Durables	20.5	51.1	163.8	106.0	245.9	148.4	137.5
Other	508.7	716.9	1,703.0	2,029.6	3,668.2	4,708.8	2,022.2
Size (persons)	6.30	6.98	4.88	5.24	5.33	5.63	5.38
Average savings ratio	0.1463	0.0814	−0.0057	0.1310	0.0839	0.1357	0.0756

162

Guayaquil (sucres)

Income	7,880.8	9,125.2	9,359.9	13,901.0	28,183.0	32,912.0	10,631.0
Expenditure	6,364.1	7,841.7	9,553.4	12,119.0	25,368.0	29,768.0	9,261.9
Food	2,832.9	3,188.7	4,409.2	4,041.9	6,460.2	5,697.8	3,592.5
Clothing	599.4	643.8	576.2	669.6	1,568.5	1,809.4	635.4
Housing	1,407.5	2,065.9	2,153.8	4,199.8	9,392.5	12,698.7	2,652.5
Durables	487.6	183.9	327.0	538.4	1,081.1	666.1	369.2
Other	1,164.3	1,682.1	2,061.2	2,634.8	7,748.5	7,465.7	2,012.3
Size (persons)	6.03	6.42	5.81	5.57	5.82	5.41	6.01
Average savings ratio	0.1925	0.1407	−0.0014	0.1282	0.0999	0.0955	0.1288

Lima (tens of soles)

Income	2,005.6	2,342.6	4,025.8	5,224.6	14,743.0	13,786.0	3,252.8
Expenditure	1,952.5	1,986.6	4,202.3	4,545.4	10,381.0	10,027.0	2,968.9
Food	765.1	783.8	1,019.0	1,092.1	1,489.1	1,519.4	884.0
Clothing	148.1	189.1	350.5	377.4	766.7	1,083.2	249.9
Housing	330.2	424.1	1,160.5	1,382.7	3,892.0	3,907.4	754.0
Durables	181.8	125.8	494.1	477.8	917.1	593.7	282.9
Other	527.4	463.8	1,178.2	1,215.4	3,316.6	2,923.7	798.0
Size (persons)	6.56	6.99	5.80	6.02	7.03	7.70	6.47
Average savings ratio	0.0265	0.1520	−0.0438	0.1300	0.2959	0.2727	0.0873

Per capita income (1968 U.S. dollars a year)[a]

Bogotá	431	507	554	857	2,089	2,925	658
Caracas	390	432	1,010	1,268	1,812	2,289	1,112
Guayaquil	467	508	576	892	1,730	2,173	632
Lima	433	475	983	1,229	2,970	2,535	712

a. Mean household income in national currency is divided by mean size, and then converted to Venezuelan bolívars of equal purchasing power by parity rates calculated to account for inflation between that date and the dates of the survey. The parities are 0.4800 (Colombia), 0.4019 (Ecuador), and 0.1593 (Peru); the bolívar-dollar free rate, used to convert to U.S. dollars, was 4.5.

163

Table 7.3. *Marginal Propensity to Consume* ($\hat{\mu}$) *in Four South American Cities*

City	Low		Middle		High		Total
	Young	Old	Young	Old	Young	Old	
Bogotá	0.9700	0.9392	0.9144	0.8546	0.8599	0.5544	0.9313
	(0.0316)	(0.0480)	(0.0352)	(0.0545)	(0.0457)	(0.0696)	(0.0171)
Caracas	0.3882	0.3368	0.7136	0.6792	0.7106	0.7465	0.7429
	(0.0661)	(0.1281)	(0.0427)	(0.0449)	(0.0427)	(0.0745)	(0.0216)
Guayaquil	0.6808	0.8090	0.9979	0.8593	0.8598	0.8737	0.7992
	(0.0325)	(0.0397)	(0.0809)	(0.0363)	(0.0490)	(0.1039)	(0.0228)
Lima	0.7906	0.2889	0.9104	0.2441	0.1487	0.6539	0.7569
	(0.0495)	(0.0907)	(0.0536)	(0.0568)	(0.0829)	(0.0446)	(0.0260)

Note: Standard errors are given in parentheses.

although the differences are not significant except at high incomes. In Caracas and Guayaquil the values for the middle and high strata, in both age groups, are not distinguishable with confidence, although there is considerable variation in the point estimates. In Lima there is no pattern to the propensities, and half of them are much too low to be reasonable. (These are all cases in which one value of β_i is negative.)

The standard errors of the estimates of μ are often rather large because the strata are small, and in any case income is observed with errors. A further difficulty is the substantial amount of transitory income and consumption. This factor explains why the very low values of $\hat{\mu}$ are concentrated in Lima, where incomes were probably abnormal in the survey period.[7] The variation in $\hat{\mu}$ among strata may also be explained by transitory income variation. Transitory income is likely to form a larger share of total income in the high and the low strata than in the middle stratum because of high unemployment in the low stratum and substantial capital receipts in the high stratum.

In summary, whenever all the estimates of μ are reasonable, the marginal propensity to consume tends to decline or remain constant with increasing income and also with increasing age. Transitory income variation in the high and—even more—in the low strata makes it difficult to get reasonable results, however.

Marginal Budget Shares

The marginal budget shares derived from ELES should always be positive. No inferior goods are allowed, which should not be a significant limitation for the aggregated categories analyzed here. Of the 140 values of $\hat{\beta}_i$ obtained, five are negative, and four of these are distinct from zero. In each of the five cases the income elasticity $(\tilde{\eta}_i)$ is also negative at the point of means, although the standard errors on the elasticities are so large that none can be distinguished from zero. In three cases (Bogotá low-old, Lima low-old, and Caracas low-young), $\hat{\beta}_i < 0$ for expenditure on durables and vehicles. This

---

7. If the linear form of the permanent income hypothesis is correct (Friedman, 1957, pp. 31–37), then μ can be expressed as $K \, \text{var}(y_p)/\text{var}(y)$, where K is the propensity to consume permanent income y_p. Estimates with the logarithmic form of the hypothesis (Musgrove, 1977, chapter 2), suggest that for Lima, $\text{var}(y_p)$ is only about 70 percent of $\text{var}(y)$, leading to low values of μ for a given K. In contrast, for Colombia (Bogotá plus three smaller cities), $\text{var}(y_p)$ appears to exceed 90 percent of $\text{var}(y)$. The same is true for Guayaquil (together with Quito).

category may be expected to have a very large transitory variance, and the marginal budget share is negative only in the low stratum, where transitory variation in income may also be especially large. The other two cases, expenditures on food in Lima (high-young and middle-old), seem to imply that at high enough incomes food becomes an inferior good, which is scarcely possible.

Tables 7.4 through 7.7 display the estimates of β_i and γ_{ij}^* by city. When all strata are analyzed together, the marginal share for food is inversely related to the income level, and the share for "other" is directly related. Housing takes a relatively constant share of marginal spending, ranging from 27 to 33 percent. Clothing shows only slightly greater variation; its share is highest in Bogotá and Lima, where personal effects are most likely to be bought as saving substitutes. The greatest variation is in durables, with a share ranging between 3 and 5 percent except in Lima where it reaches 10 percent. This is almost certainly a consequence of accelerated inflation coupled with large transitory variation in income and total expenditure.[8]

When the $\hat{\beta}_i$ are compared for young and old households in each stratum, it is evident that young families are more apt to devote the marginal budget to durables and less apt to spend on housing and "other" than are older households.[9] If the middle and high strata are considered together, young families also give higher marginal budget shares to food and clothing except in Lima; at low incomes this is true only in Bogotá and Guayaquil.[10] For necessities, the marginal budget share should fall as income rises, while it should rise for luxuries.[11] The comparison is complicated by the occasional negative estimates of β, since these raise the other marginal shares in the same stratum and age group, but the effect on the ranking of the estimates across strata seems to be slight.

8. Differences in prices among cities are probably also important in explaining marginal spending shares, but are not considered here. The explanation in terms of inflation is discussed at more length later.

9. The comparison is not reliable for Lima because a negative value of $\hat{\beta}_i$ occurs for food in the high-young and middle-old strata, and for durables in low-old. Negative $\hat{\beta}_i$ for durables in Bogotá (low-old) and Caracas (low-young) have much smaller effects.

10. If those cases are excluded in which the two estimates cannot be distinguished, then $\hat{\beta}$ (clothing) is always higher for young than for old families, and $\hat{\beta}$ (durables) is higher in all but one case.

11. No account is taken of differences in mean household size between young and old households, but, as table 7.1 indicates, these differences are usually slight.

The most consistent pattern occurs for food expenditures, where $\hat{\beta}$ (low) $>$ $\hat{\beta}$ (middle) $>$ $\hat{\beta}$ (high) six out of eight times. For clothing, $\hat{\beta}$ (low) is always highest among young households, but this pattern is less clear for older households. There is no consistent ranking of $\hat{\beta}$ (middle) and $\hat{\beta}$ (high) for either age group. For durables, the pattern $\hat{\beta}$ (high) $>$ $\hat{\beta}$ (middle) $>$ $\hat{\beta}$ (low) occurs most frequently, but in two cases $\hat{\beta}$ (low) is actually the highest estimate. There is no regular ranking for housing or for other goods and services.

Subsistence Expenditures

The Stone-Geary utility function requires that $v_i > \gamma_i^*$ for each household in the sample. Since the estimate γ_i^* obtained is an average over the sample, it can only be compared with an average level of expenditure such as $\bar{v}_i$. Since γ_i^* is estimated for two different classes of household size, an average $\bar{\gamma}_i^* = \gamma_{i1}^* \bar{z}_1 + \gamma_{i2}^* \bar{z}_2$ is used initially for comparisons, where $\bar{z}_1$, $\bar{z}_2$ are the proportions of households in the small and large classes respectively.[12] (It is this value of $\bar{\gamma}_i^*$ which enters the calculation of price elasticities, $\tilde{\eta}_{ii}$, $\tilde{\eta}_{i1}$). Of the 140 values of $\bar{\gamma}^*$, 44 exceed the mean expenditure $\bar{v}$: 20 instances in Bogotá, 6 in Caracas, 13 in Lima, and 5 in Guayaquil. Those in Guayaquil occur because the estimate of μ is almost unity; when $\mu = 1$ ELES collapses to LES and the γ^* parameters are not identified (see 2.29). In what follows this set of estimates is not considered, leaving 39 instances in which $\bar{\gamma}^* > \bar{v}$.

Except for luxuries, the value of $\bar{\gamma}^*$ may be expected to rise somewhat with income, since it is affected by habit as well as by necessity. Nonetheless it should rise less rapidly than mean expenditure, because as income rises a smaller share goes to "subsistence" expenditure. The likelihood that $\bar{\gamma}^* > \bar{v}$ should therefore be highest for the low-income stratum and should be essentially zero at high incomes.[13]

12. If $\gamma_{i1}^* > \bar{v} < \gamma_{i2}^*$ the calculation is unnecessary. An alternative is to compare γ^* with mean expenditure by size class, $\bar{v}_f = \Sigma_h v_h \bar{z}_{fh}/N\bar{z}_f$. Note that it may still happen that $\gamma^* > \bar{v}$ for many households h; in that case the variables used to estimate γ^* do not account for all the variation in minimum expenditure among households.

13. γ^* estimates based on permanent or normal income often exceed those based on current income. This is a further reason for the use of current income here, since it reduces the likelihood of $\bar{\gamma}^*$ exceeding $\bar{v}$. See Howe (1974), pp. 201–05; Belandria (1971), pp. 90–101; and Betancourt (1973), pp. 22–23.

Table 7.4. ELES Parameter Estimates, Bogotá Households, 1967–68

Socio-ecomomic stratum	Age of household head	Household size	Food	Clothing	Housing	Durables	Other	Marginal propensity to consume ($\hat{\mu}$)	$\hat{\gamma}^*$ sum
Marginal budget share ($\hat{\beta}$)									
Total			0.3274	0.0956	0.3108	0.0322	0.2430	0.9313	
			(0.0064)	(0.0018)	(0.0058)	(0.0058)	(0.0066)	(0.0048)	
Low	Young		0.3473	0.1159	0.2679	0.0458	0.2231	0.9700	
			(0.0120)	(0.0039)	(0.0092)	(0.0015)	(0.0078)	(0.0316)	
	Old		0.3900	0.0775	0.3288	−0.0001	0.2038	0.9392	
			(0.0208)	(0.0040)	(0.0715)	(0.0000)	(0.0111)	(0.0480)	
Middle	Young		0.2713	0.0946	0.3190	0.0592	0.2559	0.9144	
			(0.0111)	(0.0038)	(0.0128)	(0.0024)	(0.0104)	(0.0352)	
	Old		0.2443	0.0830	0.2870	0.0318	0.3540	0.8456	
			(0.0167)	(0.0055)	(0.0192)	(0.0021)	(0.0243)	(0.0545)	
High	Young		0.1609	0.1083	0.2986	0.0748	0.3574	0.8599	
			(0.0089)	(0.0059)	(0.0167)	(0.0042)	(0.0200)	(0.0457)	
	Old		0.1480	0.0751	0.2537	0.0570	0.4662	0.5544	
			(0.0190)	(0.0097)	(0.0342)	(0.0073)	(0.0595)	(0.0696)	

Subsistence consumption $(\hat{\gamma}^*)$

Total		Small	205.8	45.7	165.5	13.9	115.9	546.8
			(39.9)	(11.5)	(36.2)	(4.9)	(29.8)	
		Large	534.2	125.5	416.4	41.4	340.4	1,457.9
			(97.9)	(28.3)	(88.6)	(12.0)	(73.1)	
Low	Young	Small	432.4	125.4	307.1	47.2	246.2	1,158.3
			(369.5)	(121.9)	(283.4)	(49.2)	(237.7)	
		Large	1,051.2	311.6	753.8	118.2	638.6	2,873.4
			(957.8)	(315.9)	(734.7)	(127.5)	(616.3)	
	Old	Small	232.1	39.0	192.3	0.8	102.6	566.8
			(152.9)	(29.9)	(126.9)	(8.0)	(81.0)	
		Large	724.8	132.1	555.8	11.5	368.9	1,793.1
			(482.0)	(94.3)	(400.4)	(25.4)	(255.4)	
Middle	Young	Small	104.8	8.8	44.5	−4.1	32.0	186.0
			(60.4)	(22.3)	(69.3)	(15.1)	(56.8)	
		Large	416.9	97.8	352.1	50.6	260.6	1,223.0
			(84.5)	(31.2)	(97.0)	(21.0)	(79.4)	
	Old	Small	215.2	32.2	237.5	27.8	170.0	682.7
			(61.1)	(21.2)	(67.5)	(11.3)	(91.4)	
		Large	306.0	64.6	244.1	29.9	217.9	862.5
			(51.6)	(17.9)	(56.9)	(9.5)	(77.1)	
High	Young	Small	366.4	174.9	383.5	94.3	525.4	1,544.5
			(73.9)	(50.4)	(136.5)	(44.0)	(165.4)	
		Large	438.2	74.1	425.6	14.2	317.2	1,269.3
			(78.2)	(53.3)	(144.4)	(46.4)	(175.0)	
	Old	Small	132.5	17.1	118.0	−2.7	182.6	447.5
			(30.5)	(27.7)	(67.5)	(22.9)	(102.9)	
		Large	833.7	407.4	1,270.8	125.6	1,534.8	4,172.3
			(63.9)	(57.9)	(140.7)	(48.0)	(215.4)	

Note: Standard errors are given in parentheses.

169

Table 7.5. *ELES Parameter Estimates, Caracas Households, October–November 1966*

Socio-economic stratum	Age of household head	Household size	Food	Clothing	Housing	Durables	Other	Marginal propensity to consume ($\hat{\mu}$)	$\hat{\gamma}^*$ sum
Marginal budget share (β)									
Total			0.1963	0.0741	0.3282	0.0284	0.3730	0.7429	
			(0.0060)	(0.0022)	(0.0100)	(0.0008)	(0.0115)	(0.0216)	
Low	Young		0.5481	0.1550	0.0581	−0.0113	0.2501	0.3882	
			(0.0922)	(0.0273)	(0.0108)	(0.0019)	(0.0468)	(0.0660)	
	Old		0.0803	0.1662	0.4706	0.0227	0.2601	0.3368	
			(0.0344)	(0.0648)	(0.1800)	(0.0087)	(0.1079)	(0.1285)	
Middle	Young		0.1932	0.0967	0.2768	0.0465	0.3869	0.7136	
			(0.0119)	(0.0059)	(0.0178)	(0.0029)	(0.0242)	(0.0420)	
	Old		0.1631	0.0194	0.3882	0.0152	0.4141	0.6792	
			(0.0112)	(0.0113)	(0.0262)	(0.0010)	(0.0288)	(0.0440)	
High	Young		0.0993	0.0854	0.3668	0.0450	0.4035	0.7106	
			(0.0075)	(0.0064)	(0.0278)	(0.0034)	(0.0313)	(0.0522)	
	Old		0.1053	0.0313	0.4283	0.0167	0.4183	0.7465	
			(0.0108)	(0.0031)	(0.0433)	(0.0017)	(0.0442)	(0.0745)	

Subsistence consumption ($\hat{\gamma}^*$)

								Total
Total		Small	1,520.4 (75.2)	389.8 (33.9)	1,792.8 (126.4)	121.4 (25.5)	1,719.1 (152.2)	5,543.5
		Large	1,372.7 (55.1)	284.9 (24.8)	1,189.9 (92.8)	85.8 (18.7)	1,183.0 (111.8)	4,116.3
Low	Young	Small	1,159.6 (103.5)	239.5 (50.4)	550.1 (69.8)	33.2 (13.9)	827.8 (106.2)	2,810.2
		Large	944.9 (59.0)	150.3 (28.8)	440.1 (39.5)	17.1 (7.9)	403.0 (60.5)	1,955.4
	Old	Small	981.1 (124.5)	197.8 (64.5)	715.1 (121.5)	13.6 (32.2)	394.4 (151.7)	2,302.0
		Large	1,448.7 (434.9)	268.2 (77.2)	713.7 (161.1)	70.3 (34.9)	792.3 (170.7)	3,293.2
Middle	Young	Small	1,513.9 (123.1)	442.1 (63.2)	1,819.3 (212.1)	174.8 (67.0)	1,746.1 (265.6)	5,696.2
		Large	1,761.6 (121.5)	416.5 (62.3)	1,644.0 (209.2)	197.6 (66.2)	1,832.7 (262.1)	5,852.4
	Old	Small	1,382.8 (94.2)	280.8 (50.1)	1,737.7 (177.9)	89.4 (24.1)	1,526.0 (256.7)	5,016.7
		Large	1,558.3 (97.7)	317.6 (51.9)	1,599.5 (184.9)	51.0 (24.9)	1,331.8 (266.4)	4,858.2
High	Young	Small	1,510.7 (110.4)	592.5 (96.4)	2,241.4 (318.0)	174.8 (65.8)	2,434.3 (435.4)	6,943.7
		Large	1,764.5 (114.8)	474.3 (101.0)	2,236.8 (331.2)	119.3 (68.6)	2,328.7 (452.1)	6,923.6
	Old	Small	1,405.4 (291.3)	251.4 (94.5)	1,395.3 (912.6)	-4.1 (42.7)	604.4 (1,234.8)	3,652.4
		Large	1,919.5 (217.3)	273.4 (70.4)	2,907.3 (680.2)	45.7 (31.9)	2,959.5 (919.9)	8,105.4

171

Note: Standard errors are given in parentheses.

Table 7.6. ELES Parameter Estimates, Guayaquil Households, 1967–68

Socio-economic stratum	Age of household head	Household size	Food	Clothing	Housing	Durables	Other	Marginal propensity to consume (μ̂)	γ̂* sum
Marginal budget share (β̂)									
Total			0.3840	0.0724	0.2875	0.0476	0.2083	0.7992	
			(0.0118)	(0.0021)	(0.0083)	(0.0014)	(0.0062)	(0.0228)	
Low	Young		0.3586	0.1008	0.2347	0.0738	0.2320	0.6808	
			(0.0181)	(0.0049)	(0.0116)	(0.0038)	(0.0117)	(0.0325)	
	Old		0.4033	0.0727	0.3100	0.0279	0.1861	0.8090	
			(0.0205)	(0.0036)	(0.0159)	(0.0014)	(0.0100)	(0.0397)	
Middle	Young		0.4434	0.0575	0.2318	0.0491	0.2182	0.9979	
			(0.0378)	(0.0047)	(0.0189)	(0.0040)	(0.0179)	(0.0809)	
	Old		0.3565	0.0611	0.3188	0.0506	0.2130	0.8593	
			(0.0156)	(0.0026)	(0.0139)	(0.0023)	(0.0100)	(0.0363)	
High	Young		0.2801	0.0739	0.3960	0.0486	0.2015	0.8598	
			(0.0167)	(0.0043)	(0.0229)	(0.0229)	(0.0132)	(0.0040)	
	Old		0.1112	0.0535	0.5379	0.0301	0.2673	0.8737	
			(0.0135)	(0.0064)	(0.0619)	(0.0036)	(0.0325)	(0.1039)	

Subsistence consumption ($\hat{\gamma}^*$)

Total		Small	944.0 (165.5)	141.0 (23.7)	527.0 (90.2)	30.7 (23.2)	563.2 (73.3)	2,205.9
		Large	2,476.6 (191.6)	238.0 (27.4)	916.3 (104.3)	113.2 (26.8)	666.9 (84.8)	4,411.0
Low	Young	Small	1,024.5 (142.6)	48.0 (39.4)	342.3 (82.0)	−29.0 (62.7)	191.6 (93.0)	1,577.4
		Large	2,419.4 (115.3)	238.5 (31.8)	698.0 (66.1)	132.9 (50.4)	575.2 (74.8)	3,864.1
	Old	Small	974.4 (218.4)	195.4 (41.3)	646.3 (165.1)	36.7 (25.8)	655.0 (125.6)	2,507.8
		Large	2,135.6 (316.9)	216.6 (60.0)	837.7 (239.7)	43.4 (37.4)	641.5 (182.0)	3,874.8
Middle	Young	Small	—	—	—	—	—	—
		Large	—	—	—	—	—	—
	Old	Small	981.5 (304.8)	121.2 (52.0)	862.3 (264.1)	46.2 (69.7)	927.3 (218.8)	2,938.5
		Large	1,839.5 (424.3)	126.2 (72.3)	898.5 (367.4)	114.2 (96.9)	468.7 (304.4)	3,447.1
High	Young	Small	935.4 (739.9)	166.4 (187.2)	403.2 (973.7)	7.3 (172.4)	710.5 (685.1)	2,222.8
		Large	2,276.0 (680.0)	413.2 (172.1)	1,806.0 (895.4)	208.8 (158.6)	2,192.2 (629.8)	6,896.2
	Old	Small	2,847.1 (718.2)	393.5 (320.8)	2,630.1 (3,625.3)	90.3 (201.3)	1,957.4 (1,618.4)	7,918.4
		Large	3,336.1 (870.2)	279.0 (348.1)	−429.1 (3,214.0)	−80.0 (254.9)	−22.7 (1,319.7)	3,083.3

— Estimated with very large standard errors because $\hat{\mu}$ is very close to one.

Note: Standard errors are given in parentheses.

Table 7.7. ELES Parameter Estimates, Lima Households, 1968–69

Marginal budget share (β)

Socio-economic stratum	Age of household head	Household size	Food	Clothing	Housing	Durables	Other	Marginal propensity to consume ($\hat{\mu}$)	$\hat{\gamma}^*$ sum
Total			0.2237	0.1094	0.2730	0.0987	0.2952	0.7569	
			(0.0084)	(0.0038)	(0.0097)	(0.0037)	(0.0106)	(0.0260)	
Low	Young		0.2679	0.1205	0.1744	0.1442	0.2930	0.7906	
			(0.0186)	(0.0076)	(0.0112)	(0.0098)	(0.0189)	(0.0495)	
	Old		0.3115	0.1343	0.3328	−0.4015	0.6229	0.2889	
			(0.1023)	(0.0445)	(0.1078)	(0.1547)	(0.1927)	(0.0907)	
Middle	Young		0.2395	0.0875	0.3048	0.1676	0.2005	0.9104	
			(0.0145)	(0.0052)	(0.0184)	(0.0106)	(0.0134)	(0.0536)	
	Old		−0.3617	0.1989	0.7132	0.2195	0.2302	0.2441	
			(0.1109)	(0.0467)	(0.1617)	(0.0535)	(0.0572)	(0.0568)	
High	Young		−0.0142	0.0420	0.6394	0.2192	0.1137	0.1487	
			(0.0081)	(0.0238)	(0.3458)	(0.1324)	(0.0727)	(0.0829)	
	Old		0.1215	0.0814	0.4162	0.0880	0.2929	0.6539	
			(0.0086)	(0.0057)	(0.0297)	(0.0063)	(0.0207)	(0.0446)	

Subsistence consumption (ĉ*)

								Total
Total		Small	694.5 (66.6)	204.6 (27.2)	591.6 (60.2)	196.1 (37.8)	668.0 (69.4)	2,354.8
		Large	1,108.7 (82.4)	306.7 (33.6)	767.8 (74.5)	320.6 (46.8)	813.2 (85.8)	3,317.0
Low	Young	Small	544.5 (130.2)	168.1 (42.8)	329.2 (64.7)	205.7 (73.0)	498.4 (106.3)	1,745.9
		Large	1,200.0 (209.2)	301.0 (68.9)	531.5 (104.0)	375.3 (117.3)	776.1 (171.0)	3,183.9
	Old	Small	527.1 (56.9)	50.1 (41.5)	229.8 (51.5)	−10.8 (46.1)	226.3 (47.9)	1,022.5
		Large	860.0 (79.3)	245.5 (57.9)	431.2 (71.7)	124.2 (64.1)	545.1 (66.7)	2,206.8
Middle	Young	Small	2,881.9 (1,528.7)	1,029.9 (562.8)	3,555.9 (1,950.9)	1,765.8 (1,179.2)	2,772.5 (1,547.4)	12,011.0
		Large	1,490.3 (636.8)	477.8 (234.4)	1,614.1 (812.5)	801.9 (491.2)	1,183.3 (644.5)	5,567.4
	Old	Small	1,003.2 (104.1)	252.7 (33.0)	992.3 (85.2)	343.3 (79.2)	837.5 (97.5)	3,429.0
		Large	861.3 (92.1)	263.5 (29.1)	1,089.0 (75.4)	316.4 (70.0)	862.3 (86.2)	3,392.5
High	Young	Small	1,010.6 (106.5)	1,204.1 (109.1)	1,427.3 (298.1)	589.4 (330.6)	2,477.3 (371.8)	6,708.7
		Large	1,454.1 (98.2)	576.6 (168.1)	3,623.7 (274.5)	728.2 (303.9)	2,780.0 (340.9)	9,162.6
	Old	Small	1,073.5 (120.3)	515.7 (85.5)	2,817.9 (387.7)	345.3 (113.7)	1,470.7 (220.9)	6,223.1
		Large	1,267.9 (94.3)	496.0 (67.1)	2,650.2 (303.8)	363.5 (89.1)	1,713.9 (172.6)	6,490.9

Note: Standard errors are given in parentheses.

175

The results confirm this expectation. There are no instances of a too high $\bar{\gamma}^*$ in the high-income stratum, 15 in the middle, and 16 in the low stratum. (Eight instances occur when all strata are analyzed together.)

It is less obvious a priori how the occurrence of $\bar{\gamma}^* > \bar{v}$ should be distributed between young and old households, but the results are quite clear. In every city the mean expenditure for young households is closer to—or more frequently below—the minimum level. Moreover, the occurrences for old households are, with only one exception, limited to the low-income stratum, while there are many instances for younger families at the middle level of income. This can occur because $\bar{v}$ is usually smaller for young households, or because $\bar{\gamma}^*$ is higher. In the former case income is probably the most important explanatory variable. In the second case there may be important differences in need determined by family size or age structure. It may simply be, however, that younger households have different experiences and expectations, and envision a higher level of minimum acceptable consumption.

A comparison of $\bar{v}$ and $\hat{\gamma}^*$ between age groups reveals that both influences are at work. Average expenditure is more often below $\hat{\gamma}^*$ for young households in the lower two strata, except in the case of expenditure for durables. At the same time, $\hat{\gamma}^*$ is higher for young than for old households 25 times out of 35 for small families and 28 times out of 35 for large ones. Young households behave as though they had high levels of subsistence expenditure even though they usually have less money to spend than older households. Only on expenditure for durable goods does the stage in the life cycle have a clear effect; for the other categories, "subsistence" levels seem to be determined by past consumption experience, income expectations, or some other largely psychological influence.

The parameter γ^* should be positive for any category considered a necessity and negative only in the case of luxuries forgone at a low-income level. Of the 280 estimates of γ^* obtained, only eight are negative, and none differs significantly from zero. Six of these values occur for durables, one for shelter, and one for other goods and services. Small households are involved five times, at least once in each city, and large households three times (all in Guayaquil, high-old). In general, durables are the only "unnecessary" category, and they become more necessary as household size increases. When all strata are analyzed together, $\hat{\gamma}^*$ (durables) always is significantly positive for both sizes of household.

At a given income level it may be expected that $\hat{\gamma}^*$ (large) $> \hat{\gamma}^*$

(small) for all categories, but the expectation need not be satisfied in the sample since large and small households differ in income distribution and in composition. Of 140 comparisons of $\hat{\gamma}^*$, 63 show a significant difference between large and small households. For some categories, the distinction is particularly sharp. Committed food expenditures differ by household size 19 times out of 28. $\hat{\gamma}^*$ is larger for large households 101 times out of 136 comparisons (excluding four cases in which the two estimates are virtually identical, but including differences which are not statistically significant). The exceptional cases in which $\hat{\gamma}^*$ (small) $>$ $\hat{\gamma}^*$ (large) for all five categories are probably due to differences in income. Differences between $\hat{\gamma}^*$ for large and small households are most frequent in the low-income stratum (20 cases out of 40, against 11 in the middle stratum and 15 in the high). This suggests that γ^* is more closely related to physical needs, and therefore more dependent on household size, at low rather than at high incomes, which is reasonable. Finally, differences by size are more frequent for young than for old households (29 and 17 instances respectively). This may be because among older families there is more variation in composition and therefore less importance attached to the number of members.

It is also to be expected that the γ^* will vary across strata inversely to the changes in β for a given city, age class, and expenditure category.[14] There is not much consistency to the pattern. For food, it is expected that $\hat{\gamma}^*$ (high) $>$ $\hat{\gamma}^*$ (middle) $>$ $\hat{\gamma}^*$ (low), but this occurs only six times out of sixteen. The lowest $\hat{\gamma}^*$ (clothing) should occur in the low stratum for young families, and this happens six times out of eight.

If $\bar{\gamma}^*$ represents a subsistence level of spending, it should be the same in real terms in all cities. The purchasing-power parities mentioned earlier (table 7.2) are used to compare the values of $\bar{\gamma}_1^*$ (food) and $\Sigma_i\ \bar{\gamma}_i^*$ (total subsistence spending) across cities and strata in table 7.8. As before, the average values of γ^*, namely $\bar{\gamma}^*$, pool small and large households in each stratum using the proportion of households in each size class. These averages for food and total subsistence are shown first in national currency to facilitate comparison with tables 7.2 and 7.4 through 7.7; then the estimates for Bogotá, Guayaquil, and Lima are also shown in Venezuelan bolívars.

14. This is necessary if the segments of an Engel curve are to match up approximately at the strata boundaries. When the strata are based on socioeconomic characteristics rather than current income, there are of course no sharp boundaries.

Table 7.8. Average Committed Expenditures on Food and in Total for Four South American Cities

City	Committed expenditure	Total	Low Young	Low Old	Middle Young	Middle Old	High Young	High Old
National currency								
Bogotá	Food	437.3	850.3	546.2	359.6	277.8	414.5	728.7
	Total	1,189.0	2,316.5	1,348.5	1,032.6	806.7	1,360.1	3,614.7
Caracas	Food	1,437.0	1,004.8	1,324.5	1,630.7	1,470.4	1,673.3	1,741.1
	Total	4,737.5	2,193.9	3,029.9	5,769.9	4,937.6	6,930.8	6,559.8
Guayaquil	Food	1,999.5	2,043.0	1,773.0	—	1,497.8	1,939.5	3,100.5
	Total	3,724.6	3,247.1	3,447.9	—	3,244.5	5,723.1	5,412.9
Lima	Food	1,002.8	1,055.2	772.1	1,889.6	905.1	1,385.7	1,236.9
	Total	3,071.0	2,866.2	1,894.0	7,416.4	3,403.8	8,784.3	6,448.2
Venezuelan bolívars[a]								
Bogotá	Food	1,714.0	3,332.8	2,140.9	1,409.5	1,088.9	1,624.7	2,856.2
	Total	5,707.2	11,119.2	6,472.8	4,956.5	3,872.2	6,528.5	17,350.6
Guayaquil	Food	779.2	796.2	690.9	—	583.7	755.8	1,208.3
	Total	1,497.0	1,305.0	1,385.7	—	1,304.0	2,300.1	2,175.4
Lima	Food	1,622.7	1,707.5	1,249.4	3,057.8	1,464.6	2,242.3	2,001.6
	Total	4,892.1	4,565.9	3,017.1	11,814.3	5,422.3	13,993.4	10,272.0

— Estimated with very large standard error because $\hat{\mu}$ is very close to one.

Note: For comparisons of γ^* (food), the purchasing-power parities are divided by indexes of food prices relative to all prices. These indexes are 1.2246 for Colombia, 1.03142 for Ecuador, and 0.98445 for Peru, so the purchasing-power parities for food are 0.39196, 0.3897, and 0.16182 respectively. No account is taken of the fact that rates of inflation for food prices differ from those for other consumption goods.

a. As at the end of October 1966. The exchange rate was 4.5 bolívars to the U.S. dollar.

178

The definitions of strata differ sufficiently among cities and household composition can differ so much within a given stratum that a close correspondence cannot be expected. For $\bar{\gamma}^*$ (food) the estimates are fairly similar in real terms for Bogotá, Caracas, and Lima; those for Guayaquil, however, are systematically much lower. Price indexes based on the individual strata and with weights closer to consumption patterns in these countries might remove much of the variation. The correspondence is generally much less close for total subsistence expenditure, in part because this includes items such as durables, which cannot be identified with needs, and because the total may be sensitive to the alternatives for saving which households face.

The values of $\bar{\gamma}^*$ might be expected to be most nearly equal among cities in the low-income stratum, where households are closest to subsistence, but this expectation is not supported by the results. The closest correspondence occurs when all strata are pooled, perhaps because this diminishes the importance of transitory spending and of differences among definitions of the strata. The estimates are quite close for Caracas and Lima, the cities with the highest income.

Elasticity Estimates

The elasticities derived from ELES are, like the parameters, subject to certain theoretical conditions. Each elasticity can be expressed as a function of those parameters and income (or total expenditure).

Expenditure Elasticity of the Marginal Utility of Expenditure

From (2.4) and (2.7), the Frisch parameter ω can be expressed as

$$(7.3) \qquad \omega = \frac{-\bar{v}}{\bar{v} - \sum_i \bar{\gamma}_i^*}.$$

Because actual spending should exceed subsistence expenditures, the parameter should be negative and should rise in absolute value as income and total spending decline. As is evident from tables 7.2 and 7.8, however, $\bar{v}$ is frequently less than $\sum_i \bar{\gamma}_i^*$ leading to a positive value for expression (7.3). This occurs in the lowest-income groups for Bogotá and Lima, as well as for the entire sample in each city; it does not occur in Guayaquil owing to the notably low values of $\bar{\gamma}^*$ obtained there.

Table 7.9.   *Estimates of the Frisch Parameter at Mean Expenditure for Four South American Cities*

Socio-economic stratum	Age of household head	Bogotá	Caracas	Guayaquil	Lima
All households		—[a]	−4.197	−1.673	—[a]
Low	Young	—[a]	−14.240	−2.042	—[a]
	Old	—[a]	−34.666	−1.785	−21.454
Middle	Young	—[a]	—[a]	—[b]	—[a]
	Old	−3.460	−4.171	−1.366	−3.982
High	Young	−2.211	−3.294	−1.291	−6.502
	Old	−7.186	−2.098	−1.222	−2.802

a. $\bar{v} < \sum_i \bar{\gamma}_i^*$.

b. $\bar{\gamma}_i^*$ not calculated.

Table 7.9 presents estimates of ω for those cases in which the parameter is negative. The most plausible estimates are those for Caracas, where in each age class the absolute value falls as income rises. The overall value (−4.2) is also reasonable. The same pattern is evident for Guayaquil but at lower absolute values, comparable to those obtained for much richer countries (see table 4.4). Two of the three values for Bogotá are reasonable, but no pattern emerges. Reasonable estimates are derived for older households in the middle and high strata in Lima. It is not possible to estimate ω for the middle-young group in any city: this is the group that has consistently high subsistence expenditures relative to actual total spending, perhaps because of high expectations about future income.

After substituting for $\sum_i \bar{\gamma}_i^* = \sum_i p_i \gamma_i$ in (2.2), the Frisch parameter can be written as a function of average and marginal saving propensities (APS and MPS), that is,

$$(7.4) \qquad \omega = \frac{-(1 - \mu)v}{\mu (y - v)} = \frac{- \text{MPS} (1 - \text{APS})}{(1 - \text{MPS}) \text{APS}}$$

from which it is evident that the parameter estimate is extremely sensitive to errors in estimating either the MPS or the APS. For small groups of households whose incomes and expenditures are reported with small errors and may in addition contain transitory components, the margin for error in the saving propensities is large, even if the ELES parameters related to expenditures can be estimated satisfactorily.

Income and Expenditure Elasticities

Tables 7.10 through 7.13 show income and expenditure elasticities ($\tilde{\eta}_i$ and η_i) by socioeconomic stratum in the four cities under study. The right-hand columns of the tables summarize the elasticities estimated by pooling the observations for all strata. These elasticities are highest in Bogotá and Guayaquil, the cities with the lowest income. They might have been uniformly highest in Caracas, except for the larger transitory variation in income and spending; and the elasticities for durables might have been highest in Lima except for the importance of inflation. Except for food, all the elasticities are close to unity, but only five out of sixteen are indistinguishable from 1.0.

It may be of some interest to compare the estimates of $\tilde{\eta}_i$ for the whole sample (right-hand columns of tables 7.10–7.13) with some elasticities obtained with double-log Engel curves estimated using total expenditure (see table 7.14). The latter elasticities refer to all the cities surveyed in each country; only in Peru is the data base the same. More importantly, these regressions are unweighted and thus overrepresent the high stratum, except in Venezuela.

After allowance is made for all the data and procedural differences between the two sets of estimates, it is notable that the ELES results are less widely dispersed than those obtained with double-log Engel curves. Estimation within a system which guarantees the satisfaction of the budget constraint forces the elasticity estimates closer together and therefore closer to unity. In only two of the sixteen comparisons is the ELES estimate farther from one in absolute value than are the estimates shown in table 7.14.

Own-Price Elasticities

One of the reasons for estimating ELES is to obtain information about household responses to price changes.[15] Estimates are given for each stratum, since price elasticities are expected to be function of income and to differ as income rises.

Of 135 own-price elasticities presented in table 7.15 (not counting the five estimates for Guayaquil, middle-young), 28 are positive, 27 are negative but not significantly different from zero, and 80 are clearly negative. There are marked variations among cities and also

15. Information on prices paid by consumers was collected for some products (mostly foodstuffs) in some countries as part of the ECIEL survey, but these data have not been analyzed.

Table 7.10. Bogotá: Income and Expenditure Elasticities of Demand Evaluated at Point of Means

Commodity	Low		Middle		High		Total[a]	
	Income elasticity	Expenditure elasticity	Income elasticity	Expenditure elasticity	Income elasticity	Expenditure elasticity	Income elasticity	Expenditure elasticity
Young households								
Food	0.74528 (0.02599)	0.81760	0.65713 (0.03576)	0.71683	0.63501 (0.05220)	0.64485	0.79393 (0.01253)	0.82228
Clothing	1.15693 (0.04244)	1.26919	1.06713 (0.09491)	1.16407	1.07862 (0.08537)	1.09533	1.04892 (0.01948)	1.08637
Housing	0.95849 (0.02988)	1.05150	0.98001 (0.03717)	1.06904	0.92115 (0.05133)	0.93542	0.97018 (0.01141)	1.00482
Durables	1.41000 (0.10316)	1.54682	1.39510 (0.16899)	1.52184	1.34408 (0.19707)	1.36490	1.09236 (0.06456)	1.13137
Other	0.93033 (0.03599)	1.02060	1.07614 (0.04963)	1.17390	1.03811 (0.05377)	1.05419	0.97689 (0.01501)	1.0117
Old households								
Food	0.82198 (0.03378)	0.86426	0.70891 (0.05092)	0.72556	0.47383 (0.07805)	0.75637		
Clothing	0.99551 (0.06134)	1.04453	1.02282 (0.15187)	1.04684	0.49887 (0.17509)	0.79635		
Housing	0.96429 (0.03332)	1.00989	0.87307 (0.04012)	0.89357	0.53094 (0.10736)	0.84754		
Durables	−0.00609 (1.41058)	−0.00639	0.82193 (0.17573)	0.84123	1.05497 (0.31397)	1.68405		
Other	0.89856 (0.05167)	0.94281	1.10867 (0.05137)	1.3470	0.75501 (0.09258)	1.20522		

Note: Standard errors are given in parentheses.

a. Includes both young and old households in all strata.

182

Table 7.11. Caracas: Income and Expenditure Elasticities of Demand Evaluated at Point of Means

Commodity	Low		Middle		High		Total[a]	
	Income elasticity	Expenditure elasticity	Income elasticity	Expenditure elasticity	Income elasticity	Expenditure elasticity	Income elasticity	Expenditure elasticity
Young households								
Food	0.52219 (0.06238)	1.14831	0.47801 (0.03647)	0.67370	0.39294 (0.06736)	0.50659	0.56802 (0.01985)	0.70676
Clothing	0.79372 (0.18495)	1.74541	0.92324 (0.06371)	1.30119	0.87250 (0.12561)	1.12485	0.84157 (0.03718)	1.04712
Housing	0.12885 (0.16915)	0.28334	0.64737 (0.05546)	0.91239	0.86756 (0.05556)	1.11849	0.84663 (0.01933)	1.05342
Durables	−0.63232 (1.25711)	−1.39048	1.03280 (0.21795)	1.45560	1.31131 (0.25555)	1.69058	0.98928 (0.09870)	1.23091
Other	0.46521 (0.16140)	1.02301	0.88757 (0.04884)	1.25092	0.82937 (0.08187)	1.15047	0.94744 (0.02101)	1.17885
Old households								
Food	0.06884 (0.16697)	0.18777	0.47270 (0.04736)	0.60477	0.48178 (0.09480)	0.55779		
Clothing	0.70435 (0.32786)	1.92116	0.29644 (0.23696)	0.37927	0.75133 (0.16555)	0.86987		
Housing	0.69726 (0.18210)	1.90182	0.84294 (0.03164)	1.07846	0.92407 (0.04994)	1.09070		
Durables	0.44746 (0.93528)	1.22048	0.80021 (0.25713)	1.02379	1.41911 (0.19373)	1.64300		
Other	0.41408 (0.32072)	1.12943	0.98116 (0.05566)	1.25530	0.97974 (0.10626)	1.13431		

Note: Standard errors are given in parentheses.

a. Includes both young and old households in all strata.

183

Table 7.12. Guayaquil: Income and Expenditure Elasticities of Demand Evaluated at Point of Means

Commodity	Low Income elasticity	Low Expenditure elasticity	Middle Income elasticity	Middle Expenditure elasticity	High Income elasticity	High Expenditure elasticity	Total[a] Income elasticity	Total[a] Expenditure elasticity
Young households								
Food	0.61299 (0.03177)	0.72711	0.91084 (0.08244)	0.91405	0.92362 (0.02353)	0.96693	0.79213 (0.02328)	0.86351
Clothing	1.09245 (0.04798)	1.29583	1.02081 (0.04445)	1.02441	1.00683 (0.02756)	1.05404	1.01328 (0.01783)	1.10459
Housing	0.95471 (0.03238)	1.13245	1.01328 (0.02135)	1.01685	1.05439 (0.01275)	1.10383	1.02555 (0.01003)	1.11796
Durables	1.25880 (0.14154)	1.49315	1.27614 (0.09478)	1.28064	1.07367 (0.07447)	1.12402	1.15446 (0.04920)	1.25849
Other	1.05435 (0.04208)	1.25064	1.11097 (0.03333)	1.11488	0.85486 (0.05432)	0.89495	0.99191 (0.01789)	1.08129
Old households								
Food	0.82122 (0.02985)	0.87233	0.89421 (0.01916)	0.90723	0.55399 (0.08484)	0.57350		
Clothing	0.08693 (0.05849)	1.04835	1.06748 (0.03151)	1.08302	0.94978 (0.07730)	0.98323		
Housing	1.03926 (0.03335)	1.10404	1.00123 (0.01653)	1.01580	1.10732 (0.03146)	1.14632		
Durables	1.21610 (0.16752)	1.29178	1.09791 (0.09531)	1.11389	1.19348 (0.15738)	1.23552		
Other	0.91557 (0.06442)	0.97255	0.97794 (0.03886)	0.99217	1.04527 (0.03014)	1.08209		

Note: Standard errors are given in parentheses.

a. Includes both young and old households in all strata.

184

Table 7.13. Lima: Income and Expenditure Elasticities of Demand Evaluated at Point of Means

Commodity	Low Income elasticity	Low Expenditure elasticity	Middle Income elasticity	Middle Expenditure elasticity	High Income elasticity	High Expenditure elasticity	Total[a] Income elasticity	Total[a] Expenditure elasticity
Young households								
Food	0.48677 (0.05289)	0.59940	0.76320 (0.03001)	0.87507	-0.02266 (0.16908)	-0.10730	0.53280 (0.02905)	0.64249
Clothing	1.00762 (0.03840)	1.24076	0.87605 (0.04837)	1.00446	0.12960 (0.28625)	0.61369	0.91121 (0.02561)	1.09880
Housing	0.75135 (0.03887)	0.92519	0.90810 (0.02885)	1.04121	0.36398 (0.10841)	1.72353	0.88403 (0.01530)	1.06602
Durables	0.95343 (0.08272)	1.17403	1.09450 (0.06976)	1.25493	0.53336 (0.47337)	2.52559	0.88403 (0.05281)	0.96928
Other	0.90139 (0.03136)	1.10995	0.71943 (0.07816)	0.82488	0.08793 (0.25778)	0.41637	0.89006 (0.01758)	1.07329
Old households								
Food	0.25932 (0.11054)	0.76120	-0.61965 (0.38075)	-2.20850	0.60196 (0.06046)	0.66956		
Clothing	0.43039 (0.29553)	1.26336	0.72761 (0.07345)	2.59328	0.82483 (0.07171)	0.91746		
Housing	0.54388 (0.15449)	1.57008	0.66092 (0.04212)	2.35559	0.80273 (0.04348)	0.89288		
Durables	—	—	0.66291 (0.04212)	2.36269	1.01315 (0.09020)	1.12693		
Other	0.77832 (0.07493)	2.28467	0.30675 (0.12327)	1.09329	0.85731 (0.03412)	0.95358		

— Mean expenditure too close to subsistence to permit estimation.
Note: Standard errors are given in parentheses.

a. Includes both young and old households in all strata.

185

Table 7.14.   *Expenditure Elasticities from Double-Log Engel Curves*

Commodity	Colombia (four cities)	Venezuela (two cities)	Ecuador (two cities)	Peru (Lima)
Food (excluding tobacco)	0.6624	0.6098	0.6696	0.4743
	(0.0057)	(0.0116)	(0.0082)	(0.0139)
Clothing	1.2435	1.1852	1.1144	1.0495
	(0.0235)	(0.0534)	(0.0391)	(0.0453)
Housing (excluding some	0.9239	0.7608	0.9614	0.9223
services)	(0.0149)	(0.0166)	(0.0240)	(0.0316)
Durables (excluding vehicles)	1.4755	1.3082	1.3800	1.4958
	(0.0756)	(0.0898)	(0.0921)	(0.1106)

Note: Standard errors are given in parentheses.
Source: Musgrove (1977), table 6-1.

among strata, but not between the two age groups. Out of 35 estimates for each city, 11 are significantly negative in Bogotá, 16 in Lima, 23 in Caracas, and 30 out of 30 in Guayaquil. Only 15 of 40 estimates are significantly below zero in the low stratum, 18 of 35 in the middle, and 35 of 40 in the high. The variation across strata and the very clear results obtained for high-income households compensate somewhat for the rather poor results obtained when all strata are analyzed together (3 positive values, 12 negative, and 4 negative but not distinct from zero).

The expected pattern of elasticities across strata is $\hat{\eta}_{ii}$ (low) > $\hat{\eta}_{ii}$ (middle) > $\hat{\eta}_{ii}$ (high), with elasticities increasing in absolute value (becoming more negative) as income increases. The closer a household is to subsistence, the less it can respond to changes in prices. This pattern is observed 19 times out of 40. In the 12 instances in which $\hat{\eta}_{ii}$ (middle) > 0, $\hat{\eta}_{ii}$ (low) always exceeds $\hat{\eta}_{ii}$ (high). If these cases are excluded, the results are quite good. Finally, the expected pattern is observed in 13 of 18 comparisons in which the elasticity is negative in all three strata.

The estimates for Bogotá, Caracas, and Lima are usually of comparable magnitude, while those for Guayaquil are almost uniformly larger in absolute value. The smallest value in Guayaquil is —0.455 for food in the low-young group, and the largest is —0.997 for durables in high-old. This result is surprising in a low-income city like Guayaquil. The explanation appears to lie in the low ratios of $\bar{\gamma}^*:\bar{v}$ found there, since the lower this ratio, the higher is $\hat{\eta}_{ii}$. In table 7.16 own-price elasticities are averaged for both age groups, by stratum and commodity, for the first three cities together and for Guayaquil alone. Only negative estimates are included in these averages.[16] Differences between age classes are not systematic enough to warrant separate calculations. Also shown is the average of the negative elasticities calculated across all strata in each city. For Bogotá, Caracas, and Lima together, all five elasticities rise in absolute value as income rises. The elasticities for clothing and durables rise the most, as indicated by rankings in each stratum. For Guayaquil, the elasticities for food and clothing fall slightly at high incomes, and the smallest in that city (-0.542) is still above the largest average in the other cities (-0.501). It seems likely that the results for Guayaquil greatly overstate household response to price changes, but in the absence of direct estimation it is not certain that there is not some marked difference in behavior.

Positive Own-Price Responses, Inflation, and
the Dynamic Interpretation of ELES

To satisfy the fundamental theorem of demand, the own-price elasticity $\bar{\eta}_{ii}$ must be negative. Of the 28 positive estimates only one of these (durables in Caracas, low-young) is associated with a negative estimate of β_i. The remainder are a subset of the 39 instances in which $\bar{\gamma}^* > \bar{v}$.

None of the positive own-price elasticities is distinguishable from zero. Nonetheless, the point estimates suggest something about dynamic household responses to price changes. In three cases (Bogotá, low-young, and Lima, low- and middle-young) all five elasticities are positive. Of the remaining thirteen cases, six involve durables and four involve clothing; food, housing, and other goods and services each appear to have a positive elasticity only once. In all, durables are affected nine times, clothing seven times, and each of the other categories four times. Moreover, fourteen of the positive estimates occur for Bogotá and eleven for Lima; there are three in Caracas (all durables).

The rate of inflation was much higher in Bogotá and in Lima in the years immediately preceding the survey than it was in Caracas or Guayaquil.[17] In the absence of capital-market adjustments to main-

16. The averages for all four cities are not shown, because the number of positive estimates varies and therefore the weight of Guayaquil would also vary.
17. The rate ranged from 9.4 percent annually (1966) to 19.1 percent (1968) in Lima and from 5.4 percent (1965) to 20.4 percent (1966) in Bogotá (dropping to 9 percent or less in 1967–68). In Quito, Ecuador (no index is available for Guayaquil), the rate was 3.8 percent in 1967, 4.3 percent in 1968, and 6.3 percent in 1969. In Caracas the highest rate was 2.2 percent (1964). (Organization of American States [OAS], 1972.)

tain positive real interest rates, rapid inflation leads households to save less in the form of financial assets and to spend more, particularly on durable goods and on such items as jewelry and clothing. Once these goods become substitutes for saving, and consumers form expectations about future inflation, it can be expected that even when prices increase, the quantity purchased will rise. That is, households will buy as a hedge against future price increases. This does not happen with other expenditures because items such as food and services cannot be stored or used over long periods or because the data reflect consumption rather than purchases as in the case of

Table 7.15. *Own-Price Elasticities for Four South American Cities*

Socioeconomic stratum and age of household head	Food	Clothing	Housing	Durables	Other
Bogotá					
Total	−0.002	0.188	−0.040	0.008	−0.115
	(0.169)	(0.259)	(0.193)	(0.287)	(0.183)
Low: Young	1.229	2.744	1.806	2.409	1.714
	(1.959)	(3.740)	(2.667)	(3.630)	(2.578)
Old	0.336	0.900	0.487	−0.035	0.601
	(0.834)	(1.344)	(1.010)	(2.378)	(1.088)
Middle: Young	−0.151	0.036	−0.160	0.062	−0.125
	(0.146)	(0.306)	(0.207)	(0.426)	(0.240)
Old	−0.333	−0.421	−0.429	0.089	−0.615
	(0.104)	(0.238)	(0.117)	(0.308)	(0.123)
High: Young	−0.385	−0.586	−0.585	−0.725	−0.663
	(0.081)	(0.144)	(0.102)	(0.219)	(0.107)
Old	−0.166	−0.188	−0.235	−0.248	−0.388
	(0.055)	(0.105)	(0.068)	(0.281)	(0.068)
Caracas					
Total	−0.234	−0.255	−0.461	−0.279	−0.494
	(0.026)	(0.054)	(0.030)	(0.131)	(0.034)
Low: Young	−0.258	−0.131	−0.084	0.057	−0.189
	(0.035)	(0.128)	(0.061)	(0.375)	(0.074)
Old	−0.043	−0.123	−0.184	0.073	−0.126)
	(0.196)	(0.214)	(0.137)	(0.568)	(0.149)
Middle: Young	−0.091	−0.037	−0.205	0.095	−0.240
	(0.053)	(0.121)	(0.069)	(0.341)	(0.082)
Old	−0.226	−0.262	−0.459	−0.345	−0.494
	(0.035)	(0.097)	(0.043)	(0.186)	(0.063)
High: Young	−0.218	−0.307	−0.506	−0.452	−0.541
	(0.038)	(0.096)	(0.052)	(0.193)	(0.062)
Old	−0.301	−0.417	−0.672	−0.811	−0.687
	(0.067)	(0.117)	(0.071)	(0.160)	(0.103)

Table 7.15.   (*continued*)

Socioeconomic stratum and age of household head	Food	Clothing	Housing	Durables	Other
Guayaquil					
Total	−0.614	−0.692	−0.769	−0.771	−0.737
	(0.026)	(0.030)	(0.022)	(0.052)	(0.026)
Low: Young	−0.455	−0.709	−0.641	−0.826	−0.659
	(0.024)	(0.038)	(0.030)	(0.075)	(0.041)
Old	−0.625	−0.693	−0.718	−0.780	−0.674
	(0.048)	(0.063)	(0.063)	(0.144)	(0.066)
Middle: Young	—	—	—	—	—
Old	−0.741	−0.824	−0.847	−0.845	−0.798
	(0.049)	(0.068)	(0.042)	(0.115)	(0.063)
High: Young	−0.772	−0.790	−0.898	−0.860	−0.806
	(0.061)	(0.079)	(0.048)	(0.109)	(0.050)
Old	−0.509	−0.824	−0.957	−0.997	−0.904
	(0.098)	(0.135)	(0.107)	(0.249)	(0.118)
Lima					
Total	−0.058	0.029	−0.240	−0.056	−0.245
	(0.058)	(0.109)	(0.067)	(0.131)	(0.069)
Low: Young	0.087	0.660	0.271	0.646	0.041
	(0.154)	(0.371)	(0.233)	(0.479)	(0.210)
Old	−0.103	−0.015	−0.194	−0.214	−0.185
	(0.047)	(0.208)	(0.097)	(0.433)	(0.077)
Middle: Young	0.450	0.670	0.352	0.850	0.138
	(0.661)	(0.842)	(0.681)	(1.127)	(0.574)
Old	−0.098	−0.344	−0.367	−0.357	−0.336
	(0.064)	(0.063)	(0.033)	(0.116)	(0.048)
High: Young	−0.067	−0.127	−0.236	−0.255	−0.190
	(0.051)	(0.188)	(0.040)	(0.274)	(0.066)
Old	−0.251	−0.564	−0.501	−0.428	−0.537
	(0.048)	(0.053)	(0.043)	(0.128)	(0.041)

— Estimated with very large standard errors because $\hat{\mu}$ is very close to one.

housing. In short, under persistent but variable inflation, such items as durables and clothing may actually have positive price elasticities part of the time.[18] This effect should be most pronounced among

18. This cannot occur *all* the time because eventually such items would absorb the entire budget. The effect is probably strongest when prices accelerate after an interval of stable prices or after a low and steady rate of inflation. This appears to have been the case in Lima following a devaluation in 1967, when inflation was more rapid than in most preceding years. This explanation is less certain for Bogotá, although there was a sharp increase in inflation in the year before the survey began.

Table 7.16.   *Average Own-Price Elasticities for*
Four South American Cities

Socioeconomic stratum	Food	Clothing	Housing	Durables	Other
Low					
3 cities[a]	−0.135	−0.090	−0.154	−0.125	−0.167
Guayaquil	−0.542	−0.701	−0.679	−0.803	−0.667
Middle					
3 cities[a]	−0.180	−0.266	−0.340	−0.351	−0.362
Guayaquil	−0.741	−0.824	−0.847	−0.845	−0.798
High					
3 cities[a]	−0.294	−0.347	−0.456	−0.486	−0.501
Guayaquil	−0.640	−0.807	−0.928	−0.928	−0.855
Total					
3 cities[a]	−0.098	−0.255	−0.247	−0.167	−0.285
Guayaquil	−0.614	−0.692	−0.769	−0.772	−0.737

a. Bogotá, Caracas, and Lima.

low- and middle-income households, which have little or no access to those financial assets which are protected against inflation. Our results confirm this pattern: 16 positive elasticities are from the low stratum, 9 from the middle, and none from the high (the remaining three occur in the pooled data).

The preceding argument suggests strongly that the "inadmissible" result of a positive own-price elasticity may, in fact, provide valuable information about the behavior of consumers over short intervals, and that this behavior is consistent with what is known of monetary and capital market conditions in the cities studied. This argument is not easily incorporated into ELES. The original formulation of the model, as indicated in chapter 2, allows for anticipated inflation but is restricted to a constant rate of inflation affecting only permanent income. In this model it is also possible to distinguish between "permanent" and "transitory" changes in relative prices and to calculate different elasticities for these concepts. It is assumed that in an inflationary situation such changes are more likely to be perceived as permanent.[19] In the permanent-income version of ELES, however, it is still assumed that the rate of return on nonhuman wealth is constant in real terms, or that the effect of inflation is limited to permanent labor income. Even this degree of accommodation to

19. Betancourt (1973), pp. 12–15.

the presence of inflation is lost when the model is estimated on the basis of current rather than permanent income.

Despite these limitations, the ELES parameters can be interpreted in a way consistent with dynamic adjustments of expenditure to changes in the rate of inflation. A positive γ^* is usually interpreted as a minimum level of expenditure determined either by physical need or by habits which are not easily changed. For a household with a given income and composition, $\hat{\gamma}^*$ is assumed to be constant because γ is assumed constant and prices do not vary in a cross section.[20] Since durable goods are not necessities on any reasonable definition of subsistence, it is to be expected that γ^* (durables) will be small or even negative. Nonetheless, $\hat{\gamma}^*$ (durables) < 0 only six times out of 56 estimates and is never significantly below zero, whereas $\hat{\gamma}^* >$ $\bar{v}/(1 - \mu\beta)$ for durables occurs eight times in 27 estimates.

If all forms of wealth have constant rates of return, variations in the rate of saving depend primarily on variations in income. Inflation, unaccompanied by changes in nominal rates of return on some assets, reduces the total wealth of households owning those assets and provokes a shift to other assets whose value is protected in real terms. Households will be seen to behave as if there were a relatively great need to accumulate the latter kind of assets. If these include durable goods, estimation of ELES will yield high values of $\hat{\gamma}^*$ (durables). There will not necessarily be a high value of $\hat{\beta}_i$ because—as was explained earlier—the effect of inflation on wealth is concentrated among low-income households.[21]

Cross-Elasticities with Respect to Food Price

Table 7.17 presents the cross-price elasticities $\hat{\eta}_{i1}$ with respect to food price. These elasticities can, in principle, be of either sign; but given the high level of aggregation and the fact that the own-price elasticities never exceed -1, the cross-elasticity for food is expected to be less than zero. Of 112 cross-elasticities estimated, all but three are negative. All these exceptions (in Bogotá, low-old; Caracas, low-young; and Lima, low-old) reflect the purchase of durables in response

20. Although this assumption may be acceptable among households within a three-month period, it is less satisfactory for data gathered during twelve to eighteen months.

21. The reasoning here, relating flows to *desired* stocks, is similar to that used to incorporate "consumption capital" into ELES, or to explain expenditure on durables as consumption rather than as a form of saving. See Lluch (1974b) and Phlips (1972).

to changes in the price of food. This accords with the evidence presented earlier that purchase of durables is partly a form of saving and increases when inflation accelerates.

When all strata are analyzed together, the cross-elasticities with respect to food prices are significantly negative. To facilitate inter-city comparisons, these are extracted from table 7.17 and repeated in table 7.18. For each city, the four nonfood categories show very similar elasticities, although they differ appreciably among cities.

The food cross-elasticities are also usually significant (65 times out

Table 7.17.   *Cross-Elasticities and Elasticity of Average Savings Ratio with Respect to Food Price* (ξ_1) *for Four South American Cities*

Socioeconomic stratum and age of household head	Clothing	Housing	Durables	Other	ξ_1 (food)
Bogotá					
Total	−0.496	−0.479	−0.410	−0.413	—[b]
	(0.123)	(0.111)	(0.127)	(0.097)	
Low: Young	−1.605	−1.376	−1.418	−1.247	—[b]
	(1.654)	(1.381)	(1.497)	(1.259)	
Old	−0.828	−0.853	−0.005	−0.760	—[b]
	(0.675)	(0.661)	(1.128)	(0.606)	
Middle: Young	−0.434	−0.421	−0.539	−0.439	—[b]
	(0.174)	(0.145)	(0.236)	(0.154)	
Old	−0.222	−0.210	−0.285	−0.225	−0.551
	(0.084)	(0.067)	(0.157)	(0.067)	
High: Young	−0.164	−0.144	−0.193	−0.161	−0.279
	(0.053)	(0.040)	(0.075)	(0.042)	
Old	−0.073	−0.083	−0.168	−0.117	−0.645
	(0.036)	(0.026)	(0.091)	(0.027)	
Caracas					
Total	−0.189	−0.172	−0.220	−0.197	−0.722
	(0.022)	(0.014)	(0.056)	(0.016)	
Low: Young	−0.319	−0.045	0.214	−0.168	−1.762
	(0.116)	(0.064)	(0.322)	(0.077)	
Old	−0.276	−0.285	−0.198	−0.162	−3.616
	(0.188)	(0.126)	(0.503)	(0.156)	
Middle: Young	−0.271	−0.184	−0.330	0.264	—[b]
	(0.047)	(0.033)	(0.141)	(0.041)	
Old	−0.049	−0.171	−0.143	−0.204	−0.580
	(0.048)	(0.020)	(0.087)	(0.032)	
High: Young	−0.145	−0.130	−0.218	−0.131	−0.426
	(0.035)	(0.018)	(0.076)	(0.021)	
Old	−0.092	−0.113	−0.147	−0.116	−0.219
	(0.037)	(0.023)	(0.049)	(0.028)	

Table 7.17.   (*continued*)

Socioeconomic stratum and age of household head	Clothing	Housing	Durables	Other	ξ_1 (food)
Guayaquil					
Total	−0.182	−0.173	−0.206	−0.166	−0.290
	(0.019)	(0.016)	(0.034)	(0.017)	
Low: Young	−0.234	−0.232	−0.211	−0.277	−0.441
	(0.030)	(0.024)	(0.065)	(0.033)	
Old	−0.162	−0.215	−0.218	−0.159	−0.312
	(0.043)	(0.047)	(0.092)	(0.040)	
Middle: Young	—a	—a	—a	—a	—a
Old	−0.117	−0.098	−0.121	−0.104	−0.141
	(0.041)	(0.031)	(0.054)	(0.031)	
High: Young	−0.078	−0.070	−0.075	−0.043	−0.086
	(0.037)	(0.031)	(0.042)	(0.092)	
Old	−0.080	−0.112	−0.122	−0.097	−0.113
	(0.025)	(0.041)	(0.055)	(0.024)	
Lima					
Total	−0.332	−0.275	−0.265	−0.281	−5.516
	(0.041)	(0.029)	(0.055)	(0.031)	
Low: Young	−0.679	−0.441	−0.661	−0.463	—b
	(0.155)	(0.103)	(0.213)	(0.104)	
Old	−0.159	−0.175	−0.713	−0.300	−1.721
	(0.148)	(0.076)	(0.296)	(0.059)	
Middle: Young	−0.430	−0.452	−0.584	−0.293	—b
	(0.267)	(0.273)	(0.377)	(0.196)	
Old	−0.116	−0.114	−0.102	−0.042	−0.497
	(0.025)	(0.016)	(0.045)	(0.022)	
High: Young	−0.011	−0.034	−0.049	−0.007	−0.233
	(0.028)	(0.014)	(0.070)	(0.022)	
Old	−0.061	−0.086	−0.120	−0.081	−0.169
	(0.014)	(0.014)	(0.034)	(0.012)	

Note: Standard errors are given in parentheses.
a. Estimated with very large standard errors because $\hat{\mu}$ is very close to one.
b. $\bar{y} < \sum_i \bar{\gamma}_i^*$ so $\xi_1 > 0$.

of 96) when the estimation is separated by stratum and age class. Table 7.19 presents the averages by stratum, across cities and age groups. The estimates for Guayaquil, middle-young, are not included. The averages obscure both the intercity variation and the fact that young households usually respond more to price changes than do old households. Three conclusions emerge from table 7.19. The first is that all the elasticities except those for durables fall in absolute

Table 7.18.   Cross-Elasticity with Respect to Food Prices
for Four South American Cities

Commodity	Bogotá	Caracas	Guayaquil	Lima
Clothing	−0.4955	−0.1887	−0.1824	−0.3322
	(0.1228)	(0.0219)	(0.0192)	(0.0413)
Housing	−0.4793	−0.1719	−0.1732	−0.2748
	(0.1110)	(0.0140)	(0.0161)	(0.0287)
Durables	−0.4096	−0.2201	−0.2060	−0.2649
	(0.1272)	(0.0563)	(0.0336)	(0.0552)
Other	−0.4127	−0.1969	−0.1655	−0.2808
	(0.0968)	(0.0164)	(0.0165)	(0.0308)

Note: Standard errors are given in parentheses.

Table 7.19.   Food Cross-Elasticities: Average of Estimates
for Four South American Cities

Socioeconomic stratum	Clothing	Housing	Durables	Other
Low	−0.5328	−0.4528	−0.2218[a]	−0.4420
Middle	−0.2381	−0.2327	−0.3004	−0.2245
High	−0.0882	−0.0967	−0.2364	−0.0940
Total	−0.2997	−0.2748	−0.2752	−0.2640

a. −0.5412 if only negative values are averaged.

value (rise toward zero) as income rises; typically, the elasticity is about halved in passing from one stratum to another. Second, in each stratum, all the elasticities except those for durables are about equal. Third, the purchase of durables depends on food prices in a way that is very nearly independent of income.

Elasticity of the Average Savings Ratio with Respect to Food Price

Expression (2.12) makes the elasticity of the average savings ratio with respect to food price (ξ_1) a function of the saving rate and mean subsistence food expenditure ($\bar{\gamma}_1^*$). The estimate of ξ_1 can be evaluated at mean income, mean total expenditure, or mean saving (because of the way the reduced form was estimated, these values do not correspond to one another). Evaluation at mean income $\bar{y}$ leads to the saving rate $s = (1 - \mu)(\bar{y} - \Sigma_i \bar{\gamma}_i^*)$ and therefore to

$$(7.5) \qquad \xi_1 = \frac{-\bar{\gamma}_1^*}{\bar{y} - \Sigma_i \bar{\gamma}_i^*}.$$

(no standard errors are obtained). These values are shown in the last column of table 7.17.

The results parallel those obtained for the Frisch parameter, with the estimates for Caracas the most plausible and those for Guayaquil showing similar relative values but low absolute values. (These are comparable to the time-series estimates for high-income countries reported in table 4.9 and to a few estimates for urban Mexico shown in table 6.14.) There is no pattern to the results for Bogotá; those for old households in Lima are quite reasonable and agree rather well with those for Caracas. In Caracas, Guayaquil, and Lima all three socioeconomic strata can be compared for old households:

Stratum	Caracas	Guayaquil	Lima
Low	−3.616	−0.312	−1.721
Middle	−0.580	−0.141	−0.497
High	−0.219	−0.113	−0.169

The saving rate should be most responsive to food prices when real incomes are low, since food is then a larger share of the budget. This does not emerge from the comparison of Caracas and Lima, especially in the low stratum where income differences are greatest (incomes are appreciably less concentrated in Caracas than in Lima). The reason for this may be, again, that durables are a form of saving and that the saving rate is more sensitive to the price of durables.[22] There does not appear to be any consistency to differences in the value of ξ_1 between age classes in any stratum. Estimates for all strata together (in Caracas, Guayaquil, and Lima) are very dispersed. In the low stratum the elasticity often exceeds one in absolute value, while among the rich it is never more than 0.43.

Conclusions

ELES was estimated twenty-eight separate times in the four cities studied, on the assumption that all its parameters depend on income level and on age, and that in addition the subsistence expenditures vary with household size. Dividing the samples by stratum and age leads to some violations of the system restrictions on the signs and

---

22. ξ_4, the saving elasticity with respect to the price of durables, is just $-\bar{\gamma}_4^*/(\bar{y} - \sum_i \bar{\gamma}_i^*)$; it can be seen from tables 7.5 and 7.7 that $\bar{\gamma}^*$ (durables)/ $\bar{\gamma}^*$ (food) is systematically much greater in Lima than in Caracas, so that ξ_4 is larger in absolute value than ξ_1.

sizes of parameters, but these failures are infrequent and may be compensated by the additional knowledge gained from piecewise linear approximation of the demand functions.

ELES Parameters

The principal findings with respect to each of the three classifying variables may be briefly summarized.

Income. Both the marginal budget shares (β_i) and the subsistence expenditures (γ_i^*) vary rather systematically with income level, as expected, depending on whether the commodity is a necessity or a luxury. The sets of linear functions appear to capture the curvature of expenditure relationships while retaining the advantages of theoretically plausible local demand functions. Subsistence expenditures may rise with income, but they decline relative to actual spending. This shows that they more nearly represent needs at low incomes, while habits and expectations become more important as income rises. Income and expenditure elasticities also generally differ in the anticipated way. They are more nearly equal to one another and to 1.0 than elasticities estimated without the budget constraint.

Age. The effects of age are not entirely separated from those of income, since in most strata old households have higher mean incomes than do young families. There is a clear life-cycle effect only in the case of durables, where marginal spending is nearly always higher among the young; they tend to devote less of the marginal budget to housing and to other expenditures than do older households. Young households tend to have lower mean expenditures $(\bar{v}_i)$ but higher subsistence spending (γ_i^*). They behave as if their notion of a minimally acceptable standard of living, or their expectations about future income, were higher than those of older households. It cannot be determined whether this behavior merely reflects the stage in the life cycle or includes some demonstration effect or rising expectations because of the different experiences of young and old families.

Household size. This variable was not permitted to affect μ and β_i but only subsistence expenditures (γ_i^*). These generally differ between large and small households, being more often higher where there are more members. It also appears that the difference between γ_i^* (large) and γ_i^* (small) is greater for young than for old families, perhaps because of greater differences in per capita income.

Price Elasticities and Inflation

Generally, the own-price elasticities $(\bar{\eta}_{ii})$ are negative and rise in absolute value as income increases. The exceptions are concentrated in durables (and to a lesser extent in clothing) in the low- and middle-income strata, and in the cities of Bogotá and Lima. Although these results are not significant statistically, they are consistent with the idea that durables and semidurable goods have positive price elasticities under rapid or accelerated inflation, at least for those households which do not have access to assets protected against inflation. Durables are a form of saving for such households, which respond differently to dynamic price changes than they would to static changes in relative prices.

This hypothesis may be supported by the fact that the only positive elasticities with respect to food prices are for durables and among low-income households. Generally, the cross-elasticities are negative and decline in absolute value as income rises. Price elasticities also seem to rise in absolute value as the family is older. This rise is related to the fact that $\bar{v}_i - \bar{\gamma}_i^*$, uncommitted expenditure, is generally larger for older households, but the effect is not very pronounced.

Consumption and Saving

Estimation of ELES yields information about the distribution of household expenditure among commodities; the results are usually reasonable and take account of differences in behavior due to differences in income, age, and household size. The results concerning the allocation of income between consumption and saving are much less satisfactory. The elasticity of saving with respect to food prices (ξ_1) is usually negative (except in the low stratum) and of reasonable magnitude, but many of the values are rather low in absolute terms. Estimates of the marginal propensity to consume (μ) are extremely varied and often much too low. In particular, they do not always decline as income rises but are often low for very low incomes. Finally, estimates of the expenditure elasticity of the marginal expenditure utility (ω)—which can be expressed in terms of average and marginal saving rates—are satisfactory only for Caracas, with some plausible relative or absolute values in the other cities.

Two problems make it hard to use ELES to study household saving with cross-section data; both may be made worse when the sample is stratified. One is that income and expenditure are reported with errors, and some savings-related parameters (especially ω) are extremely sensitive to such errors. The other is that even if current flows are accurately reported they contain transitory elements which bias the estimates of μ and, therefore, of the Frisch parameter (ω). These problems arise more frequently for young households, whose spending may be related to expected income in the future and who may currently dissave.

Despite these difficulties—which might be reduced or overcome by a more complex model based on good estimates of permanent income—estimation of ELES offers a valuable view of spending behavior by consumers in developing countries. In particular, it offers a way to extract from rather limited household budget data information about spending as a function of income as well as about macroeconomic influences such as the level and rate of change of prices. Provided these results are interpreted with care, they can help in understanding the household sector's role in economic development.

8

Household Behavior in Chile: An Analysis of Cross-Section Data

Roger Betancourt

THE WORK ON THE CHILEAN cross-section data was done before the analysis of the other cross-section data used in this book. At that time, a number of alternatives were tried in the formulation of the model and in the empirical implementation, and the results provided guidance for subsequent research. In this chapter the alternatives considered initially are first summarized; those that were empirically implemented are compared briefly with the one actually chosen and the results that are comparable to those in the rest of the book are presented in detail.

The data base is the Cost of Living Survey for Central Chile, which covers the month of January 1964.[1] The survey contains independent information on total expenditures, by thirteen expenditure categories, and on disposable income for each household. It also contains the usual information on sociodemographic characteristics of the households. Three of the expenditure categories are treated as savings: direct saving as reported by the respondents, investment in housing (other than imputed rent), and consumer durables. The remaining expenditures are divided into three groups for the empirical analysis: rent, food, other.

1. Further characteristics of the survey are available in Betancourt (1971b).

Modifications of the Model

In chapter 2 the model underlying this book (ELES) is formulated as integrating the consumption-saving decision with decisions on the allocation of expenditures. The first modification considered was the integration of these two aspects of household decisionmaking with a third aspect, the labor-leisure decision. This extension resulted in a more general model (labeled TELES for twice extended linear expenditure system) which had ELES as a special case. The integration of the labor-leisure decision was accomplished at the theoretical level,[2] but the empirical implementation of TELES was not carried out for two reasons. First, most bodies of cross-section data do not furnish the information necessary for the implementation of TELES, although the Chilean data is an exception; consequently, it would have been impossible to compare the results for this model across countries. Second, even when the information is available, estimation problems arise that are considerably different from those involved in the estimation of ELES, for example, the errors in variables problem with respect to the wage rate.[3]

Another modification to the model in chapter 2 was the formulation of ELES using discrete time and a finite horizon. As expected, this change gave rise to only minor alterations in the model. More specifically, the marginal propensity to consume out of income (μ) is no longer δ/ρ but becomes instead $\{\delta/(1 + \delta)\,[1 - 1/(1 + \delta)^T]\}\,(1 + \rho)\,[1 - 1/(1 + \rho)^T]/\rho$ where T is the distance from the planning period to the end of the horizon. Thus, as $T \to \infty$, $\mu \to [\delta/(1 + \delta)]/[\rho/(1 + \rho)]$. In addition, it is now possible, but not necessary, to allow the subsistence parameters (γ) to vary over time. The assumption that they are constant over time, together with the assumptions listed in chapter 2, lead to equations (2.1) and (2.2), except of course for the previously mentioned interpretation of μ. The model embedding these assumptions is referred to here as the current income model. Another version of ELES which uses permanent income as the appropriate income concept was also implemented empirically. As in Watts (1960) and Ramanathan (1968), a household's permanent income was estimated from the income profile of comparable households. An extrapolative parameter, λ, was introduced to project into the future the existing deviation of an indi-

2. See Betancourt (1973a) for elaboration.
3. Aigner (1974) discusses the complications involved in solving this problem within the context of estimating the labor supply function.

vidual family's income from the mean income of the group. In a similar manner, families of above average size were assumed to maintain their relative position with respect to this variable in subsequent stages of the life cycle. The model incorporating these assumptions will be referred to as the permanent income model. This version of ELES also allows the identification of price elasticities in a cross-section context. In calculating the permanent effect of relative price changes it is assumed that changes in the initial period are expected to last throughout the time horizon of the plan.[4]

Alternative formulations with respect to the life-cycle variables were also considered. Because there is no clear-cut theoretical rationale on how age should affect the parameters of the model, its impact was captured through the stratification of the sample into six age groups (less than 25, 25–34, 35–44, 45–54, 55–64, 65 and over). With respect to family size, however, it seemed reasonable to postulate that this variable would affect the subsistence parameters. More precisely, a scheme suggested by Ando and Modigliani (1957) was adapted as follows:

$$(8.1) \qquad \gamma_{it} = \bar{\gamma}_{it}[1 + \lambda_i(f_{ht} - 1)]$$

where the bar indicates a subsistence parameter for a family of one, λ_i represents a parameter which captures economies of scale in consumption and is allowed to vary across commodities (i), and f_{ht} is the family size of the hth household in the tth period.

This specification of the family size variable introduces a substantive difference between the results for the Chilean data and those in the rest of the book—the only substantive difference that is not eliminated in the section on current income results. Information is thus obtained on the desirability of capturing the effect of family size through stratification and the use of per capita income as the independent variable, as is done elsewhere in the book, rather than directly as a determinant of the subsistence parameters. In the current income version of ELES, the main consequence of this specification of family size is to change the formulas for all the elasticities that involve the subsistence parameters. For example, the uncom-

4. The assumptions used are discussed in detail in the appendix to this chapter. In the permanent income version of ELES the subsistence parameters can be specified as growing over time at some constant growth rate, such as the expected rate of growth of income. A justification for this hypothesis is provided in Betancourt (1971a).

pensated price elasticities for ELES become

$$(8.2) \qquad \tilde{\eta}_{ij} = (1 - \beta_i^*) \{ p_i \, \bar{\gamma}_i \, [1 + \lambda_i \, (f_h - 1)] \, / \, v_i \} - 1$$

and

$$(8.3) \qquad \tilde{\eta}_{ij} = - \beta_i^* \{ p_j \, \bar{\gamma}_j \, [1 + \lambda_j (f_h - 1)] \} / v_i.$$

The rest of the formulas are similarly affected; that is, wherever γ_i appears it must be replaced by the right-hand side of (8.1). As for the problem of estimation, there is an additional parameter to be estimated (λ_i) and an additional regressor in every expenditure equation $(f_h - 1)$ of the current income version of ELES. In keeping with the other assumptions of this model, it has been assumed that the consumer expects his family size to remain unaltered over the planning horizon. This assumption was relaxed in the empirical implementation of the permanent income version of ELES.[5]

Finally, urban-rural location and occupational status or socioeconomic class (workers, self-employed, employees) were used to control for differences among consumers in tastes and preferences as well as expectations.[6] The same models were also implemented without disaggregating by occupational status in order to assess the impact on the estimates.

Permanent Income Compared with Current Income

Both permanent and current income versions of ELES were implemented with the Chilean data for households stratified by age, location, and occupational status. The estimating equation for the current income model differs slightly from the one presented in chapter 2 because of the family size variable;[7] that is, for each household

$$(8.4) \quad v_{ih} = [p_i \, \bar{\gamma}_i - \beta_i^* \, (\Sigma \, p_i \, \bar{\gamma}_i)] + [\lambda_i \, p_i \, \bar{\gamma}_i - \beta_i^* (\Sigma \, \lambda_i \, p_i \, \bar{\gamma}_i)] (f_h - 1) + \beta_i^* y_h + e_{ih}.$$

The regression results for the current income model are presented

5. Again see the appendix to this chapter for a detailed explanation.
6. A more extended discussion of the roles of these variables in the Chilean case, and possibly in other developing countries, is available in Betancourt (1973b).
7. Note that the estimation methods described in chapter 2 are still applicable in both (8.4) and (8.14).

in table 8.1 for the three expenditure functions.[8] Table 8.2 presents the estimates of the derived parameters and elasticities. The corresponding results for the permanent income model are available in Betancourt (1973a) but are not presented here in detail. Instead, the main features of both sets of results are briefly compared to provide the rationale for choosing the current income model after empirical implementation.

With respect to the statistical significance of the regression coefficients, the current income model performs better than the permanent income model. For instance, in the current income model all but one of the marginal propensities to consume (β_i^{**}) have a t ratio greater than two, as well as 38 of the 72 intercept coefficients and 29 of the 72 family size coefficients. In the permanent income model, although all but two of the regression coefficients for one of the income variables ($\beta_i^* \lambda$) have t ratios greater than two, only 9 out of 72 intercepts and 7 out of the 72 coefficients for each of the two family size variables have t ratios greater than two; finally, the regression coefficient of the other income variable $[\beta_i^* (1 - \lambda)]$ has a t ratio greater than two in only 11 out of 72 cases. The last result suggests that the appropriate value of the extrapolative tendencies parameter (λ) is unity, which implies that the household expects to retain its relative income position over the life cycle.

Other striking features of the permanent income model relate to price elasticities. The estimates of the temporary and the permanent (uncompensated) own-price elasticities are very close to each other, but the estimates for the (uncompensated) cross-price elasticities are very far apart. More importantly, for the present discussion, 32 out of the 72 own-price elasticities (either temporary or permanent) are positive. Furthermore, among the remaining 40, values smaller than minus two occur frequently. In contrast only 5 out of the 72 own-price elasticities were positive in the current income model, and none of the estimates took on values smaller than minus two. Thus the empirical results for the current income version of ELES are more consistent with the underlying theoretical restrictions of the model.

It can be seen from the appendix to this chapter that the empirical implementation of the permanent income model requires the use of

---

8. The data were stratified into twelve subsamples (six age groups for urban and rural location), and dummies on all variables were used for the three socioeconomic status groups. The first and last age groups in both sectors were dropped from the analysis, however, because of the small number of observations and the peculiarities of these stages of the life cycle.

Table 8.1. Regression Results for the Current Income Model: Expenditure Functions of Urban and Rural Workers, Self-Employed, and Employees, Chile

Age^a and expenditure	Urban workers			Rural workers		
	$Intercept^b$	β_i^*	Coefficient of f_k^c	$Intercept^b$	β_i^*	Coefficient of f_k^c
25–34						
Rent	4.7500	0.1025*	−0.4444	−2.3151	0.1617*	−0.4560
	(4.2869)	(0.0232)	(0.6938)	(1.5160)	(0.0086)	(0.2452)
Food	25.5248*	0.2789*	2.6969	10.0086*	0.4362*	1.4405*
	(9.4910)	(0.0513)	(1.5361)	(3.4467)	(0.0196)	(0.5576)
Other	−0.2537	0.2076*	−0.4466	1.9782	0.1921*	−0.5850
	(12.0020)	(0.0648)	(1.9425)	(3.1454)	(0.0179)	(0.5088)
35–44						
Rent	6.7134	0.1007*	−0.6672	3.6126	0.0792*	−0.2476
	(4.2826)	(0.0218)	(0.5766)	(2.1096)	(0.0102)	(0.2826)
Food	11.9768	0.4410*	2.4275*	36.4151*	0.2785*	1.2319*
	(8.0702)	(0.0410)	(1.0866)	(4.3429)	(0.0210)	(0.5817)
Other	−8.4985	0.3323*	−1.1981	−2.9360	0.2775*	1.2555*
	(12.3524)	(0.0628)	(1.6632)	(4.4855)	(0.0217)	(0.6008)
45–54						
Rent	9.6359	0.0976	−0.9031	5.8498	0.0779	−0.5255
	(4.5096)*	(0.0237)*	(0.7051)	(1.7786)*	(0.0094)*	(0.2376)*
Food	16.6903	0.4230	0.9771	9.8020	0.4474	1.1302
	(8.8773)	(0.0467)*	(1.3885)	(4.3749)*	(0.0230)*	(0.5845)
Other	−3.7978	0.2606	−0.6408	−1.7961	0.1937	−0.2282
	(11.0617)	(0.0582)*	(1.7302)	(3.8906)	(0.0205)*	(0.5198)

204

Age[a] and expenditure	Urban self-employed			Rural self-employed		
	Intercept[b]	β_i^*	Coefficient of f_h^c	Intercept[b]	β_i^*	Coefficient of f_h^c
55–64						
Rent	10.4694 (7.0357)	0.1356 (0.0332)*	-2.2478 (1.2077)	4.6796 (1.7241)*	0.0637 (0.0104)*	-0.3207 (0.2617)
Food	-6.4966 (11.6584)	0.4703 (0.0551)*	4.5005 (2.0012)*	20.4261 (4.5242)*	0.3734 (0.0273)*	0.4105 (0.6868)
Other	9.2878 (13.5682)	0.1942 (0.0641)*	-1.3837 (2.3290)	-2.3791 (4.7106)	0.2424 (0.0285)*	-0.6120 (0.7151)
25–34						
Rent	6.5001 (3.7670)	0.1039* (0.0101)	-0.3068 (0.7209)	2.4496 (3.0962)	0.0855* (0.0160)	-0.0802 (0.4836)
Food	9.2412 (8.3400)	0.4124* (0.0224)	2.5191 (1.5960)	14.5316* (7.0392)	0.5741* (0.0363)	-1.5886 (1.0034)
Other	-17.3348 (10.5466)	0.3268* (0.0283)	1.5812 (2.0183)	2.6676 (6.4239)	0.2505* (0.0331)	-1.0168 (1.0034)
35–44						
Rent	17.7557* (3.8568)	0.1058* (0.0083)	-1.6808* (0.6173)	6.1127* (2.9816)	0.0730* (0.0111)	-0.3601 (0.4569)
Food	27.6311* (7.2677)	0.2692* (0.0156)	4.4771* (1.1633)	31.9194* (6.1381)	0.2105* (0.0228)	1.5589 (0.9407)
Other	-33.7060* (11.1240)	0.4912* (0.0238)	-2.1092* (1.7806)	-1.5476 (6.3396)	0.2670* (0.0235)	-0.5871 (0.9716)

(*Table continues on the following page.*)

Table 8.1. (continued)

	Urban self-employed			Rural self-employed		
Age^a and expenditure	Intercept^b	β*_i	Coefficient of f_h^c	Intercept^b	β*_i	Coefficient of f_h^c
45–54						
Rent	15.5403* (3.6383)	0.0852* (0.0083)	-0.3565 (0.6146)	10.6427* (2.2115)	0.0442* (0.0061)	-0.1959 (0.3098)
Food	21.1537* (7.7621)	0.2234* (0.0164)	7.1265* (1.2099)	34.0246* (5.4399)	0.2029* (0.0151)	2.5955* (0.7620)
Other	-13.2551 (8.9243)	0.3867* (0.0204)	-2.9936 (1.5076)	-12.8761* (4.8378)	0.2423* (0.0134)	1.4539* (0.6777)
55–64						
Rent	25.1850* (4.8709)	0.0695* (0.0076)	-1.6217 (1.0853)	8.8092* (1.8481)	0.0688* (0.0076)	-0.6819* (0.3028)
Food	22.4567* (8.0713)	0.2266* (0.0126)	6.1530 (1.7983)	15.0866* (4.8494)	0.2601* (0.0200)	3.3730* (0.7940)
Other	25.9567* (9.3935)	0.2493* (0.0146)	-6.1834 (2.0929)	-2.2329 (5.0492)	0.1972* (0.0208)	0.4835 (0.8273)

	Urban employees			Rural employees		
Age^a and expenditure	Intercept^b	β*_i	Coefficient of f_h^c	Intercept^b	β*_i	Coefficient of f_h^c
25–34						
Rent	14.0860 (4.8568)	0.0991* (0.0102)	-1.0741 (0.8560)	2.9208 (4.8947)	0.1376* (0.0122)	1.6721* (0.7424)

Food	20.8791	0.2789*	5.5476*	23.5504*	0.2432*	5.1460*
	(10.7528)	(0.0227)	(1.8952)	(11.1282)	(0.0277)	(1.6880)
Other	−32.1870*	0.5346*	−4.1149	34.4107	0.1820*	−5.1969*
	(13.5977)	(0.0287)	(2.3967)	(10.1554)	(0.0252)	(1.5404)
35–44						
Rent	25.9330*	0.1013*	−2.0235*	−10.4740	0.1620*	−0.4624
	(4.4234)	(0.0074)	(0.6060)	(6.2379)	(0.0150)	(0.9006)
Food	31.2502*	0.1920*	8.3240*	34.2140*	0.1822*	5.6510*
	(8.3355)	(0.0139)	(1.1419)	(12.8419)	(0.0309)	(1.8540)
Other	−38.5125*	0.6308*	−8.4086*	38.4081*	0.5055*	−14.1485
	(12.7585)	(0.0212)	(1.7479)	(13.2635)	(0.0320)	(1.9149)
45–54						
Rent	22.0102*	0.0705*	0.3823	16.6120	0.0918*	−1.8853
	(6.8049)	(0.0101)	(0.9340)	(10.2736)	(0.0258)	(0.9367)
Food	62.6384*	0.2422*	−0.3436	47.6688	0.2264*	1.3445
	(13.3950)	(0.0199)	(1.8386)	(25.2710)	(0.0634)	(2.3041)
Other	−3.7576	0.2156*	3.4600	36.4709	0.4302*	−6.9564*
	(16.6919)	(0.0248)	(2.2910)	(22.4737)	(0.0564)	(2.0490)
55–64						
Rent	36.3305*	0.0962*	−4.0924	8.9912	0.0133	1.2419
	(12.3438)	(0.0289)	(2.4514)	(10.2670)	(0.0280)	(1.1486)
Food	24.0356	0.1345*	14.0367*	45.1081	0.1951*	3.4332
	(20.4542)	(0.0479)	(4.0621)	(26.9408)	(0.0735)	(3.0139)
Other	7.9124	0.2854*	−1.8900	63.6026*	0.3853*	12.5272*
	(23.8049)	(0.0558)	(4.7275)	(28.0508)	(0.0765)	(3.1380)

Source: Data for all tables in chapter 8 are derived from the Cost of Living Survey for Central Chile, January 1964, conducted by the Instituto de Planificación Económica, University of Chile.

Note: Standard errors in parentheses. An asterisk next to a number indicates a t ratio greater than two.

a. The age group is determined by the age of the household head.
b. The intercept in equation (8.4) adjusted because f_h rather than $f_h - 1$ was used in the regression.
c. The estimate of the coefficient of $f_h - 1$ in equation (8.4).

Table 8.2. *Structural Estimates for Current Income Model: Urban and Rural Workers, Self-Employed, and Employees, Chile*

Age[a] and expenditure	$p_i \bar{r}_i$	λ_i	$\bar{\eta}_{iij}$ j = rent	$\bar{\eta}_{iij}$ j = food	$\bar{\eta}_{iij}$ j = other	$\bar{\eta}_i$	Mean income	Mean family size
Urban workers								
25–34								
Rent	12.2430	0.0005	−0.1992	−0.5471	−0.1355	0.8535	114.4990	5.2887
Food	49.8191	0.0787	−0.0475	−0.3329	−0.0687	0.4433		
Other	15.3758	0.0303	−0.1192	−0.6556	−0.3559	1.1122		
35–44								
Rent	14.6408	−0.0149	−0.3236	−0.4451	−0.1147	0.7287	129.8434	6.2591
Food	52.0429	0.0845	−0.0705	−0.4971	−0.1074	0.6854		
Other	18.6647	0.0152	−0.1493	−0.8065	−0.5548	1.4270		
45–54								
Rent	18.5292	−0.0624	−0.4093	−0.3014	−0.0772	0.7461	147.3986	6.1103
Food	60.1252	−0.0020	−0.0592	−0.6049	−0.0704	0.7173		
Other	21.7186	−0.0606	−0.1018	−0.4796	−0.6572	1.1876		
55–64								
Rent	17.8063	−0.0931	−0.5408	−0.3495	−0.1257	0.9603	150.4861	4.9308
Food	31.2463	0.2095	−0.0849	−0.5004	−0.1509	1.1717		
Other	21.6308	−0.0249	−0.0803	−0.3822	−0.4425	1.0363		

Rural workers

25–34								
Rent	4.9837	−0.0298	−0.6555	−0.6960	−0.1453	1.4390	92.9581	5.6552
Food	32.3684	0.0701	−0.0303	−0.5923·	−0.0686	0.6828		
Other	10.6059	−0.0207	−0.0461	−0.5109	−0.5485	1.0412		
35–44								
Rent	9.7331	0.0245	0.0184	−0.5376	−0.3076	0.8286	105.5723	6.9803
Food	50.0401	0.0588	−0.0488	−0.2472	−0.1757	0.4536		
Other	20.6319	0.1434	−0.1772	−1.0850	0.5691	1.6599		
45–54								
Rent	9.2699	−0.0454	−0.4437	−0.3018	−0.0547	0.7963	116.1305	6.7362
Food	33.5926	0.0515	−0.0434	−0.6511	−0.0518	0.7538		
Other	7.7866	0.0041	−0.0716	−0.4303	−0.6647	1.1740		
55–64								
Rent	8.7721	−0.0484	−0.4085	−0.2431	−0.0469	0.5595	105.2242	5.6448
Food	46.7059	−0.0042	−0.0418	−0.5231	−0.0557	0.6531		
Other	13.8025	−0.0730	−0.1101	−0.7445	−0.5361	1.7116		

(*Table continues on the following page.*)

209

Table 8.2. (continued)

Age[a] and expenditure	$p_i \bar{r}_i$	λ_i	$\bar{\eta}_{ij}$			$\bar{\eta}_i$	Mean income	Mean family size
			$j = rent$	$j = food$	$j = other$			
Urban self-employed								
25–34								
Rent	7.6502	0.2883	−0.4294	−0.3113	−0.1331	0.7817		
Food	17.5428	0.7120	−0.0746	−0.6153	−0.1322	0.7936	185.3818	4.6456
Other	−11.1713	−0.8488	−0.1092	−0.4501	−0.7000	1.1537		
35–44								
Rent	25.8546	−0.0440	−0.4469	−0.2682	−0.0366	0.6262		
Food	56.9919	0.1028	−0.0510	−0.4177	−0.0298	0.5009	196.7757	5.6538
Other	9.5892	0.0431	−0.2017	−0.8365	−0.8824	1.9405		
45–54								
Rent	22.7937	0.0307	−0.3856	−0.1982	−0.0574	0.4881		
Food	48.2339	0.2052	−0.0568	−0.3317	−0.0573	0.4803	217.9347	4.9409
Other	18.2907	0.0984	−0.1627	−0.5501	−0.7429	1.3919		
55–64								
Rent	34.5626	−0.0542	−0.1002	−0.1899	−0.0855	0.5383		
Food	64.4721	0.0827	−0.0692	−0.3217	−0.0857	0.5678	230.8381	4.0632
Other	59.2282	−0.1197	−0.1399	−0.3939	−0.4505	1.1229		

Rural self-employed

25–34							
Rent	18.5024	−0.1424	−0.1560	−0.1858	−0.0290	0.8703	
Food	121.2697	−0.1545	−0.0689	−0.6083	−0.1117	0.9832	95.8832 4.7235
Other	48.9176	−0.1738	−0.1310	−0.7938	−0.3088	1.2827	
35–44							
Rent	11.7771	−0.0221	−0.2064	−0.3666	−0.1094	0.6823	
Food	50.8504	0.0363	−0.0388	−0.1759	−0.0696	0.4283	115.5592 5.5730
Other	19.9002	−0.0112	−0.0921	−0.5194	−0.5478	1.0084	
45–54							
Rent	13.5324	0.0102	−0.0482	−0.2240	−0.0700	0.4345	
Food	50.7844	0.0813	−0.0390	−0.2410	−0.0617	0.3834	140.1342 5.8044
Other	5.4926	0.5976	−0.1231	−0.6080	−0.4225	1.2171	
55–64							
Rent	11.7332	−0.0180	−0.2410	−0.2809	−0.0850	0.6641	
Food	32.0917	0.1594	−0.0416	−0.4223	−0.0635	0.4960	128.4644 5.0007
Other	8.5860	0.2102	−0.0874	−0.4463	−0.4763	1.0447	

(*Table continues on the following page.*)

Table 8.2. (continued)

Age[a] and expenditure	$p_i \bar{r}_i$	λ_i	$\bar{\eta}_{ij}$			$\bar{\eta}_i$	Mean income	Mean family size
			$j=rent$	$j=food$	$j=other$			
Urban employees								
25–34								
Rent	16.5685	−0.0403	−0.6200	−0.1488	0.0631	0.7511	245.7813	5.3280
Food	36.4361	0.1637	−0.0293	−0.6145	0.0635	0.5603		
Other	−17.1156	0.1123	−0.0884	−0.4650	−1.1482	1.6446		
35–44								
Rent	46.0148	−0.1051	−0.6239	−0.2023	0.1300	0.6639	325.8828	6.2116
Food	81.4717	0.0367	−0.0212	−0.4469	0.0973	0.4413		
Other	90.7296	−0.2858	−0.1456	−0.6800	−1.1820	2.2829		
45–54								
Rent	35.0053	0.0259	−0.3184	−0.1384	−0.0479	0.4549	345.3745	5.6903
Food	105.6257	0.0138	−0.0690	−0.3954	−0.1152	0.5935		
Other	38.2744	0.1322	−0.0844	−0.2423	−0.5128	0.7459		
55–64								
Rent	47.4128	−0.0526	−0.4259	−0.1084	−0.0834	0.5171	326.3501	4.5500
Food	59.2884	0.2745	−0.0292	−0.3779	−0.0536	0.2695		
Other	51.0396	0.0560	−0.0827	−0.2805	−0.6592	0.7260		

Rural employees

25–34							
Rent	24.2645	0.0899	0.0280	−0.3996	−0.2074	1.1408	231.4566	5.1301
Food	63.4648	0.0953	−0.0805	−0.3856	−0.0688	0.5167		
Other	55.2329	−0.3819	−0.1237	−0.3294	−0.4237	0.8118		
35–44							
Rent	46.3922	−0.2181	−1.2859	−0.5312	−1.0114	1.4319	279.4000	6.6499
Food	104.3420	−0.0499	0.0336	−0.4946	0.1467	0.4200		
Other	203.1461	−0.2180	0.0934	−0.4221	−1.2690	1.6328		
45–54							
Rent	48.7520	−0.0948	−0.2582	−0.4196	−0.4236	0.9708	259.7919	7.2085
Food	132.9275	−0.0406	−0.0306	−0.3421	−0.0927	0.5033		
Other	188.9663	−0.1047	−0.1221	−0.4916	−0.5973	1.1934		
55–64							
Rent	14.6491	0.1232	−0.1721	−0.0846	−0.1721	0.0992	205.1664	5.6668
Food	113.3205	0.1032	−0.0726	1.1281	−1.0673	0.6304		
Other	204.0513	0.1413	−0.1186	−0.8908	2.5892	1.3629		

a. The age group is determined by the age of the household head.

213

Table 8.3. *Estimated Values of Marginal Budget Shares (β_i) and the Marginal Propensity to Consume (μ), ELES, Chile, 1964*

Type of household[a]	Sample size	Weight of youngest subgroup[b]	Income[c]	β_i Food	β_i Rent	β_i Other	μ
Rural							
Workers							
Young	896	0.4788	100	0.499	0.168	0.330	0.709
Old	574	0.6272	112	0.597	0.104	0.301	0.704
Self-employed							
Young	237	0.3966	108	0.512	0.113	0.375	0.693
Old	321	0.6044	136	0.448	0.107	0.444	0.504
Employees							
Young	86	0.5349	254	0.309	0.214	0.477	0.696
Old	36	0.6667	241	0.310	0.095	0.595	0.697
Urban							
Workers							
Young	341	0.4575	123	0.493	0.137	0.370	0.744
Old	190	0.6211	149	0.560	0.142	0.298	0.788
Self-employed							
Young	266	0.4135	192	0.383	0.123	0.494	0.857
Old	259	0.5907	223	0.355	0.125	0.521	0.634
Employees							
Young	256	0.4648	289	0.252	0.109	0.638	0.919
Old	91	0.7802	341	0.416	0.144	0.439	0.526

a. "Young" refers to young head of household, 25–44 years old; "Old" refers to old head of household, 45–64 years old.

b. These weights are used for the youngest subgroup (25–34 for the "young" age group and 45–54 for the "old" age group) in the aggregation of the results. The weights for the other subgroups can be obtained by subtracting from one.

c. Mean monthly income per household in escudos (in 1964, 3.25 escudos = US$1.00).

explicit assumptions about expectations. Undoubtedly, more extensive experimentation with alternative assumptions might eventually lead to better results for the permanent income model. Nevertheless, this succinct summary of results indicates that the current income version of ELES provides a more reliable basis for applied work, given the present state of knowledge about the formulation of expectations.

Current Income Results

In order to facilitate comparison with the results for other countries, the data presented in table 8.1 have been aggregated to obtain two age groups, young and old, within each socioeconomic status cell for rural and urban households.[9] Again it has to be stressed that household income was the independent variable in the regressions rather than household income per capita and that family size was introduced as an additional regressor. Thus, patterns in the estimates which are the same as for other countries should be regarded as important characteristics of household behavior.

Parameter Estimates

In table 8.3 the estimates of the marginal budget shares and the marginal propensity to consume are presented for each cell. Mean household income for each cell is also included. This table as well as the next two are ordered from lowest to highest household income by location and within each location by socioeconomic status. The same order would be obtained using household per capita income. It should be kept in mind that the self-employed are those who employ less than five persons; the employers group (those who employ more than five persons) had to be excluded from the analysis because of the small number of observations.

In the case of rural households, the marginal propensity to consume is almost identical among young households regardless of income level. The marginal budget share for the category of other expenditure increases substantially with income for both young and old households, and the marginal budget share for food decreases substantially with income for old households.

The urban results reveal a very different pattern in the marginal propensity to consume (μ) for young and old households. Among young households there is a substantial increase in μ as income in-

9. See table 8.3 for the relative sample size weights used in the aggregation.

creases; among old households a substantial decrease in μ as income increases. Moreover, young urban households also exhibit a systematic variation with income in the marginal budget shares. The marginal budget share for food decreases substantially, the one for rent decreases slightly, and the one for "other" increases substantially as income increases. For old households there seems to be a break in any pattern of variation with income at the self-employed group.

Table 8.4 contains the estimates of the value of the subsistence parameters for a family of one $(p\bar{\gamma})$, the family size scale parameters (λ_i), and the household subsistence expenditures $(p\gamma)$. Parenthetically, the latter can be converted into the same units as γ^* elsewhere in the book through division by mean family size. Two features of the table stand out: in 11 out of 12 cells household subsistence expenditures are substantially larger for food than for the other two expenditure groups; and the scale parameters take on negative values quite frequently, particularly for rent and the category of other expenditure, which implies that as family size increases household subsistence expenditures decrease.

From an economic point of view, $p\gamma$ is of greater interest than $p\bar{\gamma}$. This discussion is thus restricted to the estimates of $p\gamma$ and λ_i. In the urban area $p\gamma$ tends to increase markedly with income for old households in all three expenditure categories. In the rural area the same pattern is also observed for both young and old households with respect to food and rent and for old households with respect to other expenditure. The scale parameters do not exhibit much systematic variation with income in either urban or rural areas, however.

The values of the sum of subsistence expenditures *per household* and the Frisch parameter (ω) for the household are also reported in table 8.4 for convenience. Interestingly enough, the sum of subsistence expenditures per household increases as income increases for young and old households in both the urban and the rural areas. Frisch's conjecture that ω increases with income is consistent only with the pattern for young households in the urban area, and in the rural area two of the six estimates have the "wrong" sign.

Elasticity Estimates

The estimates for the various elasticities of interest are presented in table 8.5 as well as the aggregated average budget shares (w_i).[10] Not

10. To facilitate comparison with estimates in the rest of the book, table 8.5

surprisingly, the estimates for the expenditure elasticities (η_i and η) exhibit the same pattern of variation with respect to income as the marginal budget shares (β_i) and the marginal propensity to consume (μ). The only exception is in the category of other expenditure in the rural area. Food has an expenditure elasticity less than unity, and other expenditure has an elasticity greater than unity in every cell. All but three of the rent expenditure elasticities are less than unity, and the three exceptions are for young households.

As in the disaggregated results, most of the price responsiveness of the system is contained in the own-price elasticities and the food cross-price elasticities. For the own-price elasticities, the only clear patterns of variation with income arise for expenditures on food and other in the rural area. The own-price elasticity of other expenditure increases in absolute value with income for young households, and both the food and the "other" own-price elasticities decrease in absolute value with income for old households. Note that one of the 36 own-price elasticities has the wrong (positive) sign. In both rural and urban areas the food cross-price elasticities for both rent and other expenditure show some tendency to decrease as income increases among young households, but this is certainly not the case for old households.

The elasticity of the savings ratio with respect to food price (ξ_1) is also presented in table 8.5. For both young and old households in the rural area and for young households in the urban area, this elasticity decreases in absolute value as income increases, and the decrease is quite large for young households. For old households in the urban area, however, this elasticity increases in absolute value as income increases.

Consequences of Aggregation

In the previous section discussion centered on patterns of systematic variation with income arising from the point estimates for the parameters and the elasticities. However, the effect of income on the point estimates seems to interact with the three household

contains values of η_i and η_{ij} rather than $\bar{\eta}_i$ and $\bar{\eta}_{ij}$, that is, expenditure elasticities rather than income elasticities, and price elasticities are calculated on the assumption that total expenditure rather than income is held constant. Estimates of $\bar{\eta}_i$ and $\bar{\eta}_{ij}$ are given in table 8.2 and form the basis of the discussion in the second section of this chapter.

Table 8.4. Estimated Values of Subsistence Parameters ($p_i\bar{\gamma}_i$), Scale Parameters (λ_i), Household Subsistence Expenditures ($p_i\gamma_i$), and the Frisch Parameter (ω), ELES, Chile, 1964

Type of household[a]	Total consumption expenditures[b]	Mean family size	Food			Rent			Other			Sum[d]	ω[e]
			$p\bar{\gamma}$	λ	$p\gamma$[c]	$p\bar{\gamma}$	λ	$p\gamma$[c]	$p\bar{\gamma}$	λ	$p\gamma$[c]		
Rural													
Workers													
Young	90	6.3	42	0.06	55	7	0.02	8	16	0.06	21	84	−15.0
Old	95	6.3	38	0.03	44	9	−0.05	7	10	−0.02	9	60	−2.7
Self-employed													
Young	94	5.2	79	−0.04	66	14	−0.07	10	31	−0.08	21	96	27.0
Old	112	5.5	43	0.11	64	13	0.00	13	7	0.44	21	98	−8.0
Employees													
Young	212	5.8	82	0.03	94	35	−0.05	27	124	−0.15	35	155	−3.7
Old	206	6.7	126	0.01	133	37	−0.02	33	194	−0.02	172	338	1.6
Urban													
Workers													
Young	120	5.8	51	0.08	71	14	−0.01	13	17	0.02	19	103	−7.1
Old	128	5.7	49	0.08	67	18	−0.07	12	22	−0.05	17	96	−4.0
Self-employed													
Young	182	5.2	41	0.35	101	18	0.09	25	1	−0.33	−0	126	−3.2
Old	189	4.6	55	0.15	85	28	0.00	28	35	0.01	36	149	−4.5
Employees													
Young	260	5.8	61	0.11	93	32	−0.07	21	41	−0.10	21	136	−2.1
Old	307	5.4	95	0.07	124	38	0.01	40	41	0.12	63	227	−3.8

a. "Young" refers to young head of household, 25–44 years old, and "Old" refers to old head of household, 45–64 years old.

b. Average consumption expenditures a month per household in escudos.

c. Household subsistence expenditures calculated using (8.1) and the relevant estimates and sample statistics from this table.

d. Sum of household subsistence expenditures; it may differ from sum of columns because of rounding.

e. The Frisch parameter for the household. These estimates are obtained directly from the other estimates in this table using (2.7) and (2.4).

218

Table 8.5. Estimates of the Price Elasticities (η_{ii}), Food Cross-Price Elasticities (η_{i1}), Expenditure Elasticities (η_i), and Elasticity of the Savings Ratio with Respect to Food Price (ξ_1), ELES, Chile, 1964

Type of household[a]	η_{ii}			η_{i1}			η[b]	η_i			ξ_1[c]	w_i[d]		
	Food	Rent	Other	Food	Rent	Other		Food	Rent	Other		Food	Rent	Other
Rural														
Workers														
Young	−0.05	−0.36	−0.17		−0.93	−1.07	0.79	0.72	1.53	1.74	−1.61	0.69	0.11	0.19
Old	−0.73	−0.51	−0.65		−0.38	−0.73	0.83	0.87	0.80	1.58	−1.86	0.69	0.13	0.19
Self-employed														
Young	−0.43	−0.20	−0.51		−0.67	−0.95	0.80	0.85	0.94	1.34	−1.44	0.60	0.12	0.28
Old	−0.50	−0.17	−0.55		−0.49	−1.09	0.61	0.71	0.82	1.93	−1.33	0.63	0.13	0.23
Employees														
Young	−0.44	−0.30	−0.73		−0.67	−0.66	0.83	0.57	1.53	1.49	−0.68	0.54	0.14	0.32
Old	−0.07	0.14	−0.16		−0.49	−0.97	0.82	0.65	0.73	1.49	−1.15	0.48	0.13	0.40
Urban														
Workers														
Young	−0.54	−0.28	−0.55		−0.61	−1.00	0.76	0.76	1.05	1.68	−6.02	0.65	0.13	0.22
Old	−0.62	−0.48	−0.62		−0.48	−0.65	0.92	0.93	0.89	1.24	−0.68	0.60	0.16	0.24
Self-employed														
Young	−0.39	−0.28	−1.00		−0.42	−0.98	0.90	0.68	0.77	1.76	−1.45	0.56	0.16	0.28
Old	−0.44	−0.30	−0.70		−0.30	−0.77	0.75	0.68	0.66	1.74	−0.91	0.52	0.19	0.30
Employees														
Young	−0.48	−0.55	−0.91		−0.24	−0.70	1.02	0.49	0.68	1.93	−0.26	0.51	0.16	0.33
Old	−0.50	−0.38	−0.67		−0.32	−0.51	0.58	0.87	0.80	1.25	−1.73	0.48	0.18	0.35

Note: The elasticity estimates are calculated using the formulas in table 2.2, with γ_i as defined in (8.1), and the parameter estimates from the previous tables, unless otherwise stated. In calculating price elasticities total expenditure (not income) is assumed to be constant.
a. "Young" refers to young head of household, 25–44 years old, and "Old" refers to old head of household, 45–64 years old.
b. Elasticity of total expenditures with respect to income.
c. Calculated using (2.12)
d. Average budget share obtained by aggregating the disaggregated average budget shares with the weights given in table 8.3.

characteristics determining the cells. Although the focus was on patterns across socioeconomic groups, given age and location, the effect of income on the point estimates would interact with household characteristics in the same way even if the focus were on either of the other two alternatives. Furthermore, earlier tests on the disaggregated results for the marginal propensity to consume food (β_i^*) indicated that the point estimates were significantly different for households that differed in age, location, and socioeconomic status.[11] This section examines the consequences of ignoring these determinants of household behavior in the estimation.

The age group 35–44 years old in the rural sector is taken as an illustration, and the point estimates obtained by stratifying the sample by occupational status are compared with those obtained by fitting ELES without stratifying by this variable. Occupational status was chosen because it led to the largest number of differences in the earlier tests. This particular age and location was selected because the group contained almost exactly the same set of observations for the aggregated results (657) as for the disaggregated (650).

Table 8.6 shows the two sets of point estimates for the parameters and elasticities of ELES as well as the differences in sample characteristics owing to the seven observations missing from the disaggregated sample. The weight of these missing observations in the aggregation of the disaggregated results would have been about one percent. The estimates for the marginal budget shares and the marginal propensity to consume differ less than 10 percent of the size of the disaggregated estimates. The values of the subsistence parameters for a family of one and the scale parameters sometimes differ much more, however, and in the case of the scale parameter for the category of other expenditure the values have different signs. These differences also lead to large differences in household subsistence expenditures. A similar pattern appears in the elasticity estimates where the differences in the expenditure elasticities are less than 10 percent of the disaggregated results. All the other elasticity estimates differ by a considerable margin, however; in two cases the other elasticity estimates have opposite signs, and in all cases the other elasticity estimates differ more than 10 percent of the disaggregated results.

Disaggregation brings out the fact that the aggregated results eliminate two violations of the theoretical restrictions of the model.

---

11. This was also true in the permanent income model. See Betancourt (1973b).

Table 8.6. *A Comparison of the Point Estimates Obtained
with and without Disaggregating by Occupational Status,
ELES, Chile, 1964*

Estimation procedure[a]	Expenditure group estimates			Other estimates	Sample characteristics
	Food	Rent	Other		
		β		μ	Mean income
Aggregated	0.37	0.14	0.50	0.69	122
Disaggregated	0.41	0.13	0.46	0.63	118
		$p_i\bar{\gamma}_i$			Mean family size
Aggregated	46	11	22		6.51
Disaggregated	53	12	31		6.65
		λ_i			Mean total expenditure
Aggregated	0.04	−0.04	−0.10		107
Disaggregated	0.05	0.00	0.10		103
		$p_i\gamma_i$[b]		Sum	
Aggregated	56	9	10	75	
Disaggregated	68	12	49	129	
		η_{ii}		ω	Average budget share
Aggregated	−0.57	−0.43	−0.80	−3.3	0.12 (rent)
Disaggregated	−0.40	−0.08	0.11	4.0	0.11
		η_{i1}		ξ_1	
Aggregated		−0.61	−1.14	−1.16	0.65 (food)
Disaggregated		−0.78	−1.32	−1.68	0.66
		η_i		η	
Aggregated	0.57	1.17	2.17	0.79	0.23 (other)
Disaggregated	0.62	1.18	2.0	0.72	0.23

Note: All the symbols and definitions correspond exactly to those in the previous tables. These estimates are for rural households having a head of household in the 35–44 years old group.

a. Aggregated results obtained by fitting ELES without stratifying by socioeconomic status. Disaggregated results obtained by fitting ELES to each of the three socioeconomic status groups and then aggregating the estimates using the following weights: .72 for workers, .22 for self-employed, and .06 for employees.

b. All the estimates in subsequent rows of the table are based on sample characteristics and the relevant estimates from previous rows of this table.

These violations occur in the own-price elasticity for other expenditure and in the Frisch parameter; they stem from the disaggregated estimates for workers, the group with the largest weight. These estimates contain violations that are not eliminated by aggregation of the disaggregated results.[12]

Summary

This chapter examines alternative formulations of ELES for the analysis of Chilean cross-section data, and several features of the results are worth emphasizing. Implementation of a permanent income version of ELES requires additional assumptions about expectations, and a substantial amount of experimentation may be required to find a form which yields results consistent with the underlying restrictions of the model. The household is used as the basic decisionmaking unit and family size is introduced through the subsistence parameters to provide a feasible formulation of the current income version of ELES. Moreover, the results indicate that household characteristics such as age, location, and socioeconomic status of the head of household play a role in determining the values of the parameters and elasticities of ELES which cannot be explained by income variations across these characteristics. The most systematic variation with income among the estimates arises for the sum of the subsistence expenditures *per household*. Both for young and old households in both urban and rural areas, the values of this sum increase steadily as income increases across socioeconomic status groups. Another significant regularity is the variation of the elasticity of the savings ratio with respect to food price as income increases across socioeconomic groups. In the rural area there is a negative association between the absolute value of this elasticity and income for both young and old households; in the urban area this association interacts with age, being negative for young households and positive for old households. Finally, failure to control for socioeconomic status was shown to lead to differences of less than 10 percent in the income-related estimates of ELES and substantially greater than 10 percent in the price-related estimates of ELES.

---

12. The last four rows of disaggregated estimates could have been calculated by direct aggregation of the corresponding disaggregated results. This alternative increases the number of calculations, however, and, more importantly, the resulting estimates tend to violate the restrictions of classical demand theory (as in Engel aggregation), even when these restrictions are satisfied in each of the disaggregated estimates.

Appendix. The Empirical Implementation of the Permanent Income Model

Several assumptions about expectations had to be made in the empirical implementation of the permanent income model. The model was estimated for a representative consumer who was assumed to be in the middle of his age group. The planning horizon was assumed to be twenty years for the first four age groups (less than 25 years, 25–34, 35–44, and 45–54), and fifteen years and five years for the last two age groups (55–64 and over 65) respectively. Thus, expectations span three stages of the life cycle for the first four age groups. Expectations were assumed to remain constant within a given age group or stage of the life cycle, but they were adjusted in a clearly specified manner to take account of a move from one age group to another.

The expectations to be considered first are those concerning the variation of the subsistence parameters over time. A family of one is assumed to expect its subsistence parameters to grow at the same rate as its income is expected to grow over the planning horizon. Hence, the $\bar{\gamma}_{it}$ of equation (8.1) can be expressed as

$$(8.5) \qquad \bar{\gamma}_{it} = \bar{\gamma}_{i0}(1 + \sigma)^t \qquad (t = 0, \dots T)$$

where σ is the rate at which income is expected to grow.

Specification of the permanent income variable has received the greatest attention in the literature. The method used to estimate permanent income is a variation of one first proposed by Watts (1960) and later used and modified by Ramanathan (1968). It consists of an attempt to estimate the household's permanent income (z) from the income profile of "comparable" households as follows:

$$(8.6) \qquad z = (1 - \lambda)y_j^p + \lambda \frac{y_{hj0}}{\bar{y}_{j0}}y_j^p$$

where y_{hj0} is the current income (both from work and other sources) of the hth household belonging to the jth comparable group in a given age group; $\bar{y}_{j0}$ is the mean current income of the jth comparable group in a given age group; λ is a parameter (not to be confused with the scale parameter λ_i in the text) which reflects extrapolative tendencies; y_j^p is the permanent income of a household of a given age belonging to the jth comparable group which expects its income to follow the same path as the mean income of the group, that is, the permanent income of a household for whom $\lambda = 0$. y_j^p was calculated as follows:

(8.7)
$$y^p_j = \left\{ \sum_{t=0}^{4} \bar{y}_{0j} \left[\frac{(1+\sigma)}{(1+\rho)} \right]^t + \sum_{t=5}^{14} \bar{y}_{1j} \left[\frac{(1+\sigma)}{(1+\rho)} \right]^t \right.$$
$$\left. + \sum_{t=15}^{19} \bar{y}_{2j} \left[\frac{(1+\sigma)}{(1+\rho)} \right]^t \right\} \cdot \theta$$

where σ is the rate at which the household expects its income to grow.[13] Equation (8.7) had to be adjusted for the fifth and sixth age groups by dropping the third term for the former, by dropping the second and third term for the latter, and by using the appropriate definition of θ for both.[14] Finally, education was the main variable used to determine a comparable group.

In the empirical work equation (8.7) was estimated by assuming that the household expected its income to grow at 3 percent over the horizon (except for the last age group where σ was set at zero) and by using three educational groups (no education, at least some primary education, and at least some education beyond primary school) for each cell in the three-way classification by location, occupational status, and age group.[15]

Implementation of the permanent income version with Chilean data makes it necessary to discuss price expectations. In countries with no inflationary experience, the expected rate of inflation is likely to be zero, and the usual assumption would be that the initial price level is expected to prevail. In countries with inflationary experiences, however, the expected rate of inflation is not likely to be zero. Expectations about the future thus seem to give inflation an important role in this model. This is not necessarily true, however. If the consumer does not perceive a differential rate of inflation for different commodities and if he does not perceive distributional

---

13. Different expectations for different socioeconomic status groups were also tried but did not affect the results substantially. In addition, two rates of interest (0.3 and 0.1) were tried, and the higher one was chosen because it gave results which tended to be more consistent with the theoretical restrictions of the model.

14. θ is a correction factor which converts the stock formulation into a flow formulation. It is a function of the rate of interest (ρ), and for the first four age groups it can be expressed as

$$\theta = 1 / \sum_{t=0}^{19} 1/(1+\rho)^t = \rho/(1+\rho)[1-1/(1+\rho)^{20}].$$

15. The model was also implemented with a two-way classification by location and age group.

effects through the expected behavior of wage rates, or exogenous labor income, and interest rates, then inflation will have no effect (see Betancourt 1971a). This result must be interpreted cautiously; it does not mean that inflation can be left out of the analysis but that under certain conditions it will not cloud results. In particular, it provides another incentive for stratifying the households into homogeneous groups. No attempt is made here to discuss the possible distributional effects of inflation. Instead a procedure is suggested, in the context of the permanent income version of ELES, for analyzing the systematic changes in relative prices that usually accompany an inflationary experience.

The vector of forward prices in any time period can be expressed as

$$(8.8) \qquad \hat{p}_t = \hat{p}_0 \, (1 + \pi)^t / (1 + \rho)^t (1 + \pi)^t = p_0 / (1 + \rho)^t$$

where π is the expected general rate of inflation, which drops out of the analysis unless distributional effects are assumed. Since the initial price vector affects all subsequent price vectors, however, the consumer's response to a change in relative prices in an inflationary situation is likely to be different from the response in a noninflationary situation. With inflation changes in relative prices are likely to be perceived as permanent, whereas without inflation these changes are likely to be perceived as temporary. It is therefore necessary to distinguish between transitory and permanent changes in relative prices. Such a distinction is analogous to that between transitory and permanent changes in income, but it has been ignored in the previous literature on ELES.

The transitory elasticities are:

$$(8.9) \qquad T\tilde{\eta}_{ii} = (1 - \beta_i^* \theta) \{p_i \bar{\gamma}_{i0}[1 + \lambda_i(f_0 - 1)]\}/v_i - 1$$

$$(8.10) \qquad T\tilde{\eta}_{ij} = -\beta_i^* \theta \{p_j \bar{\gamma}_{0j}[1 + \lambda_j(f_0 - 1)]\}/v_i.$$

These equations are for the uncompensated own- and cross-price elasticities respectively. The corresponding permanent income elasticities are:

$$(8.11) \qquad P\tilde{\eta}_{ii} = (p_i \bar{\gamma}_{i0}/v_i) \, \{1 + \lambda_i(f_0 - 1)$$

$$- \beta_i^* [\sum_{k=0}^{2} w_k + \lambda_i \sum_{k=0}^{2} w_k(f_k - 1)] \} - 1$$

$$(8.12) \qquad P\tilde{\eta}_{ij} = -\beta_i^*(p_j \bar{\gamma}_{0j}/v_i) \, \{\sum_{k=0}^{2} w_k + \lambda_j [\sum_{k=0}^{2} w_k(f_k - 1)] \}$$

where k refers to the stages in the life cycle. The formulas are exactly applicable to the first four age groups in each sector and need a minor modification for the fifth age group, that is, k ranges over only two stages of the life cycle. These formulas (8.9 through 8.12) also incorporate the expectational assumptions about family size.

It was assumed that a household forms its expectations of family size in the following manner. The family expects to retain its present size position relative to the comparable group over the life cycle. However, expectations of family size in a given stage of the life cycle will also be determined by the actual average family size in that stage for the comparable group to which the household belongs. For example, if in the first stage of the life cycle a household has a family size greater than the average, then it will also expect to have a family size greater than the average, by the same proportion, in the next two stages of the life cycle. This formulation leads to

$$(8.13) \qquad (f_k - 1) = \frac{(f_{hj0} - 1)}{(f_{j0} - 1)} (f_{jk} - 1) \quad (k = 0, 1, 2)$$

where the subscript j refers to the group that is determined under the same set of assumptions as in the case of permanent income, and the subscript k refers to the stages in the life cycle. Finally, the weights which apply to the family size variables presented in the previous equations are:

$$w_0 = \sum_{t=0}^{4} \left[\frac{(1+\sigma)}{(1+\rho)}\right]^t \cdot \theta; \quad w_1 = \sum_{t=5}^{14} \left[\frac{(1+\sigma)}{(1+\rho)}\right]^t \cdot \theta;$$

$$w_2 = \sum_{t=15}^{19} \left[\frac{(1+\sigma)}{(1+\rho)}\right]^t \cdot \theta.$$

Embedding all of these assumptions into the model leads to an estimating equation for each expenditure function (in the initial period):

$$(8.14) \qquad v_{ih} = p_i \bar{\gamma}_{i0} - \beta_i^* \left(\sum_t \sum_i p_i \bar{\gamma}_{i0}\right) \cdot \theta + \lambda_i p_i \bar{\gamma}_{i0} (f_{h0} - 1)$$

$$+ \beta_i^* (1 - \lambda)(y_j^p) + \beta_i^* \lambda \left(\frac{y_{hj0}}{\bar{y}_{j0}} y_j^p\right)$$

$$- \left(\sum_i p_i \lambda_i \bar{\gamma}_{i0}\right) \beta_i^* \left[\sum_k w_k (f_{hk} - 1)\right] + e_{ih}$$

where the h subscript refers to the household.

9
Consumption and Savings Behavior of Farm Households in Yugoslavia

THIS CHAPTER EXAMINES the influences of income, location, and farm type on saving and consumption expenditures of farm households in Yugoslavia. The Institut za Ekonomika Poljoprivede in Belgrade conducts an extensive farm survey annually, and the data used here are drawn from the 1972 survey. As in previous chapters households are partitioned into mutually exclusive groups of homogeneous consumers. In this case they are cross-classified by three regions (Serbia, Voyvodina, and Kosovo) and seven farm types. Since regions tend to specialize in types of farms, several cells have relatively few entries. Only three farm types are common to each region: livestock, crop, and mixed farming. We restrict our analysis to the twelve cells which contain over 100 observations. These are listed in table 9.1, together with basic characteristics of the sample data. Again, ELES is fitted separately for each cell.

A six-commodity breakdown is used: food, clothing, housing, fuel and electricity, durables, and other. Housing is defined as repairs, additions, and improvements to houses; rent is not included. With this definition, expenditures on housing and durables are likely to exhibit similar patterns.

The definition of income is complicated for some groups of farm households by the importance of remittances from Yugoslavians working in neighboring countries. Preliminary analysis showed that the demand parameters made more sense when income included

227

Table 9.1. Basic Characteristics of Farm Household Survey, Yugoslavia, 1972

Region and farm type	Income[a]	Expenditure[b]	Average propensity to save[c]	Average budget shares[d]						Sample size	Average family size
				Food	Clothing	Housing	Fuel and electricity	Durables	Other		
Serbia	7,381	4,680	0.366	0.621	0.116	0.067	0.070	0.020	0.106	2,954	4.3
1.1 Livestock	7,557	5,044	0.333	0.611	0.104	0.089	0.067	0.020	0.109	659	4.0
1.2 Industrial crop	5,789	3,755	0.649	0.525	0.178	0.054	0.093	0.021	0.129	136	7.7
1.3 Vegetable	8,997	4,678	0.480	0.593	0.133	0.070	0.056	0.021	0.127	194	4.3
1.4 Vineyards	11,145	5,884	0.472	0.618	0.131	0.022	0.061	0.021	0.147	188	4.3
1.5 Crop	7,878	4,721	0.401	0.571	0.134	0.081	0.083	0.017	0.114	277	3.5
1.6 Mixed	6,676	4,446	0.334	0.648	0.109	0.061	0.070	0.020	0.092	1,500	4.2
Voyvodina	9,656	5,716	0.408	0.611	0.120	0.066	0.062	0.019	0.124	2,384	3.2
2.1 Livestock	10,077	6,133	0.391	0.593	0.120	0.081	0.061	0.027	0.119	382	3.2
2.5 Crop	6,575	5,137	0.219	0.606	0.106	0.087	0.065	0.015	0.121	517	3.0
2.6 Mixed	10,621	5,810	0.453	0.617	0.124	0.055	0.061	0.018	0.127	1,485	3.3
Kosovo	5,440	3,500	0.357	0.627	0.129	0.050	0.057	0.023	0.113	1,606	7.5
3.1 Livestock	4,936	3,676	0.255	0.598	0.128	0.051	0.053	0.030	0.140	181	5.9
3.5 Crop	5,511	3,281	0.405	0.616	0.147	0.034	0.068	0.022	0.113	153	8.2
3.6 Mixed	5,503	3,501	0.364	0.633	0.127	0.052	0.057	0.022	0.109	1,272	7.6
Average											
Livestock	7,957	5,182	0.349	0.603	0.113	0.082	0.063	0.024	0.116	1,168	4.0
Crop	6,784	4,715	0.305	0.597	0.119	0.079	0.071	0.016	0.118	947	4.0
Mixed	7,702	4,639	0.398	0.631	0.120	0.056	0.063	0.021	0.111	4,257	4.9

Source: Data for all tables in chapter 9 are drawn from computer tapes of the 1972 farm survey of the Institut za Ekonomika Poljoprivede, Belgrade.

a. Mean personal disposable income per capita in dinars a year (in 1972, 17 dinars = US$1.00).

b. Mean total consumption expenditure per capita in dinars a year.

c. Calculated as (Income − Expenditure)/Income.

d. Alcoholic beverages are included in food; cigarettes and tobacco in other. Housing is defined as repairs and improvements to houses.

foreign remittances, and the wider definition is used in the reported results.

Price information was not available, it is assumed that all consumers in a given group face the same prices. This is likely to be a very close approximation of actuality for two reasons: First, the households included in each group live in the same geographic area, and, second, home-produced consumption, which is quantitatively quite important here, is valued at common prices.

ELES Parameter Estimates

ELES estimates are obtained by fitting equation (2.26) to individual farm household data on per capita expenditures and per capita personal disposable income for the year 1972. The method of estimation is ordinary least squares, and we ignore correlation in the errors across equations (commodities), that is, we use error specification (2.32). Estimates of the basic ELES parameters (μ, β, γ^*) are given in tables 9.3 and 9.4, together with estimates of asymptotic standard errors. In presenting results, cells are ranked in order of increasing per capita disposable income. The values of the coefficient of determination, R^2, for both the individual commodity equations (2.26) and the aggregate consumption function (2.27) are given in table 9.2. The results exhibit the usual characteristics of analyses based on individual household observations: relatively low R^2 values, but high "t values" on parameters. The explanatory power of the model is highest for the category of food, where the mean value of R^2 is 0.34. Housing and durables exhibit the lowest R^2 values. There is some tendency for the degree of fit to be lower at higher income levels.

Marginal Propensity to Consume

Although the estimates of the marginal propensity to consume (μ) given in table 9.3 are all significantly larger than zero at the 5 percent level, they are numerically small, and there is a pronounced tendency for μ to fall as income rises. At the lowest income level μ equals 0.40, falling to around 0.20 at high-income levels. The low values reflect the failure to take account of permanent income, considerations which are likely to be important here because the economic activity is farming and because of foreign remittances to households. For only one group of farm households (cell 1.2), however, was the μ estimate raised substantially by the exclusion of foreign transfer income. In

Table 9.2. R² Values, ELES, Farm Households, Yugoslavia, 1972

Region and farm type[a]	Food	Clothing	Housing	Fuel and electricity	Durables	Other	Consumption function
3.1	0.507	0.294	0.104	0.280	0.111	0.047	0.547
3.6	0.447	0.105	0.033	0.182	0.020	0.091	0.395
3.5	0.549	0.123	0.138	0.200	0.070	0.116	0.536
1.2	0.131	0.084	0.001	0.148	0.001	0.115	0.130
2.5	0.417	0.137	0.000	0.133	0.005	0.121	0.131
1.6	0.304	0.172	0.056	0.127	0.064	0.056	0.382
1.1	0.353	0.227	0.033	0.158	0.034	0.154	0.374
1.5	0.206	0.165	0.089	0.096	0.032	0.078	0.276
1.3	0.359	0.345	0.000	0.306	0.022	0.076	0.246
2.1	0.238	0.102	0.007	0.311	0.065	0.045	0.205
2.6	0.260	0.126	0.006	0.092	0.006	0.053	0.179
1.4	0.274	0.142	0.015	0.027	0.001	0.143	0.311

[a] See table 9.1 for code.

Table 9.3. *Estimated Values of Marginal Budget Shares* (β_i) *and Marginal Propensity to Consume* (μ), *ELES, Farm Households, Yugoslavia, 1972*

Region and farm type[a]	Sample size	Income[b]	β Food	Clothing	Housing	Fuel and electricity	Durables	Other	μ
3.1	181	4,936	0.539 (0.030)	0.124 (0.014)	0.137 (0.027)	0.058 (0.007)	0.076 (0.015)	0.066 (0.021)	0.404 (0.024)
3.6	1,272	5,503	0.573 (0.017)	0.082 (0.007)	0.152 (0.020)	0.056 (0.004)	0.035 (0.007)	0.102 (0.009)	0.263 (0.008)
3.5	153	5,511	0.495 (0.032)	0.084 (0.107)	0.184 (0.032)	0.073 (0.012)	0.057 (0.016)	0.107 (0.022)	0.346 (0.022)
1.2	136	5,789	0.540 (0.104)	0.119 (0.038)	-0.037 (0.145)	0.186 (0.049)	-0.020 (0.047)	0.213 (0.058)	0.143 (0.029)
2.5	517	6,575	0.583 (0.056)	0.130 (0.018)	0.008 (0.088)	0.071 (0.010)	0.024 (0.015)	0.184 (0.025)	0.194 (0.019)
1.6	1,500	6,676	0.499 (0.016)	0.098 (0.006)	0.212 (0.018)	0.056 (0.004)	0.068 (0.007)	0.067 (0.007)	0.310 (0.010)
1.1	659	7,557	0.506 (0.024)	0.100 (0.008)	0.173 (0.031)	0.057 (0.006)	0.045 (0.009)	0.119 (0.011)	0.359 (0.017)
1.5	277	7,878	0.372 (0.039)	0.106 (0.016)	0.347 (0.047)	0.049 (0.010)	0.038 (0.013)	0.087 (0.018)	0.238 (0.020)
1.3	194	8,997	0.472 (0.048)	0.226 (0.028)	0.020 (0.072)	0.107 (0.015)	0.055 (0.026)	0.120 (0.029)	0.183 (0.018)
2.1	382	10,077	0.436 (0.044)	0.115 (0.019)	0.119 (0.068)	0.115 (0.013)	0.120 (0.023)	0.095 (0.022)	0.196 (0.019)
2.6	1,485	10,621	0.507 (0.026)	0.156 (0.012)	0.121 (0.037)	0.057 (0.005)	0.028 (0.009)	0.131 (0.014)	0.183 (0.009)
1.4	188	11,145	0.506 (0.046)	0.141 (0.025)	0.054 (0.031)	0.030 (0.013)	-0.010 (0.022)	0.278 (0.042)	0.219 (0.020)

Note: Asymptotic standard errors in parentheses.
a. See table 9.1 for code.
b. Mean personal disposable income per capita in dinars a year (in 1972, 17 dinars = US$1.00).

this cell foreign remittances amounted to 31 percent of total disposable income, the highest for any cell.

Regressing estimates of μ on the common logarithm of income, $\log y$, and excluding cell 1.2, we obtain:

$$\mu = \begin{array}{cc} 2.065 & - & 0.465 \ \log y \\ (0.580) & (0.150) \end{array} \qquad R^2 = 0.518 \quad \text{(unweighted)}$$

$$\mu = \begin{array}{cc} 1.632 & - & 0.356 \ \log y \\ (0.496) & (0.128) \end{array} \qquad \text{(weighted)}$$

where standard errors are given in parentheses, and the weights used in the second regression are the standard errors of the μ estimates in table 9.3. In both cases the income coefficients are significant at the 5 percent level. The weighted results imply that as per capita disposable income rises from 5,000 to 10,000 dinars the marginal propensity to consume falls from around 0.31 to around 0.21. Conversely, the average propensity to save, s, increases significantly with rising income. Using data from table 9.1, and excluding cell 1.2, the relevant regression equation is:

$$s = \begin{array}{cc} -1.560 & + & 0.498 \ \log y \\ (0.677) & (0.175) \end{array} \qquad R^2 = 0.475$$

The equation implies that as per capita income rises from 5,000 to 10,000 dinars the average propensity to save increases, on average, from 0.28 to 0.43.

Marginal Budget Shares

The estimated values of β_i given in table 9.3 are all positive, as required by the underlying utility function, except for three estimates. None of these negative values is significantly different from zero at the 5 percent level (see housing and durables in cell 1.2, durables in cell 1.4). Overall, 64 of the 72 estimates of β_i are significantly different from zero at the 5 percent level.

Strong patterns are not apparent in the β estimates, but the marginal budget share for food tends to decline with increases in income and that for clothing increases. Regressing these β values on the common logarithm of income yields:

$$\beta \ (\text{food}) = \begin{array}{cc} 1.366 & - & 0.224 \ \log y \\ (0.514) & (0.133) \end{array} \qquad R^2 = 0.221$$

$$\beta \ (\text{clothing}) = \begin{array}{cc} -0.513 & + & 0.165 \ \log y \\ (0.338) & (0.088) \end{array} \qquad R^2 = 0.262$$

Neither relationship is significant at the 5 percent level. In each of these regressions, however, the varying precision of the β estimates across cells is ignored. Weighting variables by the standard errors of the β_i, that is, assuming that the error term on each equation has variance given by $E(u_{ij}^2) = \sigma_i^2 \operatorname{var} \beta_{ij}$ $(i = 1, 2; j = 1, ..., 12)$, yields:

$$\beta \text{ (food)} = \underset{(0.458)}{1.433} - \underset{(0.119)}{0.240} \; \log y$$

$$\beta \text{ (clothing)} = \underset{(0.249)}{-0.562} + \underset{(0.065)}{0.174} \; \log y$$

Correcting for heteroscedasticity has clearly improved the efficiency of the estimation. The coefficient of income is now significant at the 5 percent level for clothing and at the 10 percent level for food. The weighted results imply that at per capita income levels of 5,000 dinars a year the marginal budget share for food is about 0.55, declining to around 0.47 at income levels of 10,000. The corresponding β values for clothing are 0.082, increasing to 0.134.

Subsistence Expenditures

All γ^* estimates in table 9.4 are positive except one—housing in cell 3.5—but the estimate is not significantly different from zero at the 5 percent level. Only 13 of the 72 γ^* estimates are not significantly different from zero, and these all occur for two commodities, housing and durables, which are nonessentials according to the definitions given above. Estimates of "subsistence" expenditure on food are particularly well determined.

Total subsistence expenditure (γ^* sum) is in each case significantly less than actual mean expenditure. It follows that the Frisch parameter (ω) always has the "correct" sign. Estimates of the Frisch parameter are concentrated around -4.0, except for the special case (cell 1.2) where foreign receipts are very important.

Estimates of subsistence expenditure on basic commodities increase with income. Double-log regressions were preferred here, and the results are contained in table 9.5. For food and the total, the coefficient of income is significantly different from zero but significantly less than one at the 5 percent level (for both weighted and unweighted regressions). This implies that food and total subsistence expenditures increase less than proportionally to increases in income. The weighted results imply that a one percent increase in income produces an increase in both food and total subsistence expenditures of 0.74 percent. Coincidentally, exactly the same figure is obtained

Table 9.4. Estimated Values of Subsistence Parameters (γ_i^*) and Frisch Parameter (ω), ELES, Farm Households, Yugoslavia, 1972

Region and farm type[a]	Total consumption expenditure[b]	γ^{*c}						γ^* sum	ω
		Food	Clothing	Housing	Fuel and electricity	Durables	Other		
3.1	3,676	1,736 (85)	366 (24)	71 (50)	146 (11)	46 (26)	458 (35)	2,821 (149)	−4.30
3.6	3,501	1,808 (29)	386 (9)	73 (31)	159 (4)	52 (9)	310 (12)	2,788 (56)	−4.91
3.5	3,281	1,564 (85)	387 (34)	−97 (73)	140 (22)	8 (31)	251 (45)	2,253 (172)	−3.19
1.2	3,755	1,789 (75)	627 (20)	215 (79)	287 (23)	84 (26)	414 (30)	3,415 (135)	−11.06
2.5	5,137	2,443 (64)	392 (26)	435 (152)	253 (14)	51 (26)	410 (40)	3,984 (210)	−4.46
1.6	4,446	2,380 (42)	388 (10)	58 (42)	255 (7)	18 (12)	342 (13)	3,441 (80)	−4.43
1.1	5,044	2,370 (79)	385 (18)	206 (88)	258 (12)	37 (21)	380 (26)	3,636 (165)	−3.58
1.5	4,721	2,330 (95)	526 (29)	43 (142)	344 (18)	41 (25)	453 (36)	3,737 (212)	−4.80
1.3	4,678	2,318 (78)	404 (37)	244 (113)	225 (19)	45 (41)	478 (48)	3,713 (185)	−4.85
2.1	6,133	3,216 (83)	626 (33)	383 (145)	261 (17)	47 (44)	637 (42)	5,171 (215)	−6.37
2.6	5,810	3,035 (41)	550 (18)	186 (70)	291 (8)	74 (15)	594 (24)	4,731 (102)	−5.38
1.4	5,884	2,889 (133)	561 (51)	49 (63)	315 (26)	140 (41)	455 (103)	4,409 (225)	−3.99

Note: Asymptotic standard errors in parentheses.
a. See table 9.1 for code.
b. Mean total consumption expenditure per capita in dinars a year.
c. In dinars per capita a year at 1972 prices (17 dinars = US$1.00).

Table 9.5.   *Double-Log Regressions of Subsistence Parameters*
on Income, Farm Households, Yugoslavia, 1972

Commodity	Unweighted			Weighted[a]	
	a	b	R^2	a	b
Food	0.436	0.755	0.825	−0.508	0.741
	(0.426)	(0.110)		(0.339)	(0.087)
Clothing	0.970	0.437	0.331	1.152	0.392
	(0.760)	(0.196)		(0.906)	(0.236)
Fuel and electricity	−0.518	0.748	0.481	−0.492	0.742
	(0.950)	(0.246)		(0.784)	(0.202)
Total subsistence	0.820	0.708	0.753	0.701	0.739
expenditure[b]	(0.495)	(0.128)		(0.329)	(0.085)

Note: Equations are of the form log γ = a + b log y. Twelve observations are used. Standard errors
are given in parentheses.
a. The appropriate weighting factor is now the inverse of the "t ratio."
b. The negative (and insignificant) estimate of γ (housing) in cell 3.5 has been placed equal to zero when
calculating total subsistence expenditure.

for fuel, although in this case the point estimate is not significantly
less than one. Subsistence expenditure on clothing shows some
tendency to increase with income, but the relation is significant only
in the unweighted regression. No relation was detected between income and subsistence expenditure on the remaining three goods—
housing, durables, and other—and the regressions are not reported.

After allowance is made for income effects, the only regional
pattern apparent in estimates of subsistence expenditures is one of
relatively high values for food and the total in Voyvodina. The
average propensity to consume also tends to be higher in this region,
however.

Total Expenditure and Price Elasticities

Total expenditure elasticities (η_i), calculated as in table 2.2, are
presented in table 9.6. In addition, average elasticities, weighted by
sample sizes, are given for each region and for the three farm types
common to each region. Patterns are similar to those observed for
the β estimates. Key features of the table are: (a) There is a fairly
constant value for the total expenditure elasticity for food at around
0.8, with an income elasticity around 0.3. (b) The expenditure
elasticity for clothing tends to increase with income, an effect that is
most pronounced in the average values for each region: 0.68 in the

Table 9.6. Total Expenditure Elasticities, ELES, Farm Households, Yugoslavia, 1972

Region and farm type[a]	Income level[b]	Total expenditure elasticities						
		Food	Clothing	Housing	Fuel and electricity	Durables	Other	η[c]
3.1	4,936	0.90	0.97	2.68	1.10	2.51	0.47	0.542
3.6	5,503	0.91	0.65	2.92	0.99	1.59	0.93	0.414
3.5	5,511	0.80	0.57	5.44	1.08	2.57	0.95	0.582
1.2	5,789	1.03	0.67	-0.69	1.99	-0.99	1.64	0.220
2.5	6,575	0.96	1.23	0.09	1.09	1.56	1.52	0.248
1.6	6,676	0.77	0.90	3.47	0.80	3.51	0.73	0.465
1.1	7,557	0.83	0.96	1.94	0.85	2.26	1.10	0.538
1.5	7,878	0.65	0.80	4.26	0.59	2.29	0.77	0.397
1.3	8,997	0.80	1.70	0.35	1.53	2.63	0.95	0.352
2.1	10,077	0.74	0.96	1.46	1.90	4.52	0.80	0.322
2.6	10,621	0.82	1.26	2.23	0.94	1.56	1.03	0.335
1.4	11,145	0.82	1.08	2.47	0.50	-0.49	1.89	0.414
Average								
Kosovo	5,440	0.90	0.68	3.13	1.01	1.78	0.88	0.444
Serbia	7,381	0.79	0.96	2.74	0.88	2.60	0.95	0.453
Voyvodina	9,656	0.84	1.21	1.64	1.13	2.03	1.10	0.314
Crop	6,784	0.84	1.00	2.17	0.94	1.94	1.21	0.346
Mixed	7,702	0.83	0.95	2.87	0.91	2.26	0.89	0.404
Livestock	7,957	0.81	0.96	1.90	1.22	3.00	0.91	0.471

a. See table 9.1 for code.
b. Mean personal disposable income per capita in dinars a year (in 1972, 17 dinars = US$1.00).

c. η = elasticity of total consumption expenditure with respect to income. Total income elasticities are obtained by multiplying total expenditure elasticities by the cell value of η.

236

Table 9.7. *Own-Price Elasticities and Elasticity of Average Savings Ratio with Respect to Food Price, ELES, Farm Households, Yugoslavia, 1972*

Region and farm type[a]	Income level[b]	Own-price elasticities						ξ (food)
		Food	Clothing	Housing	Fuel and electricity	Durables	Other	
3.1	4,936	-0.64	-0.32	-0.67	-0.30	-0.62	-0.17	-0.82
3.6	5,503	-0.65	-0.20	-0.66	-0.25	-0.35	-0.27	-0.67
3.5	5,511	-0.61	-0.26	-1.71	-0.42	-0.89	-0.40	-0.46
1.2	5,789	-0.58	-0.17	0.10	-0.33	0.11	-0.33	-0.75
2.5	6,575	-0.67	-0.37	-0.03	-0.30	-0.36	-0.46	-1.37
1.6	6,676	-0.59	-0.28	-0.83	-0.23	-0.81	-0.22	-0.74
1.1	7,557	-0.62	-0.34	-0.62	-0.28	-0.65	-0.39	-0.60
1.5	7,878	-0.46	-0.26	-0.93	-0.17	-0.50	-0.23	-0.56
1.3	8,997	-0.56	-0.50	-0.09	-0.39	-0.57	-0.29	-0.44
2.1	10,077	-0.50	-0.25	-0.32	-0.38	-0.74	-0.21	-0.66
2.6	10,621	-0.58	-0.35	-0.48	-0.22	-0.31	-0.30	-0.52
1.4	11,145	-0.61	-0.37	-0.64	-0.15	0.14	-0.62	-0.43
Average								
Kosovo	5,440	-0.65	-0.22	-0.76	-0.27	-0.43	-0.27	-0.67
Serbia	7,381	-0.58	-0.31	-0.69	-0.25	-0.63	-0.29	-0.65
Voyvodina	9,656	-0.59	-0.34	-0.36	-0.26	-0.39	-0.32	-0.73
Crop	6,784	-0.60	-0.32	-0.56	-0.28	-0.49	-0.38	-0.99
Mixed	7,702	-0.60	-0.28	-0.66	-0.23	-0.50	-0.26	-0.64
Livestock	7,957	-0.59	-0.31	-0.53	-0.31	-0.67	-0.30	-0.65

a. See table 9.1 for code.

b. Mean personal disposable income per capita in dinars a year (in 1972, 17 dinars = US$1.00).

237

Table 9.8. *Elasticity with Respect to Food Price and Clothing Price, ELES, Farm Households, Yugoslavia, 1972*

Region and farm type[a]	Income level[b]	Food price					Clothing price	
		Clothing	Housing	Fuel and electricity	Durable	Other	Housing	Durables
3.1	4,936	−0.46	−1.27	−0.52	−1.19	−0.22	−0.27	−0.25
3.6	5,503	−0.33	−1.51	−0.51	−0.82	−0.48	−0.32	−0.18
3.5	5,511	−0.27	−2.60	−0.51	−1.23	−0.45	−0.64	−0.30
1.2	5,789	−0.32	0.33	−0.95	0.47	−0.78	−0.33	0.12
2.5	6,575	−0.59	−0.04	−0.52	−0.74	−0.72	−0.01	−0.12
1.6	6,676	−0.48	−1.86	−0.43	−1.88	−0.39	−0.30	−0.12
1.1	7,557	−0.45	−0.91	−0.40	−1.06	−0.52	−0.15	−0.31
1.5	7,878	−0.39	−2.10	−0.29	−1.13	−0.38	−0.47	−0.17
1.3	8,997	−0.84	−0.17	−0.76	−1.31	−0.47	−0.03	−0.26
2.1	10,077	−0.50	−0.77	−0.99	−2.37	−0.42	−0.15	−0.23
2.6	10,621	−0.66	−1.16	−0.49	−0.82	−0.54	−0.21	−0.46
1.4	11,145	−0.53	−1.21	−0.24	0.24	−0.93	−0.24	−0.15
Average								
Kosovo	5,440	−0.34	−1.59	−0.51	−0.90	−0.45	−0.35	−0.20
Serbia	7,381	−0.48	−1.42	−0.44	−1.35	−0.48	−0.26	−0.23
Voyvodina	9,656	−0.62	−0.85	−0.58	−1.05	−0.56	−0.16	−0.19
Crop	6,784	−0.48	−1.06	−0.45	−0.93	−0.58	−0.25	−0.19
Mixed	7,702	−0.50	−1.51	−0.47	−1.19	−0.47	−0.27	−0.22
Livestock	7,957	−0.47	−0.92	−0.60	−1.49	−0.44	−0.17	−0.27

a. See table 9.1 for code.

b. Mean personal disposable income per capita in a year (in 1972, 17 dinars = US$1.00).

lowest income region, Kosovo; 0.96 in Serbia; increasing to 1.21 in the highest income region, Voyvodina. (c) The elasticity of total consumption expenditure with respect to income is higher for high-income farm types: 0.35 for crops, 0.40 for mixed, and 0.47 for livestock.

The price elasticities (η_{ij}) given in tables 9.7 and 9.8 are calculated using the formulas in table 2.2 which assume total expenditure constant. Table 9.7 also contains estimates of the elasticity of the average savings ratio with respect to food price (ξ_1) as defined in equation (2.12). Key features of table 9.7 are: (a) Of the 72 own-price elasticities (η_{ii}) only three have "incorrect" signs. The positive values occur for housing and durables in cell 1.2 and durables in cell 1.4, and they are associated with the negative but insignificant estimates of β_i in table 9.3. (b) There is remarkable stability in the own-price elasticities for food (around -0.6) and clothing (around -0.3). (c) The elasticity of the average savings ratio with respect to food price is higher in absolute terms for crop farming (-1.0), where mean incomes are lower.

Of the cross-price effects, those for food dominate and the elasticities (η_{i1}) are reported in full in table 9.8. In contrast to other findings in this book there is no tendency for the food cross-price elasticities to decline in magnitude as income levels rise. Changes in the price of clothing appear to have considerable influence on the demand for housing and durables (see last two columns of table 9.8) but not on the demand for food and fuel, where numerical values were generally less than 0.1 in absolute value and are not reported.

When the numerical values of the three key elasticities $(\eta_i, \eta_{ii}, \text{and } \eta_{i1})$ are compared the food cross-price elasticity (η_{i1}) is always close to half the total expenditure elasticity for all commodities (other than food). This substantial cross-price effect is more important than the own-price effect for all commodities (other than food). For the nonfood categories the average results show that own-price elasticities tend to be around one-third of total expenditure elasticities; for food the ratio is about three-quarters.

The dominant feature of the results is the stability in elasticities across groups of farm households, even though the mean income of the richest group is more than twice that of the poorest group. Since the β estimates also showed less than usual variation, it can be concluded that farm households in Yugoslavia are reasonably homogeneous with respect to demand behavior. Savings behavior, however, is influenced by income levels.

10
Summary and Conclusions

TIME-SERIES AND CROSS-SECTION data from a total of twenty-six countries spanning the development spectrum have been used to investigate demand and savings patterns. The aggregate time-series results provide broad measures of movements in demand and saving behavior as levels of per capita GNP rise. The results obtained using disaggregated cross-section data enable quantification of the effects of location, socioeconomic characteristics, and demographic features of households. While controlling for these attributes it is also possible to examine how demand and saving vary across households with per capita income levels and thus to establish a link with the aggregate time-series results.[1] The key findings for each of the measures of demand and savings responsiveness are summarized and discussed below. In all reported results the use of a dollar sign ($) in front of a value implies that the unit of measurement is 1970 U.S. dollars. All values are expressed on an annual basis.

Savings Responses

The most pronounced characteristic of the marginal propensity to save is that it is markedly larger for farmers. Estimates based on a time series of aggregate cross-section data for Korean farm house-

1. Aggregate time-series results for different countries may also be used to examine the influence of demographic factors (see Parks and Barten, 1973). When aggregate data are used, however, these effects are likely to be much more difficult to pick up than when using disaggregated cross-section data.

holds indicate a marginal propensity to save of 0.54. Similarly, dis-aggregated cross-section data for Yugoslavian farmers yield values of around 0.75. In contrast, rural households as a whole exhibit savings responses which are similar to those for urban households: The marginal propensity to save averages 0.11 among rural households in Mexico compared with 0.25 for urban households; for rural house-holds in Chile the values tend to be around 0.30, with slightly lower levels for comparable urban households.

It has been argued (especially in chapter 5) that the relative instability of farm income and the permanent income hypothesis of consumption behavior jointly imply that the marginal propensity to save out of current income is likely to be higher for farmers than for other socioeconomic groups distinguished in this study. Within the context of ELES it was also noted in chapter 5 that if farmers face higher interest rates than do other occupational groups this situation might be expected to produce a higher marginal propensity to save among farmers. The Latin American cities analyzed in chapter 7 offer the only other examples of a high marginal propensity to save be-ing associated with socioeconomic classes whose incomes are judged likely to have a high transitory component. There is no pronounced tendency for the marginal propensity to save to be high for self-employed households in Mexico and Chile.

Some permanent income effects are noticeable in the aggregate time-series results in chapter 3. Here the marginal propensity to save is positively associated with the rate of growth of income. Re-placing current income by various measures of permanent income in time-series analysis for Taiwan does not affect estimates of the long-run savings response. It is an open question as to how general this result is, although it is an encouraging finding because both in-come growth and the estimated marginal propensity to save out of current income are high for Taiwan, and the estimate of the long-run savings response might therefore be expected to be particularly sensitive to the income measures used.

Attempts (briefly referred to in chapters 7 and 8) at introducing measures of permanent income (other than those implicit in the socioeconomic classifications adopted) into the cross-section work yielded results, for the model as a whole, inferior to those obtained using current income. Nevertheless, transitory influences affect the cross-section estimates of savings behavior; for this reason, and because of the simplicity of our treatment, the results should be used circumspectly in predicting over time.

Other patterns in estimates of savings responses are less marked.

There is some tendency in the cross-section results for the marginal propensity to save to increase with income and age, but interaction effects are important here. In Chile, for example, it increases uniformly with income for old households (as defined by age of household head) but decreases uniformly for young households. In the four Latin American studies in chapter 7 the marginal propensity to save tends to increase with age in each socioeconomic stratum; only in Bogotá does it rise with socioeconomic stratum within a given age group.

A useful feature of ELES is that it permits estimation of the responsiveness of saving to changes in relative prices. Saving is found to be sensitive to the price of food, although this effect declines with income. The aggregate time-series results presented in chapter 4 suggest that at levels of GNP a head of between $100 and $500 the elasticity of the average savings ratio (and of total saving) with respect to the price of food (ξ_1) is around -1.8, declining to -0.3 at per capita GNP levels around $3,000. A decline with income is also evident in the cross-section results, although irregularities occur. In urban Mexico, for example, estimates of ξ_1 are centered around -1.3 at low income levels and around -0.4 at high income levels. Broadly comparable results are obtained for Yugoslavia, Chile, and the Latin American cities studied in chapter 7. Cross-section estimates for Korea range from -4.4 to -0.9, but these higher absolute values are to be expected given the lower income levels. There is thus broad consistency between the time-series and cross-section results. This is of particular interest since the latter were calculated without using price data.

Subsistence Expenditure

Estimates of the γ_i terms of ELES are consistent with an interpretation of these parameters as measuring subsistence consumption, but only in the sense of *perceived* minimum requirements. At low income levels the estimates more closely represent "subsistence" in the sense of that which is necessary to survive. In both the time-series and cross-section work the key overall findings for estimates of the γ parameters are: (a) They are almost always positive for the basic commodities of food, clothing, and shelter but are sometimes negative for nonnecessities such as durables. (b) They increase with income levels, but those for food and total subsistence decline relative to actual spending. (c) Total subsistence expenditure for large families is higher than for small, but on a per capita basis it tends to be less, confirming the presence of some scale economies in household consumption.

From the time-series results total subsistence or committed expenditure (γ sum) is estimated to be around 62 percent of GNP at per capita GNP levels of $100 to $500, but this falls to around 25 percent at levels of GNP per capita of about $2,500. Subsistence expenditure on food falls as a percentage of total subsistence expenditure from around 63 percent in the per capita GNP interval of $100 to $500, to 50 percent at higher levels.

Cross-section results suggest that the age of the household head is a relevant determinant of the γ estimates. There is evidence that in Mexico and the four South American cities studied in chapter 7 subsistence expenditure on durables is higher for young households (after allowance is made for other factors). In the South American cities young households also have a higher ratio of committed to actual expenditure than do older households.

The most detailed cross-section analysis of behavior of the γ parameters was undertaken for Mexico. Here socioeconomic class appears to be the key determinant of the γ estimates, and income adds nothing further to the explanation of their variation over household groups. The γ estimates appear to measure an acceptable minimum standard of consumption as perceived by households in a given socioeconomic class. These estimates (and those for other countries) might therefore provide some guide to minimum levels of private consumption in prudent economic planning.

Demand Responses to Income Changes

In fitting our linear model to any given body of data, marginal budget shares are assumed constant. By partitioning the data bodies into subgroups, however, it is possible to estimate sets of marginal budget shares (β)—in time-series analysis, for example, to arrive at separate estimates for countries at different income levels, or in cross-section analysis separate estimates for different socioeconomic groups. The empirical result that occurs with most frequency and strength is a fall in the marginal budget share for food as income levels rise. In the time-series results the marginal budget share for food in high-income countries is only half that for low-income countries: 0.39 for per capita GNP less than $500, 0.18 for per capita GNP over $1,500. The same phenomenon occurs in the cross-section studies. In Korea, which is typical, the marginal budget share for food declines from about 0.4 for low-income urban wage earners (also the estimate for farm households) to around 0.16 for high-income urban salary earners (the values are lower for large families). Since mean per capita disposable income for the high-income earners in Korea is always less than $400, the estimates for this group are lower than would be expected on the basis of the time-series results discussed above. For low-income rural households in Chile and Yugoslavia the food marginal budget share sometimes exceeds 0.5. There is no evidence, however, of specific rural-urban effects over and above those due to income differences.

The marginal budget share for clothing tends to be irregular, although in Korea and Yugoslavia there is some tendency for it to increase with income. In the time-series results it is highest at middle income levels, and in the cross-section studies there is some tendency for it to be higher for young households. When the time-series results are averaged for four income classes (table 3.11), the marginal budget share for clothing ranges from about 0.08 to 0.14. This spread encompasses the majority of estimates in each of the cross-section studies except Korea where the values are higher (up to 0.30 for young households in Seoul) and Guayaquil, Ecuador, where they tend to be lower.

Estimates of the marginal budget share for housing based on national accounts data increase with income, doubling from 0.12 at low levels of per capita GNP to 0.21 at high levels. Comparison of cross-section estimates is complicated by the different definitions used in the surveys studied. The only strong patterns occur in urban Mexico where, interestingly, 80 percent of the values fall in the range given above for the national accounts results (the definitions of housing are equivalent in both cases). In Mexico, the effect of income alone on housing's marginal budget share is negative, but estimates of this share are significantly higher in high-income Mexico City, and for given per capita income the values are lower for large families.

Only limited overall comparison of the results for durable goods may be made because of differences in definition and treatment. In chapter 8 (Chile), for example, durables are not included in consumption but are regarded as saving. In chapter 7 (South American cities) they are included in consumption, but estimates of the marginal budget share differ substantially across cities in a manner which is consistent with the purchase of durables as assets and a hedge against inflation. Both in the four South American cities and in Mexico those in high socioeconomic classes have a high propensity to spend on durables. In the four cities young families tend to spend more on durables at the margin than do old families, but this is not evident in Mexico. The time-series results show that the marginal budget share for household durables is lower for countries with per capita GNP below $500, but the marginal budget share for transport, which includes expenditure on motor vehicles, increases significantly with income levels over the whole development spectrum (doubling in value from 0.10 to 0.20).

The elasticities of demand with respect to total expenditure or income tend to be less dispersed than the corresponding estimates of the marginal budget shares, but weaker versions of the patterns outlined above for the β values are evident. In other words, since the expenditure elasticity is the ratio of the marginal to the average budget share, average budget shares tend to move in the same direction as marginal budget shares but less strongly.[2]

The expenditure elasticity for food derived from national accounts data declines with increases in per capita GNP, except that the mean value of 0.66 for the lowest income countries (GNP a head between $100 and $500) is less than the mean value of 0.82 obtained for countries in the next highest income range ($500 to $1,000); the average value in the highest income group (over $1,500 per capita GNP) is 0.50. In the Korean cross-section study the expenditure elasticity for food falls from about 0.90 to 0.45 as incomes rise; family size exerts a negative influence on the values. In Mexico the expenditure elasticity for food falls with income from about 0.85 to 0.45 for rural households and from about 0.75 to 0.30 for urban households, where incomes are above those in rural areas. For the South American cities studied in chapter 7, the values tend to vary inversely with socioeconomic class; two-thirds of the estimates lie in the range 0.6 to 1.0. Similar results are obtained for Chile. The cross-section results for farmers in Yugoslavia show a fairly constant value for the expenditure elasticity for food of around 0.8. Interestingly, the cross-section estimates conform broadly to those obtained by Clark (1957). Using mean data for different classes from prewar family budget studies in eleven countries, he fitted an average relationship which implies a decline in the value of the expenditure elasticity for food from 0.77 at per capita income levels of $100 to

2. The major exception is the time-series results for transport. There the average budget share increases markedly with income, leading to a fall in the total expenditure elasticity even though the marginal budget share increases with GNP per capita.

0.41 and 0.26 at income levels of $500 and $1,000 respectively.[3]

Time-series estimates of the expenditure elasticity for clothing tend to be above unity at middle income levels and below unity at both low and high income levels. However, if the low Korean figure of 0.66 in table 3.12 is replaced by the estimate of 1.42 obtained using a more recent time period[4] (table 5.15), then there is more of a tendency for the expenditure elasticity for clothing to fall uniformly with income. The cross-section results for Latin America exhibit a remarkable tendency for η_i values (clothing) near 1.1 to occur. This is the estimate for average values in both rural and urban Mexico and in Bogotá, Caracas, Guayaquil, and Lima individually when single estimates are obtained from nonpartitioned data. Korean cross-section estimates are higher—several estimates for urban households are around 2.0. In Yugoslavia the cross-section estimates show the expenditure elasticity for clothing increasing with income, averaging 0.7 in the low-income region and 1.2 in the high-income region.

Estimates of the expenditure elasticity of demand for housing tend to be centered on unity. The national accounts estimates average at 1.0; they display a weak tendency to increase with levels of GNP per capita, which becomes stronger if the lowest income countries are excluded. Estimates of the expenditure elasticity for housing in the four South American cities tend to be a little above unity, those in Mexico marginally below. In Chile nine of the twelve estimates lie below unity; the three above unity all relate to young households. In Mexico the estimates are higher in Mexico City and for those in the higher socioeconomic classes, but within these groups income appears to have a negative impact on the expenditure elasticity for housing.

The effects of income levels on estimates of the expenditure elasticities of demand for food, clothing, and housing are not as pronounced as those discerned by Russell (1967), who regressed Houthakker's (1957) cross-section estimates from different countries on per capita consumption and relative price. For each of the three goods Russell found that the expenditure elasticity declined significantly (at the one percent level) with increases in per capita consumption. The section of our formal analysis which is closest to that

---

3. These values are calculated from the equation reported in Clark (1957), p. 453, table V, using a conversion factor (kindly provided by Colin Clark) of one International Unit to US $2.76 (1970).

4. A change of this magnitude occurring in estimates as a result of changes in the estimation period is very atypical. It may be partly explained by the substantial changes in the Korean economy over the 1955–72 period.

of Russell is in chapter 3, where we regress time-series estimates of expenditure elasticities on per capita GNP. Although there are a number of reasons why these findings may differ from those of Russell—the obvious one of cross-section as against time-series estimates, different methods of converting to a common currency, different explanatory variables[5]—a contributing factor would seem to be that our values are estimated within the context of a demand system which satisfies the budget constraint, whereas the values used by Russell were estimated using a double-log model which does not satisfy such a constraint. In chapter 7 the expenditure elasticities derived from cross-section data for South America show less dispersion under ELES and are closer to unity than is the case for estimates obtained using a double-log formulation. Similarly, in Deaton's (1975) work using time-series data for the United Kingdom, there is a tendency for the expenditure elasticities calculated using LES to be closer to unity than those calculated using a double-log model.[6]

If systems estimates of expenditure elasticities tend to under-estimate their variation, this is not evident for the remaining commodity groups, which for convenience may be labeled "nonnecessities." In the time-series results expenditure elasticities for durables, personal care, transport, recreation, and other services nearly always exceed unity and for low-income countries are frequently around 2.0. The estimates for durables, transport, and recreation decline significantly (at the 5 percent level) as GNP per capita increases.

The nonnecessities are subdivided into fewer commodity groups in the cross-section work, but values of expenditure elasticities between 1.0 and 2.0 predominate, with higher values for durables than for services. In Mexico, estimates of the expenditure elasticities for durables are higher in Mexico City and positively related to socio-economic class; in Yugoslavia they are particularly high for livestock farmers, averaging 3.0.

Spending on durables and nonessential services may vary substantially from country to country (as, for example, when motives are affected by high rates of inflation in Latin America) and among different household types in a single country. More complicated

5. The price effect in Russell's analysis was never large and was significant (at the 5 percent level) only in his equation for clothing. It seems possible to rule this out as an explanation of the difference. Our use of GNP rather than consumption as an explanatory variable should have the effect of moving our findings toward those of Russell since private consumption tends to fall as a proportion of GNP as income levels rise.

6. See, in particular, Deaton (1975), figure 5.4, p. 72.

models and richer data would therefore be required to analyze more adequately the responsiveness of demand for nonnecessities to changes in income.

The Frisch Parameter and Overall Price Responsiveness

In his classic paper on demand analysis Frisch (1959) suggested that it would be extremely useful to construct a universal "atlas" of the values of the expenditure elasticity of the marginal utility of expenditure (ω) for different countries and for different types of population. These values would then be used judiciously, in the context of an additive utility model, to calculate own- and cross-price elasticities in situations where only expenditure elasticities were known. Frisch conjectured that the absolute value of ω would decline as incomes rise. More recently, Sato (1972) has emphasized the role of the inverse of the Frisch parameter, in directly additive models, as a measure of the overall elasticity of substitution and of the average price responsiveness of demand (as noted here in equation 2.4), although he still recognizes the important role played by ω or its inverse in linking price and expenditure responses. In keeping with the analysis in the rest of the book, this overview of our findings concentrates on estimates of ω rather than its inverse, which in the context of ELES and LES is ϕ, the negative of the supernumerary ratio. Clearly, statements about ω can be immediately transformed into statements about its inverse.

Estimates of ω from national accounts data have been discussed in some detail in chapter 4. There the relation between ω and GNP per capita in 1970 U.S. dollars, denoted by X, is:

$$(10.1) \qquad \omega \simeq -36\,X^{-0.36}.$$

The implied values of ω at different levels of GNP per capita are: -7.5 at \$100, -4 at \$500, -3 at \$1,000, and -2 at \$3,000. Thus at low income levels estimates of the Frisch parameter are much higher in absolute terms than the value of -2.0 which is frequently reported by others (and ourselves) for high-income countries.[7]

For cross-section results in Korea, the absolute values of ω tend to fall as incomes rise. The range for urban households is from -13.5 at the lowest level of per capita disposable income (around \$140 per year) to -5.3 at the highest income level (around \$330). These

7. For a summary of estimated values see Brown and Deaton (1972) and Sato (1972), p. 111.

estimates are higher in absolute value than the −4.9 predicted from equation (10.1). (Korean per capita GNP at the time of the household survey was about $250.) The results from using time series of Korean aggregate survey data suggest a specific farm effect on estimates of ω: $\hat{\omega} = -5.3$ for farm households and −6.8 for urban wage and salary earners. Since incomes are higher for urban households the obtained ranking is the reverse of that expected on the basis of income alone.

In all the cross-section studies for Latin America (chapters 6–8), some difficulties were experienced in obtaining reliable estimates of ω, particularly at low income levels where values frequently have the "wrong" (positive) sign.[8] Values of ω for rural areas in Mexico and Chile are unreliable, and a comparison of Latin American results must be confined to those for urban households. In Guayaquil estimates of ω decline in absolute value as incomes rise, but they are very low, lying between −1.0 and −2.0, if the one positive value is excluded, even though per capita GNP in Ecuador is only a little above the Korean figure. It should be borne in mind, however, that the mean income of sample households in Guayaquil is above the national average. In Bogotá and Lima the estimates straddle the values implied by equation (10.1) of −4.5 for Colombia and −4.0 for Peru, but no strong patterns emerge. The time-series relationship (10.1) implies a value of ω of −3.5 for Mexico and Chile (per capita GNPs around $620 and $650 respectively in the years of the sample surveys). In urban Mexico the cross-section results yield a median value of ω of −5.2 for per capita disposable incomes below about $800 a year, and a median value of −3.3 for incomes above this. In urban Chile values of ω range from −7.1 at low incomes to −2.1 at high; the income effect is most pronounced when young households are considered separately. Thus the cross-section results for Mexico and Chile are consistent with the value expected on the basis of time-series estimates for other countries. The remaining set of Latin American estimates of ω are those for Caracas. They show, for the two age classes considered separately, a decline in the absolute value of ω as incomes rise. The overall estimate of −4.2 compares with an implied value of −3.1 from equation (10.1) (per capita GNP in year of survey was around $890).

8. Note from the definition of ω (equations 2.7 and 2.4) that as $\Sigma p_i \hat{\gamma}_i$ approaches v from below, $\hat{\omega}$ becomes large negative, changing to large positive for $\Sigma p_i \hat{\gamma}_i > v$. Thus in many cases positive values of ω are not significantly different from the (large) negative values of ω expected at low-income levels.

From equation (10.1) the expected value of ω for Yugoslavia is -3.5, the same as for Mexico and Chile. Cross-section estimates show no marked patterns, but the median value of -4.6 is not inconsistent with the predicted value since the cross-section results refer only to farm households. Unlike Korea, Yugoslavia offers no evidence of a specific farm effect on estimates of ω.

Overall, then, the Frisch conjecture of a negative relation between $-\omega$ and income is supported. In fact, the estimated relation is not only negative but also relatively stable. The cross-section evidence is in general agreement with the relation between the expenditure elasticity of the marginal utility of expenditure and the level of income which was established using national accounts data. The applicability of this result is enhanced by the fact that the countries included in these two data sets are disjunct (except for Korea). The cross-section analysis suggests that factors other than income are, in general, of much less importance in influencing estimates of ω. Finally, it follows from considering estimates of the inverse of ω that demand, both within and between countries, is much more responsive to prices at high income levels, where there is a wider latitude of choice in decisions to purchase.

Specific Price Effects

The underlying theoretical model requires that own-price elasticities (η_{ii}) be negative. In general our estimates satisfy this condition, with the exception of cross-section values for lower income families in Mexico and in Bogotá and Lima. In the time-series analysis only one out of the 134 estimates of own-price elasticities is positive. This represents a major improvement on the results obtained by Weisskoff (1971) who, working outside a demand systems framework and using a double-log model and data from sixteen low- and middle-income countries, obtained positive own-price elasticities in 28 percent of the cases. Within LES and ELES, however, price effects depend very heavily on model specification, on estimated income effects, and on the estimated Frisch parameter. Patterns perceived in price elasticities, therefore, inevitably reflect to a substantial extent the patterns already discussed in the previous two sections.

In our cross-section study of urban households in Korea no positive values of η_{ii} occur; in Chile only one out of 36 η_{ii} estimates are positive, while in Yugoslavia three out of 72 are positive. For urban Mexico 90 percent of own-price elasticities are negative; but, with the exception of own-price elasticities for food, rural estimates are unsatisfactory for two reasons. First, positive values occur because estimates of subsistence expenditure exceed mean actual expenditure; and, second, in two household groups the γ parameters and own-price elasticities are not identifiable because estimates of the marginal propensity to consume are very close to one. The latter problem was also encountered in obtaining estimates for one household group in Guayaquil, but otherwise all η_{ii} estimates are negative in that city, as are all but three of the 35 estimates for Caracas. In both Bogotá and Lima about one-third of own-price elasticities are positive. The positive values are concentrated in the commodity groupings of durables and clothing (which includes personal effects), and none occur in the high socioeconomic stratum. It is argued in chapter 7 that the positive values may reflect the high rates of inflation in Bogotá and Lima in the years immediately preceding the household surveys. Taken as a whole, however, the results of the cross-section studies indicate that our model has been reasonably successful in providing estimates of own-price elasticities with the correct sign from data on income and expenditures only.

Consistent with the finding that overall price effects are more important at high levels of income, the time-series results reported in chapter 3 show that for most commodities own-price elasticities increase in absolute value as per capita GNP rises. The increases are significant at the 5 percent level for housing, personal care, and transport, and at the 10 percent level for other services. The notable exception to this phenomenon is the own-price elasticity for food, which is relatively stable.

Among the cross-section estimates of own-price elasticities, those for urban Mexico and the four South American cities show a clear tendency for all own-price elasticities to increase in absolute value as incomes rise (see, in particular, tables 6.11 and 7.16). Few clear patterns are evident, however, in the other cross-section studies. In Yugoslavia, for example, each set of own-price elasticities shows remarkable uniformity across types of farm households. In urban Korea the own-price elasticity for fuel and light appears to increase in absolute size with household income, but the reverse is true for the own-price elasticity for food. The phenomenon of $-\eta_{11}$ (food) decreasing in value as incomes rise is also observed for rural families in Chile, particularly among old households.

The following summary of point estimates of own-price elasticities is limited to the important categories of food, clothing, and housing. The mean value of the own-price elasticity for food based on national accounts data is —0.47. This compares, for example, with mean values of —0.32 for urban wage earners and —0.18 for urban salary earners derived from Korean cross-section data, and —0.46 for Korean farm households from a time-series of aggregate survey data. Mean values of η_{11} (food) from other cross-section studies are: —0.59 for Yugoslavian farmers, —0.31 for rural and —0.27 for urban households in Mexico, and —0.45 and —0.50 for rural and urban households in Chile. Averaging results for the cities of Bogotá, Caracas, and Lima yields a range of from —0.14 for the low socioeconomic class to —0.29 for the high socioeconomic class, but these values are not strictly comparable with the other results. They are estimates of $\tilde{\eta}_{11}$ rather than η_{11}, that is, they are calculated on the assumption that income rather than total expenditure is held constant.

The national accounts estimates of the own-price elasticity of demand for clothing exhibit a marked jump at per capita GNP levels of around $500. Below this income level the average is —0.30, whereas above this level the average is —0.52. Mean values of η_{22} (clothing) from household survey data are: urban Korea, —0.37; Korean farmers, —0.32; urban Mexico, —0.37; and Yugoslavian farmers, —0.31. These estimates show considerable uniformity and are consistent with the time-series results. The values of $\tilde{\eta}_{22}$ (clothing) for Latin American cities corresponding to those given above for $\tilde{\eta}_{11}$ (food) range from —0.09 for the low socioeconomic group to —0.35 for the high socioeconomic group.

The regression equation developed in chapter 3 from national accounts estimates of the own-price elasticity for housing (see table 3.18) implies an increase in $-\eta_{33}$ (housing) from 0.29 at a per capita GNP level of $200 a year to around 0.65 at $2,000. The cross-section studies for Mexico and the four South American cities use a definition of housing corresponding to that used in the national accounts. In both these cross-section studies the demand for housing becomes more responsive to changes in its price as incomes rise, and the point estimates are broadly comparable with those obtained using time-series data. In urban Mexico the mean value of η_{33} (housing) for the poorest third of households (as measured by per capita disposable income) is —0.23, compared with —0.49 for the richest third. Values of $\tilde{\eta}_{33}$ (housing) for the cities of Bogotá, Caracas, and Lima, averaged by socioeconomic class, range from —0.15 for the low stratum to —0.47 for the high stratum. In Chile the housing category includes only rent, but there are no clear patterns in estimates of the own-price elasticity; mean values are —0.23 for rural households and —0.38 for urban households.

Cross-price effects can, in principle, be of either sign, but positive values rarely occur in our analyses. This is to be expected since we consider only broad commodity groups—the income effect dominates the substitution effect. In both the time-series and cross-section results the dominant cross-price effects are those related to the price of food. Particularly at low levels of income the average budget share for food is relatively large and therefore the income effect of any change in its relative price is also large.

The national accounts results show a clear tendency for cross-elasticities with respect to the price of food, η_{i1}, to decline in absolute value as the level of per capita GNP rises. The falls are all significant at the 5 percent level except for housing. If housing is excluded, mean values at the highest income levels (per capita GNP over $1,500) range from one-half (personal care and other services) to one-quarter (durables and recreation) of the mean values at low income levels ($100 to $500). Average estimates of η_{i1} at these low levels of per capita GNP range from a moderate -0.46 and -0.54 for clothing and housing respectively to a high -1.01 and -1.25 for durables and transport.

In the cross-section study for Mexico the absolute values of η_{i1} decline significantly as incomes increase. Mean estimates for urban households are -0.37 for clothing, -0.32 for housing, and -0.43 for durables; values for rural households, where mean incomes are much lower, are nearly double those for urban consumers. Estimates of η_{i1} in urban Mexico also tend to be lower in absolute value for large families. Average values for the four South American cities show that each cross-elasticity with respect to food price, $\tilde{\eta}_{i1}$, declines in magnitude by about half in moving from the low to the middle socioeconomic stratum, and halves again in moving to the high socioeconomic stratum (see table 7.19). The ranges for clothing, housing, and other are very similar—from about -0.5 to -0.1—whereas the values for durables are a little higher in absolute value. Mean values of $\tilde{\eta}_{i1}$ for a given city are relatively constant across commodities but differ across cities in a fairly consistent manner. Absolute values are much lower in high-income Caracas than in Bogotá and Lima, as expected, but the values for low-income Guayaquil are unexpectedly similar to those for Caracas. A non-income effect is also observed: Values of $-\tilde{\eta}_{i1}$ tend to be larger for young households. In the cross-section results for Korea and Chile there is only a weak tendency for estimates of $-\tilde{\eta}_{i1}$ to fall as incomes rise. Estimates for Yugoslavian farm households are irregular and no clear patterns emerge.

Comparison of the Magnitudes of
Expenditure and Price Elasticities

It follows from the homogeneity property of the model that for a given commodity the expenditure elasticity is equal in magnitude to the sum of the price elasticities. Our empirical results show that in comparing the relative magnitudes of elasticities it is useful to partition the consumption categories into food and nonfood. In the time-series analysis of chapter 3, for example, the own-price elasticity for food is relatively stable at around three-quarters of the expenditure elasticity at all levels of per capita GNP. For the nonfood categories own-price elasticities vary considerably as a proportion of the expenditure elasticity, but the proportion has a tendency to be similar for different commodities at a given level of per capita GNP, and the sum of the own-price and the food-price cross-elasticity is relatively stable at around three-quarters. Thus for all commodities the nonfood cross-price elasticities tend to be about one-quarter the magnitude of expenditure elasticities, except at high levels of GNP per capita (over $1,500) where they fall to around one-fifth. To facilitate comparison with cross-section results we note that own-price elasticities for commodities other than food are around one-quarter of expenditure elasticities at per capita GNP levels of $100 to $500, rising to nearly one-half at income levels of between $500 to $1,000. Conversely, the ratio of the food-price cross-elasticities to the expenditure elasticities (our model forces them to be the same for each good) falls from 50 to 27 percent over the same income range.

At the individual cell level in the cross-section studies the ratios of price elasticities to expenditure elasticities are much more irregular than was the case with the national accounts estimates. In a number of cross-section studies, however, the food own-price elasticity is around half the expenditure elasticity for food; this is the case for urban households in Mexico (at mean values) and Korea, and for farm households in Yugoslavia. For Korean farmers the ratio is 60 percent; values in both rural and urban Chile tend to be higher but they exhibit substantial variation; estimates for Yugoslavian farmers tend to be around 75 percent and are therefore closest to the national accounts findings. For urban households in Korea the food-price cross-elasticity tends to be about one-third of the corresponding expenditure elasticity in the case of salary earners and 40 percent for wage earners; there is no pronounced tendency for the ratio of η_{ii} to η_i to be constant across commodities. The Mexican results are irregular at the individual cell level but at mean values for urban households the own-price elasticity, the food-price cross-elasticity, and the sum of the remaining (nonfood) cross-price elasticities are each about one-third of the total expenditure elasticity for all commodities other than food. The estimates for Yugoslavian farm households show greatest uniformity across cells; for each of the nonfood categories the own-price elasticity tends to be around one-third of the expenditure elasticity, whereas the food-price cross-elasticity is always about one-half. These food cross-price effects are higher than those obtained for other cross-section studies and are similar to the national accounts estimates for low-income countries.

At the disaggregate level the results for the four South American cities tend to be irregular, but a few remarks can be made. In Guayaquil the ratio of the own-price to income elasticity for food tends to be around 75 to 80 percent, but in the other cities it averages around 50 percent. On the basis of aggregate data for each city, food cross-price effects are most pronounced in Bogotá, where these elasticities approach 50 percent of the income elasticities; in Guayaquil and Caracas the ratio is only around 20 percent; in Lima it is 36 percent. Again with aggregate data, Guayaquil is the only case in which own-price elasticities tend to be the same proportion (around 75 percent) of income elasticities for all goods—clearly all cross-price effects are small here.

In summary, the cross-section results tend to lie halfway between those obtained for the two lowest income groups in the national accounts analysis (per capita GNP $100 to $500 and $500 to $1,000 a year), except that the own-price elasticity for food is a lower proportion of the expenditure elasticity. The only exception to this general finding is Yugoslavia, where the cross-section results correspond to those obtained for the lowest income class. There is only limited support for Deaton's (1974, 1975) claim that additive models in general, and LES in particular, restrict the ratios of own-price to expenditure elasticities to be the same for all goods. It seems that this potential limitation of the model is less important at the relatively high levels of aggregation (three to eight commodities) considered in this book. Certainly the restriction does not hold for a food-nonfood breakdown of consumption, the subdivision which we regard as most crucial at low and middle income levels.

Consumer Disaggregation

National accounts (time-series) data were used in chapters 3 and 4 to provide estimates of demand and savings behavior on the basis of a single representative consumer in each of the seventeen countries studied. In subsequent chapters the behavior of sets of representative consumers was studied by using household survey data for eight countries with per capita GNP below $1,000, only one of which was included in the time-series analysis. In previous sections of this chapter the results obtained from the cross-section studies were noted to be in general conformity with those obtained from the national accounts, at least after the characteristics of special groups such as farmers are taken into consideration. There seems to exist considerable uniformity in demand and savings behavior.

Korea is the only country for which estimates are derived from both national accounts and household survey data. Although the sample surveys do not cover the whole population, a time series of aggregate survey data for urban wage and salary earners was available together with disaggregated data on individual urban households for one time period. In chapter 5 the results obtained for six representative consumers in the detailed cross-section analysis are aggregated and compared with those obtained using the time series of the aggregate survey data. Estimates of expenditure and own-price elasticites are similar in 60 percent of the cases. The exceptions are the expenditure elasticities for food, fuel and light, and housing and the own-price elasticity for housing; but in all four cases the results obtained by aggregating the estimates from the cross-section results are closer to the estimates obtained using national accounts data than are results from the time series of aggregate cross sections.[9] The weakness of the cross-section analysis for Korea is that on aggregation it yields a comparatively low estimate for the marginal propensity to consume.

Within countries with per capita GNP below $1,000 where do the greatest differences in demand and savings behavior occur? It has long been recognized that the savings behavior of farmers differs substantially from that of other types of consumers, and the difference is clearly confirmed here. There is also some evidence (from Korea) that consumption behavior of farmers differs from that of urban consumers. According to our results, however, nonfarm rural households do not seem to differ appreciably from urban households in

9. In Korea the subgroups each yielded acceptable point estimates of parameters and elasticities. Compare these results with those reported for Chile in chapter 8, where one rural subgroup contained a positive own-price elasticity which was carried through in aggregating over socioeconomic class, but which was not present when the model was fitted to less stratified cross-section data.

either savings or consumption behavior once income differences have been allowed for.

All our cross-section studies suggest that some classification by socioeconomic class is very important, much more so than a classification by income. A comparison of results for Latin America (chapters 6–8) suggests that it is probably preferable to classify according to the economic function of the family head (wage earner, salary earner, entrepreneur), as was done in Mexico and Chile, rather than by a proxy for permanent income (such as housing standards), as was done in the four Latin American cities, at least if current income is to be the explanatory variable in the model.

Age of household is also quite important: Demand and savings patterns tend to become clearer when age is held constant. Throughout the book we have incorporated the age variable by a simple two-way classification of families into young and old. If enough data (and computer time!) are available, further disaggregation would seem to be desirable.

When cross-section estimates are obtained for families of different sizes the greatest differences occur in the γ parameters. Thus the effects of family size may be conveniently incorporated directly into the estimating equations as was done in chapters 7 and 8. This approach seems called for once categorization goes beyond a simple subdivision into small and large households. There is some evidence from Korea and Mexico of the effect of urban size as well: Demand patterns in large metropolises seem to be different from those in small urban concentrations, even after income differences are allowed for.[10] Because Seoul and Mexico City are two of the largest cities in the less developed world, however, it would be rash to generalize.

Future Research

Directions for future research lie in three main areas: widening the data base and estimation framework, extending the theoretical model, and incorporating the results into economywide models.

Although our national accounts data for low-income countries were confined to east Asia, this limitation was overcome to some extent by the cross-section analysis which included six Latin American countries and one from eastern Europe. The most noticeable remain-

10. Howe (1974), chapter 5, finds significant differences in LES estimates for cities of different sizes (Bogotá, Barranquilla, and Medellín) in Colombia.

ing gap in the coverage is Africa, and the analysis should be extended to countries from this continent as suitable national accounts and household survey data become available. It would also be desirable to undertake cross-section work with data from developed countries to see to what extent results are consistent with our time-series findings.

In searching for demand and savings patterns we deliberately refrained from pooling data from different countries. If demand and savings responses vary substantially across countries, then simple pooling of data from different countries is likely to produce serious specification error, especially in the context of a model such as ELES, which is only mildly nonlinear and is parsimonious in its use of parameters. In addition, there are difficulties in converting incomes and prices to common units of measurement (which admittedly applies to the international comparison of incomes made in this book). Now that estimates for individual countries have been obtained and certain patterns in demand and savings behavior noted, however, a judicious pooling of data (including time-series and cross-section data) would be possible which would provide statistically more efficient estimates. The recent work of Kravis and others (1975) on international price comparisons would facilitate conversion of income and price data.

The main theoretical weakness of our model appears to lie in its fairly simple treatment of the allocation of consumption over time. Certainly the empirical results were poorest when they related to the consumption-saving choice. The model proved inadequate to explain demand and savings behavior of those household groups with negative mean saving; estimates of the marginal propensity to consume were particularly low in several cross-section studies; and estimates of own-price elasticities for durables in Latin American cities were frequently positive. Although the limited attempts to consider permanent income in the empirical work did not improve results, further work in this area is warranted. Also important for extending the range of the analytical framework would be explicit attention to the integration of production and consumption decisions by the self-employed; in particular, the basis of the savings function should be broadened to incorporate investment decisions. A promising attempt to extend the model to deal specifically with durable goods has recently been made by Dixon and Lluch (1975). Finally, a further useful extension of the model not implemented in this monograph is Lluch's (1974b) introduction of habit formation, with the consequent dynamization of the model.

Although the assumption of direct additivity does not appear to have been excessively restrictive at the level of aggregation used in this book, extension of the empirical work to a more detailed breakdown of commodities would require a more general utility specification. The task is a difficult one, however. Even in atemporal analysis, much remains to be done in estimating at fine levels of disaggregation within a systems approach.[11]

Economywide development models require, for their closure, the detailed specification of links between the input-output framework, the functional distribution of income, the personal distribution of income, and personal saving and consumption expenditures. A growing concern in the literature of development economics is how to achieve growth and simultaneously improve the equity of income distribution in less developed countries (Chenery and others, 1974). Changes in the distribution of income must be expected to change the consumption and savings patterns typical of consuming units in a developing country. It is hoped that the present work will give guidance on the likely magnitude of these changes in demand and saving and hence facilitate realistic modeling of the consumption-induced feedback from projected changes in the income distribution. Although work on detailed economywide models is proceeding within the World Bank and elsewhere (Norton, 1975; Adelman and Robinson, 1975), only limited experience is available so far. In the meantime, experimentation with simple economywide models such as those of Kelley, Williamson, and Cheetham (1972, 1974) and Lluch's extension thereof (1974a) would seem to be warranted. These models are extremely highly aggregated with respect to both commodity split-up (food-nonfood) and classes of households (rural-urban). Without sacrificing the simplicity of the two-way commodity split, our parameter estimates could be used for experimentation with a finer disaggregation of consumer types in order to put orders of magnitude on the potential importance of disaggregation by consumers for the behavior of quantitative development models.

11. For recent major advances in this area, see Brown and Heien (1972), Christensen and Manser (1975, 1977), and Manser (1975).

Bibliography

Adelman, I., and S. Robinson. 1975. A wage and price endogenous general equilibrium model of a developing country: Factors affecting the distribution of income in the short run (restricted circulation document). Washington, D.C.: The World Bank. Forthcoming as *Income distribution policy in developing countries* (Stanford: Stanford University Press, 1977).

Aigner, D. 1974. An appropriate framework for estimating a labor supply function from the SEO file. *International economic review*, 15: 59–68.

Allen, R. G. D., and A. L. Bowley. 1935. *Family expenditures*. London: Staple Press.

Ando, A., and F. Modigliani. 1957. Test of the life cycle hypothesis of savings. *Bulletin of the Oxford University Institute of Statistics*, 19: 99–124.

Balassa, B. 1973. Just how misleading are official exchange rate conversions? A comment. *Economic journal*, 83: 1258–67.

———. 1974. The rule of four-ninths: A rejoinder. *Economic journal*, 84: 609–14.

Bard, Y. 1967. Nonlinear parameter estimation and programming. IBM Contributed Program Library 360D–13.6.003.

Barten, A. P. 1964. Family composition, prices and expenditure patterns. In *Econometric analysis of national economic planning*, ed. P. E. Hart and others. Proceedings of the 16th Symposium of the Colston Research Society. London: Butterworths.

————. 1968. Estimating demand equations. *Econometrica*, 36: 213–51.

————. 1969. Maximum likelihood estimation of a complete set of demand equations. *European economic review*, 1: 7–73.

————. 1974. Complete systems of demand equations: Some thoughts about aggregation and functional form. *Recherches économiques de Louvain*, 40: 1–18.

————. 1975. The systems of consumer demand approach: A review. Paper presented at Third World Congress of Econometric Society, Toronto, Canada.

Belandria, F. 1971. An empirical study of consumer expenditure patterns in Venezuelan cities. Ph.D. dissertation, Northwestern University.

Berndt, E. R., and N. E. Savin. 1975. Estimation and hypothesis testing in singular equation systems with autoregressive disturbances. *Econometrica*, 43: 937–58.

Betancourt, R. R. 1971a. Intertemporal allocation under additive preferences: Implications for cross-section data. *Southern economic journal*, 37: 458–68.

————. 1971b. The normal income hypothesis in Chile. *Journal of the American Statistical Association*, 66: 258–63.

————. 1973a. Household behaviour in a less developed country: An econometric analysis of Chilean cross-section data. College Park, Md.: Department of Economics, University of Maryland.

————. 1973b. The analysis of patterns of consumption in under-developed countries. Paper presented to the ECIEL Conference on Consumption, Prices, and Economic Development, Hamburg, West Germany. In *Consumption, prices, and economic development*, ed. R. Ferber. Washington, D.C.: Brookings Institution, forthcoming.

Blitzer, C. R. 1975. Development and income distribution in a dual economy: A dynamic simulation model for Zambia (restricted circulation document). Washington, D.C.: Development Research Center, The World Bank.

Blitzer, C. R., P. B. Clark, and L. Taylor, eds. 1975. *Economy-wide models and development planning*. London: Oxford University Press.

Bridge, J. L. 1971. *Applied econometrics*. Amsterdam: North-Holland.

Brown, A., and A. Deaton. 1972. Surveys in applied economics: Models of consumer behaviour. *Economic journal*, 82: 1145–1236.

Brown, M., and D. Heien. 1972. The S-branch utility tree: A generalization of the linear expenditure system. *Econometrica*, 40: 737–47.

Brown, T. M. 1952. Habit persistence and lags in consumer behaviour. *Econometrica*, 20: 355–71.

Buse, A. 1973. Goodness of fit in generalized least squares estimation. *The American statistician*, 27: 106–08.

Byron, R. 1974. Empirical demand analysis: An informational approach. Paper presented at the Fourth Conference of Economists, Canberra, Australia.

Carlevaro, F. 1971. Formulation et estimation des fonctions de consommation semi-agrégées. *Canadian journal of economics*, 4: 441–70.

Carlevaro, F., and E. Rossier. 1970. Le Programme LINEX pour l'estimation des paramètres du système linéaire de dépenses. Geneva: Centre d'économétrie, University of Geneva.

Cheetham, R. J., A. C. Kelley, and J. G. Williamson. 1974. Demand, structural change, and the process of economic growth. In *Nations and households in economic growth*, ed. P. A. David and M. W. Reder. New York and London: Academic Press.

Chenery, H. B. 1960. Patterns of industrial growth. *American economic review*, 50: 624–54.

———. 1965. The process of industrialization. Paper presented to the First World Congress of the Econometric Society, Rome.

———, ed. 1971. *Studies in development planning*. Cambridge: Harvard University Press.

———. 1975. The structuralist approach to development policy. *American economic review*, 65: 310–16.

Chenery, H. B., and W. J. Raduchel. 1971. Substitution in planning models. In *Studies in development planning*, ed. H. B. Chenery. Cambridge: Harvard University Press.

Chenery, H. B., and others. 1974. *Redistribution with growth*. London: Oxford University Press.

Chenery, H. B., and M. Syrquin. 1975. *Patterns of development, 1950–1970*. London: Oxford University Press.

Christensen, L. R., and M. E. Manser. 1975. Cost of living indexes and price indexes for U.S. meat and produce, 1947–1971. In *Household production and consumption*, ed. N. E. Terleckyj. New York: National Bureau of Economic Research. Studies in income and wealth, no. 40.

————. 1977. Estimating U.S. consumer preferences for meat with a flexible utility function. *Journal of econometrics,* 5: 37–53.

Clark, C. 1940; 3d ed. 1957. *The conditions of economic progress.* London: Macmillan.

Clements, K., M. Evans, D. S. Ironmonger, and A. A. Powell. 1975. A linear expenditure system with adjustment costs. Paper presented at Third World Congress of Econometric Society, Toronto.

Clower, R. 1965. The Keynesian counter-revolution: A theoretical appraisal. In *The theory of interest rates,* ed. F. M. Hahn and F. P. R. Brechling. London: Macmillan.

David, P. A. 1972. Just how misleading are official exchange rate conversions? *Economic journal,* 82: 979–90.

————. 1973. A reply to Professor Balassa. *Economic journal,* 83: 1267–76.

Deaton, A. S. 1974. A reconsideration of the empirical implications of additive preferences. *Economic journal,* 84: 338–48.

————. 1975. *Models and projections of demand in post-war Britain.* London: Chapman and Hall.

de Janvry, A., J. Bieri, and A. Nuñez. 1972. Estimation of demand parameters under consumer budgeting: An application to Argentina. *American journal of agricultural economics,* 54: 422–30.

Dhrymes, P. J. 1970. *Econometrics.* New York: Harper and Row.

Dixon, P. B. 1975. *The theory of joint maximization.* Amsterdam: North-Holland.

Dixon, P. B., and C. Lluch. 1975. Durable goods and the theory of consumer demand (restricted circulation document). Washington, D.C.: Development Research Center, The World Bank.

Duloy, J. H., and R. D. Norton. 1973. CHAC, a programming model of Mexican agriculture. In *Multi-level planning: Case studies in Mexico,* ed. L. M. Goreux and A. S. Manne. Amsterdam: North-Holland.

ECIEL. 1974. P. A. Musgrove, ed. Urban household income and consumption patterns in Latin America. Washington, D.C.: Estudios Conjuntos sobre Integración Económica Latinoamericana, mimeographed.

Evans, M. 1969. *Macroeconomic activity.* New York: Harper and Row.

Fama, E. F., and M. H. Miller. 1972. *The theory of finance.* New York: Holt, Rinehart and Winston.

Fisher, I. 1930. *The theory of interest.* New York: Macmillan.

Friedman, M. 1935. Professor Pigou's method for measuring elasticities of demand from budgetary data. *Quarterly journal of economics,* 50: 151–63.

———. 1957. *A theory of the consumption function.* Princeton: Princeton University Press.

Frisch, R. 1959. A complete scheme for computing all direct and cross price elasticities in a model with many sectors. *Econometrica,* 27: 177–96.

Gamaletsos, T. 1973. Further analysis of cross country comparison of consumer expenditure patterns. *European economic review,* 4: 1–20.

Geary, R. C. 1950–51. A note on "A constant utility index of the cost of living." *Review of economic studies,* 18: 65–66.

Goldberger, A. S. 1964. *Econometric theory.* New York: Wiley.

———. 1967. Functional form and utility: A review of consumer demand theory. Systems Formulation, Methodology and Policy Workshop Paper 6703. Madison: Social Systems Research Institute, University of Wisconsin.

Goldberger, A. S., and T. Gamaletsos. 1970. A cross-country comparison of consumer expenditure patterns. *European economic review,* 1: 357–400.

Green, H. A. J. 1964. *Aggregation in economic analysis.* Princeton: Princeton University Press.

Hicks, J. R. 1939; 2d ed. 1946. *Value and capital.* Oxford: Clarendon Press.

Hoel, M. 1975. A note on the estimation of the elasticity of the marginal utility of consumption. *European economic review,* 6: 411–15.

Houthakker, H. S. 1957. An international comparison of household expenditure patterns, commemorating the centenary of Engel's law. *Econometrica,* 25: 532–51.

———. 1960. Additive preferences. *Econometrica,* 28: 244–57.

———. 1965. New evidence on demand elasticities. *Econometrica,* 33: 277–88.

Houthakker, H. S., and L. D. Taylor. 1970. *Consumer demand in the United States: Analyses and projections,* 2d ed. Cambridge: Harvard University Press.

Howe, H. J. 1974. Estimation of the linear and quadratic expenditure systems: A cross-section case for Colombia. Ph.D. dissertation, University of Pennsylvania.

――――. 1975. Development of the extended linear expenditure system from simple saving assumptions. *European economic review,* 6: 305–10.

Howe, H. J., and R. Pollak. 1975. Time series estimation of the quadratic expenditure system. Paper presented at the Third World Congress of the Econometric Society, Toronto.

Iacono, J. 1976. Durables in the consumption function. M.Ec. thesis, Monash University.

Johansen, L. 1969. On the relationship between some systems of demand functions. Liiketaloudellinen Aikakauskirja. Reprinted in Reprint Series no. 47, Institute of Economics, University of Oslo.

――――. 1974. *A multi-sectoral study of economic growth,* 2d ed. Amsterdam: North-Holland.

Johnson, H. G. 1968. The transfer problem and exchange stability. In American Economic Association, *Readings in international economics,* ed. R. E. Caves and H. G. Johnson. Homewood: Irwin.

Jorgenson, D. W., and L. J. Lau. 1975. The structure of consumer preferences. *Annals of economic and social measurement,* vol. 4, no. 1, pp. 49–102.

Kelley, A. C. 1969. Demand patterns, demographic change, and economic growth. *Quarterly journal of economics,* 83: 110–26.

Kelley, A. C., J. G. Williamson, and R. J. Cheetham. 1972. *Dualistic economic development.* Chicago and London: University of Chicago Press.

――――. 1974. *See under* Cheetham.

Klein, L. R., and H. Rubin. 1947–48. A constant-utility index of the cost of living. *Review of economic studies,* 15: 84–87.

Klijn, N. 1974. The specification of the extended linear expenditure system: Some alternatives. Department of Economics, Research School of Social Sciences, Australian National University.

Kravis, I. B., and others. 1975. *A system of international comparisons of gross product and purchasing power.* Baltimore: Johns Hopkins University Press.

Kuznets, S. 1962. Quantitative aspects of the economic growth of nations: VII. The share and structure of consumption. *Economic development and cultural change,* vol. 10, no. 2, pt. 2, pp. 1–92.

————. 1966. *Modern economic growth*. New Haven, Conn.: Yale University Press.

Lewis, W. A. 1954. Economic development with unlimited supplies of labour. *Manchester School of Economic and Social Studies*, 22: 139–91.

————. 1955. *The theory of economic growth*. London: Allen and Unwin.

Liviatan, N. 1961. Errors in variables and Engel curve analysis. *Econometrica*. 29: 336–62.

————. 1964. *Consumption patterns in Israel*. Jerusalem: Jerusalem Academic Press.

Lluch, C. 1971. Consumer demand functions, Spain, 1958–1964. *European economic review*, 2: 277–302.

————. 1973a. The extended linear expenditure system. *European economic review*, 4: 21–32.

————. 1973b. Functional form for utility, demand systems, and the aggregate consumption function. *IEEE transactions on automatic control*, 18: 385–87.

————. 1974a. Development in segmented economies (restricted circulation document). Washington, D.C.: Development Research Center, The World Bank.

————. 1974b. Expenditure, savings and habit formation. *International economic review*, 15: 786–97.

————. 1974c. Some ELES estimates of the subjective rate of discount (restricted circulation document). Washington, D.C.: Development Research Center, The World Bank.

Lluch, C., and A. Powell. 1975. International comparisons of expenditure patterns. *European economic review*, 6: 275–303.

Lluch, C., and R. Williams. 1974. Household savings and demand patterns in Korea: Some evidence from the national accounts. Bank of Korea, *Quarterly economic review*, pp. 19–25.

————. 1975a. Consumer demand systems and aggregate consumption in the USA: An application of the extended linear expenditure system. *Canadian journal of economics*, 8: 49–66.

————. 1975b. Dualism in demand and savings patterns: The case of Korea. *Economic record*, 51: 40–51.

————. 1975c. Cross country demand and savings patterns: An application of the extended linear expenditure system. *Review of economics and statistics*, 57: 320–28.

Manser, M. E. 1975. Systems of demand equations and cost of living indexes for U.S. food consumption, 1947–1973. Paper presented at Third World Congress of Econometric Society, Toronto.

Marschak, J., and W. H. Andrews. 1944. Random simultaneous equations and the theory of production. *Econometrica*, 12: 143–205.

Mattei, A. 1973. An intertemporal model of consumer behaviour. Institute for Economic Research, Swiss Federal Institute of Technology.

McLaren, K. 1976. A dynamic model of the firm-household with an imperfect capital market. Impact of Demographic Change on Industry Structure in Australia, Preliminary Working Paper no. OP–06. Melbourne: Industries Assistance Commission.

Meullbauer, J. 1974. Household composition, Engel curves and welfare comparisons between households. *European economic review*, 5: 103–22.

———. 1975. Identification and consumer unit scales. *Econometrica*, 43: 807–09.

Meyer, A. C. 1973. International comparison of consumption patterns. Paper presented to the ECIEL Conference on Consumption, Prices and Economic Development, Hamburg, West Germany.

Mikesell, R. F., and J. E. Zinser. 1973. The nature of the savings function in developing countries: A survey of the theoretical and empirical literature. *Journal of economic literature*, 11: 1–26.

Moore, H. L. 1914. *Economic cycles: Their law and cause.* New York: Macmillan.

Musgrove, P. A. 1977. Income and spending of urban families in Latin America: The ECIEL study. Washington, D.C.: Brookings Institution, forthcoming.

Norton, R. D. 1975. A computable general equilibrium framework for structuralist models of economic development (restricted circulation document). Washington, D.C.: Development Research Center, The World Bank.

Nurkse, R. 1959. *Patterns of trade and development.* The Wicksell Lectures. Stockholm: Almquist and Wiksell.

Oksanen, E. H., and B. G. Spencer. 1973. International consumption behaviour: Tests of alternative consumption function hypotheses using national accounting data for twelve countries. *International statistical review*, 41: 69–76.

Organization of American States (OAS). 1972. *Boletín estadístico*, vol. 79.

Pak, K. H., and K. C. Han. 1969. *An analysis of food consumption in the Republic of Korea, 1964–67, with projected trends, 1968–71.* Seoul: Yonsei University.

Parks, R. W. 1969. Systems of demand equations: An empirical comparison of alternative functional forms. *Econometrica*, 37: 629–50.

———. 1971. Maximum likelihood estimation of the linear expenditure system. *Journal of the American Statistical Association*, 66: 900–03.

Parks, R. W., and A. P. Barten. 1973. A cross-country comparison of the effects of prices, income and population composition on consumption patterns. *Economic journal*, 83: 834–52.

Pasinetti, L. 1962. Rate of profit and income distribution in relation to the rate of economic growth. *Review of economic studies*, 29: 267–79.

———. 1974. *Growth and income distribution: Essays in economic theory.* Cambridge: Cambridge University Press.

Phlips, L. 1972. A dynamic version of the linear expenditure model. *Review of economics and statistics*, 54: 450–58

Pigou, A. C. 1910. A method of determining the numerical value of elasticities of demand. *Economic journal*, 20: 636–40.

Pollak, R. A. 1971. Additive utility functions and linear Engel curves. *Review of economic studies*, 38: 401–14.

Pollak, R. A., and T. J. Wales. 1969. Estimation of the linear expenditure system. *Econometrica*, 37: 611–28.

Powell, A. A. 1969. Aitken estimators as a tool in allocating predetermined aggregates. *Journal of the American Statistical Association*, 64: 913–22.

———. 1973a. An ELES consumption function for the United States. *Economic record*, 49: 337–57.

———. 1973b. Estimation of Lluch's extended linear expenditure system from cross-sectional data. *Australian journal of statistics*, 15: 111–17.

———. 1974. *Empirical analytics of demand systems.* Lexington, Mass.: D. C. Heath.

———. 1975. The dynamics behind the linear expenditure system. Monash University.

Prais, S. J. 1959. A comment. *Econometrica*, 27: 127–29.

Prais, S. J., and H. S. Houthakker. 1955, 2d printing 1971. *The analysis of family budgets*. Cambridge: Cambridge University Press.

Ramanathan, R. 1968. Estimating the permanent income of a household: An application to Indian data. *Review of economics and statistics*, 50: 383–87.

Rosenstein-Rodan, P. N. 1943. Problems of industrialization of eastern and southeastern Europe. *Economic journal*, 53: 202–11.

Russell, R. R. 1967. International disparities in income elasticities. *Review of economics and statistics*, 44: 579–82.

Saito, M. 1972. A general equilibrium analysis of prices and outputs in Japan, 1953–64. In *The working of econometric models*, ed. M. Morishima and others. Cambridge: Cambridge University Press.

Samuelson, P. A. 1947–48. Some implications of "Linearity." *Review of economic studies*, 15: 88–90.

Sanderson, W. C. 1974. Does the theory of demand need the maximum principle? In *Nations and Households in Economic Growth*, ed. P. A. David and M. W. Reder. New York and London: Academic Press.

Sato, K. 1972. Additive utility functions and double-log consumer demand functions. *Journal of political economy*, 80: 102–24.

Saxonhouse, G. R. 1976. Estimated parameters as dependent variables. *American economic review*, 66: 178–83.

Schultz, H. 1938. *The theory and measurement of demand*. Chicago: University of Chicago Press.

Slutsky, E. 1952. Sulla teoria di bilancio del consomatore. *Giornale degli economisti*, 51 (July 1915), 1–26. English trans. in *Readings in price theory*, ed. G. Stigler and K. Boulding. London: Allen and Unwin.

Solari, L. 1969. Sur l'estimation du système linéaire de dépenses par la méthode du maximum de vraisemblance. Centre d'econometrie, University of Geneva.

———. 1971. *Théorie des choix et fonctions de consommation semi-agrégées, modèles statistiques*. Geneva: Dros.

Stone, R. 1954. Linear expenditure systems and demand analysis: An application to the pattern of British demand. *Economic journal*, 64: 511–27.

———. 1970. *Mathematical models of the economy and other essays*. London: Chapman and Hall.

Summers, R. 1959. A note on least squares bias in household expenditure analysis. *Econometrica*, 27: 121–26.

Taylor, L. 1969. Development patterns: A simulation study. *Quarterly journal of economics*, 83: 220–41.

Taylor, L., and S. L. Black. 1974. Practical general equilibrium estimation of resource pulls under trade liberalization. *Journal of international economics*, 4: 37–58.

Taylor, L. D., and D. Weiserbs. 1972. On the estimation of dynamic demand functions. *Review of economics and statistics*, 54: 459–65.

Theil, H. 1954. *Linear aggregation of economic relations*. Amsterdam: North-Holland.

Thurow, L. 1969. The optimum lifetime distribution of consumption expenditures. *American economic review*, 59: 324–30.

Uzawa, H. 1968. Time preference, the consumption function, and optimum asset holdings. In *Value, capital, and growth*, ed. J. N. Wolfe. Chicago: Aldine.

Watts, H. 1960. An objective permanent income concept for the household. Cowles Foundation Discussion Paper no. 99.

Weisskoff, R. 1971. Demand elasticities for a developing economy. In *Studies in development planning*, ed. H. B. Chenery. Cambridge: Harvard University Press.

Yaari, M. E. 1964. On the consumer's lifetime allocation process. *International economic review*, 5: 304–16.

Yang, C. Y. 1964. International comparisons of consumption functions. *Review of economics and statistics*, 46: 279–86.

Zellner, A. 1962. An efficient method of estimating seemingly unrelated regressions and tests for aggregation bias. *Journal of the American Statistical Association*, 57: 348–68.

Author Index

Subject Index